How to Win at Cricket

OR

The Skipper's Guide

E.M. ROSE

How to Win at Cricket

OR

The Skipper's Guide

Cartoons by Albert Rusling

Hodder & Stoughton
LONDON SYDNEY AUCKLAND TORONTO

British Library Cataloguing in Publication Data

Rose, E. M.
How to win at cricket: or the skipper's guide.
1. Cricket – Team captains
I. Title
796.358 GV927.5.T4

ISBN 0-340-40171-0

 Photoset by Rowland Phototypesetting Limited, Bury St Edmunds, Suffolk. Printed in Great Britain for Hodder & Stoughton Limited, Mill Road, Dunton Green, Sevenoaks, Kent, by St Edmundsbury Press Limited, Bury St Edmunds, Suffolk. Hodder & Stoughton Editorial Office: 47 Bedford Square, London WC1B 3DP.

Foreword
by Trevor Bailey

In the same way as many people secretly fancy their chances at managing a football team, or hosting a TV chat show, most cricketers, especially those who have never had the job, believe that they would make a good captain – certainly far better than the present incumbent at their club, or the clowns currently leading their county and national elevens. Fortunately few have the opportunity to translate a lovely dream into reality, as none of these occupations is as easy as it appears.

The ideal skipper is a great player, master tactician, natural leader with a strong character, an enthusiast, a brilliant psychologist, and born lucky; but to be highly successful in terms of matches won, and for which, most unfairly, he is liable to be judged, the vital factor is a team considerably stronger than the opposition. A glance at seven of the finest post-war international captains reveals that there is no standard model. Sir Donald Bradman, Sir Len Hutton, Sir Frank Worrell, Richie Benaud, Tony Greig, Mike Brearley and Ian Chappell were entirely different in personality, character and approach but all possessed a deep knowledge of the game and a presence, so that they commanded respect and could, when necessary, distance themselves from those under their command. In addition they were, apart from Mike, outstanding as players. Don was both a living legend and father figure. Len, Frank and Mike were older than their players. Richie was a master of public relations. Tony was a flamboyant front leader who, like so many South Africans and Australians, had retained more of his schoolboy enthusiasm than the average English player. Ian was an aggressive fighter, rebel and a natural Australian folk hero, likely to be highly decorated in war, but certain to clash with the establishment in peacetime.

The alternative title for 'How to Win at Cricket', *The Skipper's Guide*, provides an accurate description of this book. Ted Rose has examined and analysed in depth the art and the importance of captaincy. His findings and conclusions will interest and intrigue any cricketer, and it will be of special value to the young, and the not-so-young club skipper taking on the responsibility for the first time. It should help with his field placings, and contains numerous useful tactical suggestions, like arriving early for an away fixture in order to carry out a reconnaissance of the battleground.

Unquestionably Chapter 7 is the most vital, because it deals with probably the biggest weakness in the game of cricket, the dull draw, and shows how many draws could, and should, have been avoided. Any player, county, or club who doubts the menace of the 'bore-draw' has only to examine last season's fixtures and count the number, not those due to the weather, which occurred. If the percentage is as high as I expect, think of those matches which might, with a little more imagination by the captains, have produced a result as well as more enjoyment for all concerned. If this book persuades just a few more skippers to make realistic declarations and to pursue victory for a little longer, it will have done the game a great service.

The sporting declaration which gives both teams a good chance to win seldom occurs in a Test, because it is part of a series, but it is not employed enough or, to be accurate, is not made sufficiently tempting in county and club cricket. Like the author, I believe that setting a realistic target is one of the most vital and fascinating features of captaincy, but you must be prepared to lose. Irrespective of the outcome I reckoned that, whenever a match finished in the penultimate or the final over, my declaration had been right. Both county and club skippers are so frightened of defeat that they are prepared to settle for a draw too early. All too often they take the negative view that the fewer overs bowled the less runs will be scored, rather than the positive one of the higher the number of overs, the greater the chance of taking wickets.

No two captains will ever be in complete agreement about every aspect of cricket, indeed it would be very dull if they were. Therefore it is to be expected that I do not concur on some of the points with Ted Rose. I found 'the bowler who wishes to set his own field is not helping himself, or his side' rather surprising, as it must surely depend on the bowler concerned. Throughout my career I invariably set my own field for the good reason that I knew considerably more about my requirements than any of my skippers who included several outstanding ones. All I wanted from them were their tactics but I welcomed their suggestions.

A sweeping statement like 'there are more good captains in club than first-class cricket' is dangerous. In one respect, Ted Rose is completely correct as there obviously must be more good club captains as there are thousands of clubs and only seventeen first-class counties. However, most club skippers would at first be lost if put in charge of a three-day game, let alone a Test match, whereas the majority of county cricketers, who spend most of their lives playing cricket, will do a reasonable tactical job of leading a club team on a Saturday afternoon. This view was certainly substantiated by what occurred on numerous occasions when, in the amateur and professional days, a club cricketer was put at the helm of a county XI. The outcome, unless he led an exceptionally powerful eleven, was usually disastrous.

About the bouncer, Ted Rose writes, 'Used sparingly it is certainly an effective wicket-taker', but sadly it has secured even more wickets when it has been used excessively, tactics which we both deplore. Finally, there is no comparison between an Australian 'sticky wicket', and an English one. On the former, batting against a couple of accurate seamers is almost impossible and a lottery, while, on the latter, good batsmen can and have made runs.

These are minor differences, however, in an excellent book, written by somebody who not only feels deeply about the game but also fully appreciates the large part a captain should play both on and off the field; and he gives much sensible advice.

December 1987

Contents

List of photographs

(Between pages 160 and 161)

List of cartoons
by Albert Rusling

List of diagrams

Part One

1

Is a captain really necessary?

'You're a lucky devil. I really thought we'd got you today. What did we need . . . another 30 to win with 4 wickets in hand? I told them you'd never bring back the quickies; and when Joe hit you for that enormous six there were still half a dozen overs to go.'

We had reached my favourite stage of a Saturday evening at the Limpsfield Club. As captain I had seen that all the chores were done: the local paper had been phoned, the tea-ladies paid, the umpires had their pints, the telegraph boys their coke and crisps. We had eleven men for tomorrow, and the Second XI had telephoned to say that they had won, too. All that lay ahead was an hour or so of talking cricket with old friends. The best of all possible worlds.

'Well batted, Joe! What's that, the sixers' jug? You owe me a slurp of that then!'

'Yes, I caught hold of that one. Who pays for the tiles on the roof?'

'The Club does. But what went wrong with the next one: same ball, wasn't it?'

'Yes, pity that; old Frank didn't have to move, did he? You know, I don't think I've ever seen him drop one. Short boundary, too, really.'

As far as I was concerned, we had won the match the way I had planned to win it and the way the team was accustomed to win. But during the conviviality of the evening I had a serious seed to sow in our opponents' minds; I wanted them to bring a good side again next year, and to be really keen to win. That way we should have another cracking good day's cricket lined up for ourselves.

John came over and joined our group. With an eye to the future we encourage some of the younger members to run one or two of the Sunday fixtures, against the less onerous opposition. It was his turn tomorrow.

'Don't you think you declared a bit early, Skipper?' he said. 'They jolly nearly won, you know. That chap that Frank caught on the boundary . . . '

'I reckon he won us the game,' I replied. 'Their two fast bowlers were so determined to hit me farther out of the ground than he had, that they never even looked at the ball. But that doesn't really answer your question, does it?'

It was at that moment that the idea of this book came into my mind.

Had John's question been about Geoff's technique, some point of law, or what should have been bowled at Jack, a ready enough answer would have been available: *The M.C.C. Coaching Book* or *Wisden* or Bradman's *The Art of Cricket* provide ultimate authority.

Yet when the talk turns to captaincy, practical captaincy on the field of play, there is no guide. Not even Brearley's *The Art of Captaincy*! There is even a problem of recognition. Club cricketers who have seen Vivian Richards bat or Dennis Lillee or Richard Hadlee bowl are unanimous that what they saw was superlative. Yet some of those same cricketers, who watched England's successful performances under Mike Brearley's leadership, especially during his benefit season of 1978, could be heard to say that, since Test bowlers know their fields, a captain is no more than a figurehead and England would have been better served by a more accomplished opening batsman.

Brearley's failure with the bat that summer, with all the pressures that it entailed, was greeted with a clamour for his replacement which perfectly exemplifies that failure to understand what captaincy is about.

For in Brearley England had a captain who, even if he had never scored a single run, did almost as much to win every Test he played in as the rest of the side put together. (Admittedly the captain has to make some runs or he loses the respect of his side, but the way he conducts himself through a lean spell also increases his team's affection for him.)

The first point which pundits will often make is that England should have made 400 or 500 runs on such and such a day instead of, say, 350. Batsmen always think in terms of runs: in reality the number does not matter so long as it is one run more than the other side. So what made the other side keep on failing? Because someone was manipulating his bowlers, encouraging them and setting the field correctly and keeping the pressure on the batsmen; because there are no easy runs to be had or tired bowlers to hit; because the captain can see beyond the present state of play to the requirements of a different set of circumstances four hours, or four days, later.

The problem about making judgments on captains is not only the lack of a satisfactory 'norm', although that makes it difficult enough. But since we measure the excellence of batsmen by the number of runs they score, we tend to assume that a side which scores 500 runs is better than one which scores 350 (in comparison, not in opposition!). Since the 350 side may well win more often than the 500 side, this is not necessarily true.

The core of this conundrum often lies in the question of the declaration, for the concept of a side apparently winning and yet voluntarily conceding a proportion of its advantage to its opponents, presents an intellectual problem with which many cricketers find it impossible to come to terms. And there is precious little light thrown on the subject by the famous captains in their memoirs.

Mike Brearley's fascinating books endorse his thoughtful, intellectual aura, but they do not actively help the rest of us not endowed with his genius and charm. None of them explains his methods. Cricket rebels may be quick to criticise their leaders, yet are ill-equipped to explain the alternatives. *The M.C.C. Coaching Book* is naïve in the extreme on the subject. Perhaps the marvellous Bradman is the most perplexing of all, for in *The Art of Cricket* he has only this to say about declarations:

> Fine judgment must often be exercised. The risk of losing must be balanced against the possibility of a win – the time factor being all-important. Due appraisal must be made of the relative skills of the two teams; whether a wicket will be easier or more difficult with the passage of time.

That may be a succinct summary of the major items in a

declaration equation. But Bradman, greatest of cricketing brains, makes little attempt to solve it.

Colin Cowdrey, in *M.C.C.*, merely quotes Bradman on the subject. Noble, Fender, Warner, Jardine: they, too, spend pages identifying the qualities (often their own) that they look for in a good captain, even that he should win the toss!

This is not that sort of book. It assumes that you are, or are about to be, a captain, whatever your faults or foibles. It aims to be a textbook of the nuts and bolts of the job. So let us begin by looking at two games of cricket in order to examine their components and see how they actually worked.

2

Two Tests analysed – the captains' view

During their tour to England and Holland in 1981, Sri Lanka were elected full Test-playing members of the International Cricket Conference. So in March of the following year, 1982, when they visited Pakistan, it was their first-ever overseas tour as a Test-playing nation.

One can imagine the feelings of anticipation, pride, ambition and sheer heart-quickening excitement among not only the tour party, but their thousands of supporters who followed their deeds on transistor radios at home.

The first Test had been evenly enough contested for the opening four days: Pakistan 396 and 301 for 4 declared, to which the visitors had replied with 344 in their first innings. Javed Miandad's declaration then invited Sri Lanka to score 353 on the last day, a perfectly sensible move in the context of the opening salvoes of a three-match series. It was designed to establish a platform of strength, with the hope of exerting a little pressure on the batsmen and of exposing weaknesses for possible exploitation in more favourable circumstances later. Miandad did not expect to win this match, rather to ensure against defeat and perhaps to create a psychological superiority for the other two matches of the series.

In the event, though, through a mixture of inexperience, misplaced bravado and lack of discipline, Sri Lanka allowed themselves to be hustled out for a disappointing total of 149. Sadly, the circumstances must have been more or less predictable, and further reinforced when Pakistan won the toss and batted. Again, the whole way through Pakistan's second innings every player must have been doing his own sums, anticipating the equation. The failure to meet that first challenge of the series makes the student of cricket wonder what the Sri Lankans talked about in the team hotel on that fourth night.

One down and two to play: and it is with the second Test that this story really begins. The result was a draw, common enough in that part of the world; it was also an improvement over the first Test, which should have been a welcome relief. The scores look as ordinary as the result: Sri Lanka 454 and 154 for 8 declared; Pakistan 270 and 186 for 7. With Warnapurna, the captain, injured and Duleep Mendis at the helm for the first time, one might conclude that the result represented just the sort of points victory for Sri Lanka that Pakistan themselves had looked for in the previous encounter: characteristic Indian subcontinental fare. But take another look.

Sri Lanka needed to win one of the last two tests to square the series. Their lead of 184 on the first innings clearly put them in a position from which they must have had every reason to expect to force a victory. So how did Pakistan escape? What went wrong? (See scorecard, page 26.)

In their first innings, Sri Lanka had scored at a rate of 3.17 runs per over. Pakistan in reply struggled through 92 overs for their 270. It seems clear that the wicket was no longer quite as good as at first, because when Sri Lanka batted in their second innings they took 63 overs to score 154 for 8 (2.4 runs per over). Normally, of course, one expects a side with a substantial first-innings lead, looking to set up a declaration, to score much faster than in their first innings.

If you had been Duleep Mendis on the fourth day, contemplating your declaration, there would have been two things you needed to know. The first, always, is the state of the wicket; the second is the amount of time. In Pakistan the standard over rate is about 13 overs per hour, and this is borne out by *Wisden*'s arithmetic of this match: five hours on the last day, a drinks interval every hour.

When would you have declared?

At this stage of the book, that is perhaps not a fair question. However, Mendis's answer was: half an hour into the last day. This asked Pakistan to score 339 in four and a half hours. With the advantage of hindsight we know that Sri Lanka bowled 59 overs or 13 overs per hour, so the asking rate was 5.7 runs per over.

Mendis knew the number of overs he expected to bowl, so

he was aware that he was asking Pakistan to score at double the rate of their first innings in worse conditions. Could it have been that he thought the pitch so bad that with men clustered round the bat he would simply roll Pakistan over?

Two interesting quotations from *Wisden*, 1983:

> The second Test might have been won had Sri Lanka switched to attack sooner, rather than using de Mel to bowl to a defensive field, with one slip, long after all possibility of defeat had vanished.

> The match was proceeding quietly to a draw until D. S. de Silva took three wickets in an over which spanned the tea interval, and dismissed Miandad, in the fourth of the last twenty overs.

I believe that Mendis had the opportunity to become one of those 'who wore at their hearts the fire's centre and left the vivid air singed with their honour'. But I reckon he funked it.

I asked earlier what the Sri Lankans could have discussed on the fourth evening of the first Test. I asked myself again how they could have failed to scheme and plan for victory on this occasion. How could they possibly be bowling to defensive fields, having declared, unless someone was tearing their attack apart? What 'possibility of defeat'?

They could have been frightened only of Miandad (and rightly, as he was close to joining the select band of those with Test averages of 60); but if this is the case they deserved to fail.

What I consider Mendis should have done is the following:

First, he should have made an accurate assessment of the situation. One hardly gains the impression that he had analysed the scoring rates in sufficient detail, because if he had, he would have known that, in the target he intended to set, he had provided himself with a massive cushion, compared with anything previously achieved, of about 2.5 runs per over. Translated into four and a half hours that meant no less than 147 runs. So, in the team room that very night he already had enough runs. All he needed was time to bowl Pakistan out. He should have declared overnight.

Second, he was apprehensive of Miandad. Understandably, but the arithmetic indicates that he was wrong here, too.

If Miandad was to win the match against all the odds, he was going to have to play one of the greatest Test innings of all time. Wouldn't you love to be able to tell your grandchildren, 'I was there!'? Good luck to him.

Third, he should have encouraged the Pakistanis to believe that it was worth their trying to win, rather than giving them no option but to defend. This is a difficult and complex concept which I explain more fully later in the book.

Fourth, he should have worked out, with each of his bowlers, field-placing options and preferences designed to give them the best possible chance of taking those 10 wickets. He should have spent the night planning his bowling changes. Who would prefer to operate from which end, in long spells or short. He should have worked his way through the Pakistan batting order mentally, imprinting their individual styles and weaknesses on his mind, looking to inflict the maximum pressure on each. He should have planned for three or four close catchers *all the time*.

Finally, he should have said this to his team: 'Don't try *too* hard. It will be a long day, with all the pressure on the batsmen. So let them be the ones to feel tense. But remember this: a good Test team will always have the capacity to fight back. Don't get despondent when it happens. Stay alert and confident and concentrate all day. Enjoy it.'

Having done all this he would find himself bowling to defensive fields *only* if the batsmen forced him to do so.

It is easy, of course, to criticise errors of captaincy from the safe distance afforded by hindsight. And, to be fair to Mendis, he was the stand-in captain. But a more difficult question to answer is, 'What would a great captain have done in the same circumstances?'

The man who led the Australians in England in 1961 was Richie Benaud. He brought with him as part of his credentials a half-share, as it were, of the 1960 Brisbane Test: the match which was tied with Frank Worrell's West Indians. Nor was it a coincidence that the captains on that then unique occasion were Benaud and Worrell: two of the very best of their own, or any other, generation.

The Australian 1961 tourists came to England as holders of the Ashes, wrested from England's grasp in 1958/9 with the help of such as Ian Meckiff, whose arm was bent and Gordon Rorke who had a 4-yard drag. Terrifying! Thus there was a need for chivalry, sportsmanship, respect and friendship in this series even more than usual. And one cannot praise the two captains (actually four, as injuries to May and Benaud forced Colin Cowdrey and Neil Harvey to take over at times) enough for the fact that they not only displayed these qualities in abundance, but also met each cricketing challenge as it arose, head-on and unflinching.

The first Test at Edgbaston, interrupted by rain, was drawn after England, bowled out for 195 and with a deficit of 321, had salvaged pride and the match at 401 for 4.

The second Test at Lord's was dominated by the fast bowlers and the infamous 'ridge', which made England's selection of Lock and Illingworth seem inappropriate, to say the least. England 206 and 202; Australia 340 and 71 for 5. Bill Lawry's 130 in Australia's first innings won the match for them.

England gained ample revenge in 'Trueman's match' at Leeds. The pitch had been infected by and treated for Fusarium, and was two-paced and crumbly. Two devastating spells by Trueman, one fast, in the first innings, and in the second bowling cutters, caused Australia to collapse. Australia 237 and 120; England 299 and 62 for 2.

All square. With Old Trafford and The Oval to come, England desperately needed another win. One more victory for Australia, however, would make the Ashes secure for them.

At Old Trafford Benaud won the toss and batted, but after 'Fiery Fred' on his home pitch now came genial 'George' Statham on his: Australia were all out for 190.

England grafted steadily to establish a first-innings lead of 177. By the close of play on Saturday Lawry and Simpson had reduced this to 114.

In contrast to hot, dusty Faisalabad, there is no shortage of documentation as to what the teams thought and planned for damp, murky Manchester – not only *Wisden*, but Benaud's own *A Tale of Two Tests* and Peter May's *A Game Enjoyed*. Benaud's planning had begun months before on the boat out of Perth: an advantage denied the Sri Lankans in return for the speed of air travel.

Benaud was also going to be able to reach back into his own rich granary of experience for the seeds of an idea when the time came. First, though, Australia had to produce the stern, backs-to-the-wall rearguard action that England had managed in the first Test. This they did, up to a point, but despite 100 from Lawry, when their ninth wicket fell at 334 they were still only 157 ahead. David Allen's off-spin had accounted for three wickets without cost in just fifteen balls at the very start of the final day. In spite of an inordinate number of dropped catches, Peter May had juggled well with his bowling resources and was now apparently poised on the brink of victory.

Once again in this marvellous series, desperate plight induced a resoundingly forthright response. Alan Davidson, now partnered by the young, untried Graham ('Garth') McKenzie, assaulted David Allen and hit 20 runs off one over, every run as valuable as gold-dust.

Peter May's response was immediate and soundly reasoned: the runs had come off the middle of the bat, no risky edges. He took off Allen and offered something perhaps less palatable. Numbers 8 and 11 are not usually notable for their ability to handle every type of bowling with equal facility. But on this occasion no one made any difference until Flavell, with the new ball, undid McKenzie. By then the triumphant pair had not only added 98, but occupied vital time. So England needed 256 to win in 3 hours 50 minutes: a rate of 67 runs an hour.

Only an hour before Peter May had felt confident of victory. Now he knew it was no longer a realistic proposition: heartbreakingly bitter after England had dominated the match for so long.

Benaud, on the other hand, was elated. Not only did he foresee escape with a draw, but that last stand had fired his team with adrenalin – and he had formed the germ of an idea.

Watching Allen bowl into the fast bowlers' footmarks the previous afternoon, Benaud recalled how Tony Lock had exploited the same conditions one day in Sydney. He had bowled left-arm-over-the-wicket to Neil Harvey and then stayed on the same line to the right-handers as well. He had been virtually unplayable.

On the fourth evening of this Manchester Test there had

been no mystery about Benaud's thoughts, nor about Peter May's for that matter. May had only to keep a firm, unyielding squeeze on the Australians and surely, they were doomed. He had a good solid professional side who knew exactly how to do just that. A pleasant evening talking cricket with his bowlers from a position of strength: make the Aussies work for every single run.

Benaud spent that evening testing the validity of his memories with Ray Lindwall, gathering his courage, for all the world like Henry V before Agincourt. There were five left-handers in the England side – Pullar, Subba Row, Close, Statham and Flavell – and he was looking forward to bowling to them.

The actual events did not quite follow the pattern either captain had planned: they seldom do. However England's openers, Pullar and Subba Row, put on 40, on either side of lunch, in even time. Ted Dexter then arrived to play one of the finest short Test innings ever seen; 76 in only 85 minutes and, in the curious contrary way that is cricket's greatest fascination, practically won the game for Australia.

Look at it this way. At the start of England's innings the odds were on a draw, with a win for Australia the next most likely result. At 150 for 1, and with Dexter in full flow, Australia no longer had the option to force a draw: they could only lose or win. So Benaud needed no encouragement to bowl round the wicket to the right-handers. Dexter had forced him into a corner. At the same time Dexter had dispelled the cold, bitter, cruel reasoning in the England dressing-room that they could no longer win. The golden wand of his bat promised them that the victory, which had been so close for so long, was once again within reach.

Just as the mathematics of the situation gave Benaud no option but to go all out to win, so it was that the collective desire of the England players drove them headlong and helpless into Benaud's trap. Dexter's innings enabled them to believe what they wanted to believe.

May was bowled round his legs by Benaud, out of that rough, for 0, England's last seven wickets fell for 51, and Australia won by 54 runs; Benaud 6 for 70.

Now perhaps you can see why Mendis should not have feared

Pakistan v. Sri Lanka

Second Test Match, 1982

Sri Lanka

S. Wettimuny b Raja	157	– c Ashraf b Tahir	13
†H. M. Goonatillake c Salim b Qasim	27	– b Qasim	56
R. L. Dias c Salim b Qasim	98	– c Mohsin b Tahir	7
R. S. Madugalle not out	91	– lbw b Qasim	12
*L. R. D. Mendis b Qasim	16	– run out	0
A. Ranatunga b Qasim	0	– c Ashraf b Tauseef	2
A. N. Ranasinghe c Miandad b Qasim	6	– c Miandad b Tauseef	5
A. L. F. de Mel c Salim b Qasim	4	– (9) not out	25
D. S. de Silva lbw b Rizwan	25	– (8) st Ashraf b Tauseef	8
L. W. Kaluperuma b Rizwan	0	– not out	11
G. R. A. de Silva lbw b Rizwan	5		
L-b 11, w 2, n-b 12	25	L-b 9, w 1, n-b 5	15
1/77 2/294 3/304 4/341 5/341 6/355 7/385 8/446 9/448	454	1/19 2/44 3/82 (8 wkts dec.) 4/82 5/86 6/104 7/114 8/114	154

Bowling: *First Innings* – Tahir 26–4–108–0; Rashid Khan 13–3–52–0; Qasim 65–18–141–6; Tauseef 12–3–35–0; Raja 26–6–66–1; Miandad 1–0–1–0; Rizwan 12–3–26–3. *Second Innings* – Tahir 13–3–53–2; Rashid Khan 1–0–4–0; Qasim 30–9–51–2; Rizwan 5–2–13–0; Tauseef 14–4–18–3.

Pakistan

Rizwan-uz-Zaman b G. R. A. de Silva	36	– b de Mel	16
Mohsin Khan c Wettimuny b de Mel	12	– c de Mel b D. S. de Silva	74
Salim Malik b de Mel	23	– lbw b de Mel	4
*Javed Miandad c Ranatunga b D. S. de Silva	18	– c Madugalle b D. S. de Silva	36
Wasim Raja c Madugalle b D. S. de Silva	22	– c Wettimuny b D. S. de Silva	0
Haroon Rashid c de Mel b D. S. de Silva	25	– b D. S. de Silva	0
†Ashraf Ali b Ranasinghe	58	– not out	29
Tahir Naqqash c de Mel b G. R. A. de Silva	1	– c sub b D. S. de Silva	13
Iqbal Qasim run out	5		
Rashid Khan not out	43	– (9) not out	3
Tauseef Ahmed c Madugalle b D. S. de Silva	18		
L-b 1, n-b 8	9	B 3, l-b 7, n-b 1	11
1/19 2/54 3/83 4/116 5/124 6/154 7/156 8/185 9/222	270	1/24 2/40 3/132 (7 wkts) 4/132 5/132 6/137 7/174	186

Bowling: *First Innings* – de Mel 23–4–73–2; Ranasinghe 7–1–23–1; D. S. de Silva 32–3–103–4; G. R. A. de Silva 24–10–38–2; Kaluperuma 6–0–24–0. *Second Innings* – de Mel 17–2–71–2; Ranasinghe 5–0–17–0; D. S. de Silva 18–2–59–5; G. R. A. de Silva 19–4–28–0.

Umpires: Javed Akhtar and Khizer Hayat.

England v. Australia

Fourth Test, 1961

Australia

W. M. Lawry lbw b Statham	74	– c Trueman b Allen	102
R. B. Simpson c Murray b Statham	4	– c Murray b Flavell	51
R. N. Harvey c Subba Row b Statham	19	– c Murray b Dexter	35
N. C. O'Neill hit wkt b Trueman	11	– c Murray b Statham	67
P. J. Burge b Flavell	15	– c Murray b Dexter	23
B. C. Booth c Close b Statham	46	– lbw b Dexter	9
K. D. Mackay c Murray b Statham	11	– c Close b Allen	18
A. K. Davidson c Barrington b Dexter	0	– not out	77
*R. Benaud b Dexter	2	– lbw b Allen	1
†A. W. T. Grout c Murray b Dexter	2	– c Statham b Allen	0
G. D. McKenzie not out	1	– b Flavell	32
B 4, l-b 1	5	– B 6, l-b 9, w 2	17
1/8 2/51 3/89 4/106 5/150 6/174 7/185 8/185 9/189	190	1/113 2/175 3/210 4/274 5/290 6/296 7/332 8/334 9/334	432

Bowling: *First Innings* – Trueman 14–1–55–1; Statham 21–3–53–5; Flavell 22–8–61–1; Dexter 6.4–2–16–3. *Second Innings* – Statham 44–9–106–1; Trueman 32–6–92–0; Flavell 29.4–4–65–2; Allen 38–25–58–4; Dexter 20–4–61–3; Close 8–1–33–0.

England

G. Pullar b Davidson	63	– c O'Neill b Davidson	26
R. Subba Row c Simpson b Davidson	2	– b Benaud	49
E. R. Dexter c Davidson b McKenzie	16	– c Grout b Benaud	76
*P. B. H. May c Simpson b Davidson	95	– b Benaud	0
D. B. Close lbw b McKenzie	33	– c O'Neill b Benaud	8
K. F. Barrington c O'Neill b Simpson	78	– lbw b Mackay	5
†J. T. Murray c Grout b Mackay	24	– c Simpson b Benaud	4
D. A. Allen c Booth b Simpson	42	– c Simpson b Benaud	10
F. S. Trueman c Harvey b Simpson	3	– c Benaud b Simpson	8
J. B. Statham c Mackay b Simpson	4	– b Davidson	8
J. A. Flavell not out	0	– not out	0
B 2, l-b 4, w 1	7	– B5, w 2	7
1/3 2/43 3/154 4/212 5/212 6/272 7/358 8/362 9/367	367	1/40 2/150 3/150 4/158 5/163 6/171 7/171 8/189 9/193	201

Bowling: *First Innings* – Davidson 39–11–70–3; McKenzie 38–11–106–2; Mackay 40–9–81–1; Benaud 35–15–80–0; Simpson 11.4–4–23–4. *Second Innings* – Davidson 14.4–1–50–2; McKenzie 4–1–20–0; Benaud 32–11–70–6; Simpson 8–4–21–1; Mackay 13–7–33–1.

Umpires: John Langridge and W. E. Phillipson.

Javed Miandad so much at Faisalabad and why I consider he chickened himself out of his golden chance there. If you do understand, you are already well on the way to holding the Holy Grail of cricket captaincy in your hands. The rest of this book describes how you go about finding it.

3

Key objectives

One day, on tour with my club and after I had written most of this book, I found myself criticising a young friend of mine for what I felt was inept management of a match. Once again I was doing it from a safe distance, and a deckchair.

We had lost the game in question, an all-day one, fielding second. My point was that he had used only four bowlers when he had three or four others of assorted styles, but none of them rubbish, fretting in the wings. Why had he not used them?

His exasperated reply prompted a conversation about objectives: a good example of why captaincy is so difficult. Even experienced sources of help may overlook the most obvious factors.

So, tomorrow, you are captaining your side. What are you actually going to try to do?

'Win, of course!'

Fair enough. But plenty of people, if they are honest, will reply instead that their opponents won by an innings last time and anyhow they themselves have never skippered a side before so the best they can hope for is a draw. Nonsense. Winning is much more fun than a draw and very, very much more fun than losing. So, whatever else you do, and for the rest of your life, fix your sights firmly on winning. Always. If you are not prepared to do that there is nothing in this book for you.

Next objective? This depends a bit on what sort of match it is: prep school, under-15 house match, school, club, league, or wandering all-day club, let alone county or Test match. But surely cricket is a game and therefore by definition meant to be fun, even in Yorkshire?

Right: so your next task is to try and see that everyone enjoys the game.

Everyone, opposition as well?

Yes, of course.

How can they have fun being beaten by an innings and 500 runs?

Difficult, admittedly, but at least you can all be friendly, sporting, play the game in a good spirit. Thank goodness one can say, 'copy Allan Border', particularly after the Australian 1985 Tour of England and the tied Test with India in 1986.

As to your own side, it is not difficult to ensure that most of the players enjoy the game once you have overcome the biggest hurdle: recognising that as a positive, prime objective. But it is difficult to make sure that everyone enjoys it.

First, however, try to let all the batsmen bat and all the bowlers bowl. Both are easier when you bat first. However, if you bat second, the batsmen who fail to get in will not be upset: the earlier men's job was to win the match and they have done it. Not your fault.

Similarly, if your two opening bowlers run through the opposition at the start of the match, well done them. For goodness' sake, though, do not take them off, 'to make a game of it'. Also, the one time it is usually wrong to try every bowler is on a 'green top'. Slow bowlers then cannot induce the ball to grip and it will just come invitingly on to the bat: in a low-scoring game they would probably lose it for you.

So the best game, in fact, is where you win the toss (which you will achieve for 50 per cent of your career), make about 200 for 9 declared and win by 10 runs in the last over. A lovely day out.

However, precisely because you have been deliberately trying to get everyone into the game, you will know with whom you have failed. Go and apologise to them. More than that, try and make sure that you do something about it next time. It will also make you much keener to change the bowling when nothing much seems to be happening!

Do not, though, put Smith, who did not get a knock yesterday at no. 8, in to open today. When he is clean bowled by the new ball his weekend tally will read, 'Did not bat, and 0'. No help to anyone. Try instead to make sure that he goes in when the bowling is easier and gets some runs under his belt.

If you are in charge of your side for a club season or a school term the achievement of these objectives will need the continuing collaboration of your team-mates. They cannot all blossom under your leadership, but some of them will and all should have the chance to do so. They must become aware that the team's success depends on each of them, even the least able, and that their contribution is vital.

Keep these objectives not at the back but at the forefront of your mind as you use this book. You will quickly realise that by making constant use of all of your players, their keenness, enjoyment, enthusiasm and confidence will reward you with both better results and more fun than you have ever imagined possible.

Part Two

4

Captain's homework

Good cricket captaincy begins long before the game starts. The captain should be involved in selection, although at school he may not always be. Either way he should think hard about the make-up of his side for as long as possible before the match.

A week before England played the first Test of the 1961 series against Australia, Colin Cowdrey was asked to take over the captaincy from an unfit Peter May. Cowdrey had not been involved in the selection. England was therefore faced with an almost impossible task. Why? Because Cowdrey, as he says himself, simply did not have enough time, given his county commitments, to do his homework properly. What a way to lose a Test series: before it started!

May seemingly has failed to learn from this episode. As chairman of selectors he took no positive decision about the captaincy for the three-match series against India in 1986. Gower's side had suffered (*sic*) a 5–0 'blackwash' at the hands of the West Indies the previous winter. The players were all 'shell-shocked', and the wet spring prevented any proper rebuilding of confidence. All the selectors offered was to give Gower the captaincy for two limited-over internationals and the first Test. This might almost have been deliberately designed to put Gower's successor on the wrong foot since, by definition, he would start his tenure one down in a three-match series.

Naturally, the captain wants to field the strongest possible side. But strongest means balanced. Lots of opening batsmen, or a bowling attack that is virtually all seam or all spin, can be embarrassing. Similarly, good outfielders, as well as close catchers and vice-versa, are vital. Whether you win or lose the toss, if the wicket is green or dusty, fast or slow, with a well-balanced side you will hold plenty of trump cards.

The history of Test cricket abounds with examples of imbalance (which shows that good balance is not easy to achieve with always limited resources). India in the past, with her host of spinners so lethal at home, used to find series abroad almost impossible to win. The arrival of Kapil Dev and his like gave them balance. The value of players like Kapil Dev, Richard Hadlee, Ian Botham and Imran Khan, is underlined starkly enough if one reads of the perennial problems England have had in the past in trying to find a genuine sixth batsman among five bowlers and a wicket-keeper. The bowling, and more usually the spin bowling, so often suffers. The side for the fourth Test in 1961 (see page 28) is a case in point. Dexter, in spite of his figures then, never regarded himself as a genuine Test bowler.

The success of the West Indies' all-fast attack throughout the years 1976–86 was achieved by cheating. (This is a criticism of the authorities, not the players.) It involved slowing down the over rate to keep the bowlers fresh, and persistent intimidation. Without these ingredients they would have met the same fate that befell England in the first Test in Australia in 1954–5. Bedser, Statham, Tyson, Bailey and Edrich were picked as bowlers, England fielded first, and Australia declared at 601 for 8! In this series, incidentally, the enigmatic captaincy of Hutton, and the technical achievements of the players, together with the violent swings between disaster and eventual triumph, make it a fascinating study, especially for Englishmen. But to set the record straight after that initial disaster at Brisbane, I should quote Cowdrey on the second Test at Melbourne: 'No captain, before or since, could have handled his bowling or set his fields more effectively . . . [Hutton] was manipulating everything as though playing a very tight and ruthless game of chess.'

For the third Test of the 1986–7 tour in Australia, the problem that faced the England selection committee was that Ian Botham's rib injury forced him to withdraw. England had won handsomely at Brisbane, and drawn comfortably at Perth; now Adelaide promised perfect batting conditions. The management thinking, therefore, was to pursue another draw here and try to win at Melbourne and Sydney where conditions were more likely to assist the bowlers. Since England held the Ashes and Australia would need to win the last two Tests to wrest them back, this seemed logical enough, and England chose to pack the batting by giving James Whitaker his first cap and played only four bowlers. But is not cricket a more subtle game than that suggests?

If I had been on that management committee I should have asked questions on several levels: in the first place, the obvious ones such as what happens when one of those four bowlers breaks down? What happens if one of those bowlers (or worse, one of the three remaining!) has a poor spell? More particularly, DeFreitas had played adequately in two Tests as the third seamer, but he was not yet a genuine Test opening bowler even as one of a trio, let alone one of a pair. Could he cope? If not, what would be the effect on him for the remainder of the tour?

For that matter, although the two spinners, Edmonds and Emburey were good, reliable, experienced professional bowlers, in the context of the whole series they were likely to be one of the crucial factors if England was to win. Could England afford to use them as stock bowlers? What would happen if Dilley or DeFreitas was injured and well-set batsmen took a chance with an all-out assault? If England were to win the series it was important that the spinners maintained a web of mystique and superiority over the batsmen. How important was the timing of spells in this?

On another plumb wicket, like Perth, did England actually need an extra batsman? It is always good to blood a youngster like James Whitaker when conditions are ideal, but England already had a batsman wicket-keeper, and all the top order, except for Lamb, were making runs.

Finally, Australia had been astonished and shattered by their comprehensive defeat at Brisbane. At Perth they had managed to avoid following-on by a whisker. Thereafter England had lost their way slightly, but enough to allow some of the Australians a glimmer of confidence and self-esteem. Might it not be dangerous to relax the pressure on their batsmen and allow them to score runs? The psychological balance can tilt extremely quickly.

The answers to those questions led me to believe that the Adelaide selection was wrong: but I was more worried by the negative reasoning, or even lack of it, that lay behind it.

Team selection is, in fact, the captain's first step in developing a strategy. Look at the cards in your hand. What are the strengths and weaknesses? What is likely to be your biggest chance of winning? What are the risks? Go a step farther. Do you know anything about the opposition, or the likely weather, or the state of the wicket? Look at last year's scorebook to refresh your memory. Speak to anyone who has recently played against the same side. Read the press reports to see how they have been doing and who has been doing it. How do you set about making the most sensible use of all the information you assemble? A few suppositions may help.

Suppose you have a strong batting side, a bit thin perhaps in bowling, and that you then win the toss. Do you bat first, attack hard all the way and let the weight of runs made create the pressure to help the bowlers? Or, do you put the opposition in, hope for a reasonable declaration and then knock off the runs?

You are in charge of the match

Clearly the former is the more positive policy, since for you to win when batting second presupposes a certain amount of help or goodwill or at least some positive action on the part of your opponents. This leads immediately to a most important premise. It is your job to run the game. You are not just the skipper of your side; *you are in charge of the match*.

No matter how boring or defensive, bad-tempered or just plain incompetent the opposition, you must take control and retain that control as far as you possibly can. By letting the opposition decide when to declare you are passing that control over to them. In this particular instance they may well exercise their control by simply taking a differing view of 'a reasonable declaration' from your own. They will probably know all about your glittering batting line-up and not be too keen to hand you the match on a plate. So if you do put them in and fail to bowl them out, you will find yourself out on a precarious limb.

But on hard mid-season wickets, particularly if there is only one new ball for the match, it may well be the case that the side batting second has the better chance of winning. Certainly, first-class limited-overs games have vastly widened the club player's concept of what is possible when chasing runs. The many junior school and club competitions, which now form part of the staple diet of all young cricketers, have also given them much more confidence than their forebears in this respect. So if your own club has a good wicket you may justifiably aim to bat second. In that case, though, there are various factors to bear in mind.

The first requirement is that your opponents should somehow be persuaded to declare early enough. They are unlikely to underestimate your batting strength, but they might not realise what one might call the mean scoring rate for the ground. Let me give an example. Many sides, who have played against us at Limpsfield in the past, have declared at, say, ten minutes after half-time for about 180/200 runs, with no. 3 or no. 4 having just completed an enjoyable century, and 6 or 7 wickets down. We have then won fairly comfortably with about 5 overs to spare and about the same number of wickets down.

How does this come about? There are three main factors. In the first place the opposition did not score too well against the new ball; many times in this sort of match the score at the end of the first hour is in the region of 40 or 50 for 3. Compare this with the typical first hour of our innings, batting second against the old ball, when the score would be 70 for 1, and we had a considerable advantage.

Second, although one of their batsmen played splendidly later on, there would nearly always have been a lack of urgency about the batting. One batsman a bit out of touch, or just 'a not very good player', occupying the crease for too long without doing anything positive, would have taken another 10 or 20 runs off what they might have scored. Again, contrast this with the approach of our side: constant clock-watching and discussion between the batsmen as to the run rate. We had a specific deadline to meet; they did not.

Finally, once we had got off to a reasonable start and were up with the clock, and with wickets in hand, the fielding captain simply had to experiment. Two poor overs from a change bowler and the score might leap from 130 to 150. Which could really settle the issue.

There is a world of difference between experimenting, and deploying our own planned variety of bowling in the same circumstances. It depends on who is running the match, or that part of it, the batsmen or the fielding captain.

In the case just mentioned the change was forced by the batsmen both by scoring at a good rate and by not losing their wickets. In fact, when we field second we actually want the batsmen to score at a fair but comfortable rate, but it is vital to us that they lose one or two wickets reasonably early on so that there are about five for us to take in the last 20 overs. If we are failing to get wickets, then we try and exert pressure another way, by putting the throttlers on as hard as possible.

When these matches unfold in this way they are so simple that the pitfalls are easily overlooked. What, for example, will happen next year in the same circumstances? One local club once left us two hours to get 170 and we won by 9 wickets with a quarter of an hour to spare. This year they won the toss, batted much better and left us 200 to make in the same time: a very dull draw ensued. So you have to be selective or you make a rod for your own back.

Incidentally, if the opposition puts you in, assume that it is a defensive move, unless you have definite indications to the contrary. Expect, then, to have to bat more positively, and declare even earlier, than usual.

Many people take the attitude: 'You put us in, you jolly well bowl us out'. This is a mistake, in my view, in that for their part they are failing to take advantage of the difficulties in your batting second; for you will be in honour bound to chase hard whatever target you are set or be charged with a totally negative attitude to the whole match. So the pressure would be on you, with all its attendant suicidal risks, right until the target really becomes impossible, by which time the tail may be fighting for survival. But you do not want the pressure on you. You want it on them.

Let us suppose, on the other hand, that your side's strength is in bowling. If you have seamers they will be itching to get their hands on that bright, shining, new 'cherry'. But the caveat as to failure still applies. If, conversely, you have spinners, they are more likely to be at their best weaving their subtle spells in the evening. So, given a sensible view of the conditions, the lines of attack are fairly obvious.

When Surrey used consistently to win the County Championship under Stuart Surridge and Peter May, they possessed the best bowling attack, and the best close catching in the country. They were seldom greatly concerned who batted first. The prime requirement, from their far from modest batting, was to give the bowlers time to win the match.

Similarly if you have a reasonably balanced side, and the playing conditions are good, you can approach the toss without trepidation. In fact I actually prefer my opponent to win the toss in these circumstances. If, over a lifetime, I am going to win 50 per cent of tosses I shall be very happy to lose on all the days it does not matter. In a freakish sort of way it becomes a long-term advantage to lose it on those days!

Of course, in the event, things seldom prove to be quite so clear-cut. Inconsistency is, after all, one of the hallmarks of club cricket. You might also have to allow for the fact that X's wife is doing the teas, so he must play, even though he insists on opening the batting and is a ghastly plodder. Or Y has just returned from his honeymoon and is consequently unlikely to generate his usual 'nip' with the new ball. So you have to allow for the 'human' factor when reviewing your real strength on that day.

Having given some thought to your own side and your best chances of winning, what of the other factors, the opposition and the weather?

Do not make the common error of misinterpreting information about your opponents: there is *always* some key player or other missing from their ranks. Just keep it in the back of your mind that they may not be quite as aggressive as normal and be alert to back-up signals to that effect.

On the other hand . . . we were playing the Metropolitan Police and our captain told us that seven of their First XI were attending a colleague's wedding: easy win in prospect. What he did not tell us was that there were two or three young men just itching to seize this opportunity to force their way into the side – in particular one new recruit who had chosen the police instead of county cricket as a career. And of course the four who were left were their regular bowlers. When stumps were drawn we had our last pair together at the crease!

The moral is, first, to make sure that your information is in context; and, second, to be guarded about broadcasting it.

For example, the opposition may have one batsman who is a cut above the rest. By reminding your own side of his excellence and how vital it is to get him out, you put them under pressure rather than him. Instead of that, always look forward first to the enjoyment of watching a class player in your midst. Then, however, do not assume he will inevitably dominate the match.

Finally, look for subtle ways of thwarting him: try to give him as little of the bowling as possible, but do not make a big show about it. Do the following:

Make sure first that when he has the strike your boundary fielders are the ones who will save two runs without your having to shout at them or bring them fifteen yards off the line. Also, see that mid-on and mid-off are deep enough to give him a single. Again, it does not have to be very obvious.

When the lesser players have the strike you try to achieve a balance. On the one hand you want to get them out just as you normally would, and second, you want them to continue to have the strike for most of the time, frustrating both them, if they have the wit for it, and the star.

Do not revert to the totally negative all-saving-one field, nor deliberately give away runs. What you are attempting to do is to *deny* the good player the fours that he is accustomed to collect, even though that entails apparently 'giving' him singles. It is extremely irritating after a while for a batsman to see his best shots repeatedly go for one only. Do not forget, either, that a star will, if only subconsciously, expect batting to be easy at your level and may not be prepared to keep working as he would normally.

Similarly never give a poor player a single at the end of an over to keep a better player away from the strike at the start of the next. What will inevitably happen, and jolly well serve you right, is that he will strike yet another single off the first ball of the next over, too. He is not a very good player, so keep trying to get him out. Why let him relax?

There are different standard ploys aimed at counteracting your opponents' known strength. For example: they have a leg-spinner who is normally a thorn in your flesh, so it might make sense to deploy any left-handed batsmen you have to face him. Another thought about leg-spinners. (There are not many of them about, so a good one becomes more of a problem than he would be otherwise, which is why he is worth some thought.) If you win the toss, bat first, especially in a one-new-ball match. He then probably will not be on as early in a first innings as he might be in a second. Also there is not the same pressure on your batsmen to score off him as when they are chasing a total; you merely have a lower-scoring match.

The opposition may have a renowned hitter whose favourite arc is in the direction of mid-wicket. So you might try to tie him down with accurate seam bowling, and then tempt him with your left-arm spinner so that he has to hit against the tide and gets a top edge to short third man.

There can, too, be a positive advantage to you in the opposing big hitter. You will mostly find him coming in at about no. 6, 7 or 8. His presence in the side will tend to discourage the earlier batsmen from worrying about keeping right up with the clock. You have the opportunity, therefore, of squeezing them a bit more tightly than normal. He for his part, sitting in the pavilion, will be fretting a little more. If you then confront him, when he does arrive at the crease, with your gentlest spinner instead of trying to keep him quiet for a while, he has a chance of going berserk at once and overreaching himself. With him out of the way you then have few worries about feeding the genuine tail generously.

Since most club games are played with one new ball for the match, rather than one for each innings, it is worth asking yourself, even if you do not have anyone to use it effectively, have they? On firm wickets in mid-season it is surprising how often the new ball can govern the outcome of the match. It is under precisely those conditions that early pace and bounce may give way to an amiable softness for the side batting second. In those circumstances, denying the opposition the use of their strongest suit may well be even more advantageous than the full exploitation of your own.

Personally, I find the pressures in this type of game rather tedious. In the first place your new-ball bowlers have to bowl well. If they do not you are in trouble because it is always difficult to reduce the striking rate. They have to be aware of their responsibilities.

Then there is a tricky decision to make on how soon to go entirely on the defensive. Some days you always look likely to take another wicket yet it does not quite happen, so then you have given away more runs than you intended by attacking too much. On other days, perhaps, you go too defensive too early, allow the batsmen to settle and then they have the confidence to take liberties. It is so very easy to fall between these extremes and fail to do much one way or the other.

Finally there is the problem of the team's interest and morale. There is little opportunity to give your 'bit' bowlers a turn without losing that vital tight grip on affairs; but it is also simple to fall into the rather boring pattern of long spells of seam-up, length-and-line bowling with a corresponding lack of shots being played. The fielders gradually fall asleep and the afternoon seems inordinately long. To crown it all, the innings is apt to end in a flurry of shots and hectic running of short singles which the listless fielding side is now in no position to counter.

To build a relationship such that everyone knows the pressures and responsibilities before they happen requires a great deal of hard work off the field. Once that is done there is no reason why the cricket should not be bright and entertaining; but your players have to work at it and help you.

So you have to be sensible and careful about fielding first, since although it is positive in concept, it is negative in execution. You can come unstuck. For example, you might have misinterpreted the nature of the wicket. Suppose it turns out to be benign at the start and then breaks up, leaving you at the mercy of their spinners? Not quite what you had in mind.

Most wickets in fact behave predominantly in a certain fashion day in and day out, so you can find out about that before the game. Do not fall into the trap, however, of slavishly believing what you have heard, rather than the evidence of your own eyes. The logical integration between wickets and weather can often be used to your advantage as well. Weather forecasts are a traditional Aunt Sally, but it is usually obvious these days when a forecast is dubious or definite. There is a world of difference between, say, sunny intervals and showers, and a belt of rain spreading from the West and expected to reach SE England by mid-afternoon. You may or may not get any rain in the former case, but in the latter it is only a question of time. So there is the opportunity to make sure that you do not get caught on 'a flier' or have to bowl with a wet ball.

The experience of poor Mike Denness at Edgbaston in 1976 against the West Indies furnished a woeful example of faulty analysis of the information available to him before the match. He was, understandably, concerned at the prospect of what the West Indies fast bowlers might do if the wicket gave them some help on the first morning of the Test. As the Edgbaston wicket usually gets slower and easier as a match progresses, he put West Indies in to bat.

In the event the wicket was hardly green at all, and by all accounts did not look it. In the second place the weather forecast was quite definite that the match would be interrupted by rain before the weekend. So what happened was predictable: West Indies made a comfortable tidy score and then caught England on a horrible wicket after the rain.

The reports of this match also furnish an interesting example of how not to use advice. When you get it wrong it is no good saying that your players agreed with your decision. The right way to use advice is to make up your own mind first and then use your colleagues' views to check that (a) you have not missed some factor or (b) you have not put the wrong weight of interpretation on the facts. This is not at all the same as the Willis or Gower system of captaincy by committee.

It will frequently be the case that all your prior information and experience tell you that your side is much stronger than your opponents'. They, for their part and knowing your strength, will quite reasonably be thinking that, if they can get away with a draw, they will have done well. You do not have to be very brilliant to put them in first, bowl them out for nothing much and win by 10 wickets. Unfortunately, there is a big temptation, backed up by advice from your run-hungry batsmen, to bat first and make 400 for 3 declared. But you are the person who will have to live with the chagrin afterwards of their being 60 for 9 at the close of play and, possibly, laughing at you all year because someone dropped a sitter in the final over!

Conversely, if your side is very weak, pray for the opposition to bat first if they win the toss. With any luck they will enjoy themselves so much at your expense that they leave you with refreshingly little time to hold out for a draw.

One such occasion that gave me enormous satisfaction was when with a side of genuine no-hopers, we visited near neighbours who laughed at us before the match. We won the toss and fielded. We had only two gentle medium-paced bowlers who changed ends occasionally, but otherwise performed non-stop for three hours. We achieved a draw that should never have been remotely possible. The headlines in the local paper made sweet reading: 'Visiting skipper ruins local Derby'.

Playing against the same club a few years later we had a very different sort of game. Our own club had a new captain, a genial, gentle man, inexperienced in captaincy but with considerable hidden depths of character and determination. During the week before the fixture he asked two of us ex-captains, separately, our advice as to how he should play it. We had a good side out and he received the same advice from both of us: 'They never chase any total you set them, so win the toss, put them in, bowl them out fast and knock the runs off.'

In the event he won the toss and batted. A couple of hours later he was asking our opinion as to the timing of his declaration. Quite naturally he did not get much help!

We comfortably topped the 200-mark for about 6 wickets and then bowled them out for 60 in only 26 overs.

In the bar afterwards the captain took my arm and said, in his gentle way: 'Now that's the way to play cricket properly you know.' Quite right, too – if you can do it.

I failed to derive much satisfaction, however, from the following encounter when the boot was firmly on the other foot; but it demonstrates the need for courage.

A local village side, with a long tradition of always having a few useful cricketers, suffered an internal upheaval some years ago when their best players left. The remainder soldiered on, but obviously, with weak sides, totally bereft of self-confidence; and, indeed, the whole club had a chip on its shoulder, as it were. Since then we have beaten them decisively until last year when most of our regular players opted for a more jovial, competing 'country-house' day out, and they beat what was essentially our Second XI. This year, when we visited them they were still crowing about it. For our part we had our big guns out, seeking revenge, and they knew it.

Our fixture card indicated a 2.00 p.m. start; they turned up at 2.15 for a 2.30 start. (Fixtures secretaries always exchange fixture cards at the beginning of the season as a check against errors such as this!) The shorter the match the more likely is a draw, so the red lights were flashing already. Their captain announced that tea was fixed at 5.00 p.m.; more red lights; 2.30 to 7.30 = 5 hours, less 20 minutes for tea means half-time is 4.50 p.m. With the normal tea between innings we should be looking to declare before that, say 4.40. Then they won the toss and put us in. Now if we wanted to declare early we should lose a further 10 minutes between innings. So the match started with their having done their homework with due diligence and set up their desired draw in every way possible.

The only effort we made to break out of this strait-jacket was to declare at 4.55 to ensure a prompt start after tea. By then we were 183 for 6 made off only 36 overs. (A slow over rate is another weapon deliberately exploited by draw-minded sides.) At the close they were 87 for 5 off our 40 overs. Unfortunately we dropped three catches thus providing the captain with an alibi. 'If we had caught all our catches we should have won.' But club cricket sides do not catch all their catches.

So what should we have done? We should have declared at about 4.35 when the score was 140! Ridiculous? They would then have had 15 minutes before tea and 130 minutes after; 145 minutes to get 140 against a good bowling side with lots of variety, and assuming tea was strictly 20 minutes. We could in fact have knocked even another five minutes off for say 135!

What would their reaction have been? Probably, 'Arrogant sods; they've overdone it. Hey, we can get these runs you know.' In those circumstances I should put my shirt on our winning by a clear 50 runs.

To return to the beginning of this example – our captain made a very significant remark when I suggested that such a declaration had been possible: 'After last year I was not prepared to lose it.'

This betrayed, it seemed to me, a total misunderstanding of the situation. We had a very, very much stronger side than they, in every department, so a draw to me was as complete a failure as defeat.

Of course, in strict philosophical terms, if you are not prepared to lose a match you should not play it in the first place. More interestingly, though, the suggestion that a run-a-minute equation would persuade them that it was 'on' also persuaded him. In fact, the relative bowling and batting resources of the two sides were so disproportionate that the proposition was never remotely feasible.

So often in cricket you have first to win the mental battle with yourself before you can win the physical one with the opposition. Second, there is the technical problem that batsmen committed to defence are much more difficult to dislodge than those who are playing shots. I shall go further: bowlers in club cricket simply do not do enough with the ball to demolish sides that are committed to drawing, almost regardless of the state of the wicket. Therefore, you must make them think that they can win.

Notice, finally, that it is vital, if you want all the possible time available to bowl them out, to make sure that the umpires are in position, and the field ready set, 18 minutes after the start of the tea interval. Make sure your own umpire is out strictly on time. Give him the onus of getting his opposite number out there with him.

But I digress.

In school cricket the problems of analysis are greater, and not solely because of the inexperience of the captain. Your own side, too, will have changed considerably since the previous year; so will that of your opponents. Your leg-spinner, so devastating last year, has grown a foot; as has his length.

Young batsmen need the confidence of runs behind them to overcome glaring faults. Half the side are longing for their 'ribboned coats', despite what the poem says, so they will not commit suicide for you in headlong pursuit of victory. If they did, you could hardly drop them for the next match in spite of some Second XI star making three hundreds in succession. (The same applies to the young batsmen of the opposition; so take note of who does and does not have his colours.)

You should also realise that each of your batsmen has a choice. He can either plough on at his own rate, putting runs in the bank for himself, or get out having a real go. You, too, have a problem: to be fair and honest with young players reaching for the stars. You have to help them all you can to learn their trade.

Every school captain does have one ace up his sleeve, though – the master in charge. There are not many good captains about and he is *unlikely* to be one of them. He will, however, possess experience and a sense of continuity. He will know his opposite number and the long-standing traditions of the opposition that are likely to influence their attitudes to the fixture. How, for instance, have they usually responded to declarations? So, although you may not take his word as gospel, at least if you do your homework it will make him do his. Nowadays, with so little cricket being taught in many schools, you may well have to work doubly hard to get the help you desire.

Wandering cricket clubs, again, operate within completely different parameters. You do not necessarily want the strongest side you can raise; balanced, yes, but of a different nature. Ideally you would like to win by 1 wicket or by 5 runs out of the 500 scored in the day. Many of your side will have had to travel some distance. Some might have even given up a precious day's holiday to play for you. It is therefore important that everyone has a good day out, and is involved somehow. A walk-over for either side is the last thing you want. So you can afford a few passengers, but you must have the reliable hard men to do the work; a star or so would be fun.

Selection is just as vital, so you cannot leave it until the last moment. Analysis is not wholly concerned with winning (although it will help to scrape home by the skin of your teeth), but also with ensuring that everyone gets into the game. So, a couple of overs before lunch for dear old Fred.

'Harry, would you mind opening the batting with Jack Hobbs?' Harry, of course, will miss the first straight (or otherwise) ball wherever he bats, so it does not materially affect the game whether he is no. 1 or no. 11, but it will make his day. Provided you do not forget the port at lunch-time it will also make it that much easier to raise a side again next year.

Len Newbery, one-time managing director of Grey-Nicholls and in his youth the very highest class of club batsman, was a genius at this sort of fixture. He would have Test players and cricket-mad, but hopeless, old friends in his sides. To cap it all, everyone of his team invariably went home knowing they had enjoyed their best day of the summer.

One year Dennis Atkinson played for Len's XI against our club. Who? Look him up in *Wisden*: he had quite a partnership for the West Indies in 1954–5 against Australia and then celebrated with five wickets.

The following year I arrived at our ground bright and early only to find that Dennis, having spread his washing out in the sun to dry, had already swept the visitors' changing-room, was in the process of doing ours, and had placed a crate of light ale in each. 'Just a "thank you" to Len.' Two delicious characters.

How do you measure up to that?

The final process in pre-match preparation is communication; not just with the regular key players, but also with those on the edge of the team. For the most part this takes place as a matter of course between people you see regularly and frequently. Even so, there will often be a young or a new player coming into the side, nervous about his likely position in the batting order, or terrified lest he should throw the game away if he does come on to bowl. You might have an out-of-form opening bat, secretly praying for a less-taxing slot further down the batting order. Again, your third seamer, who has had no chance to contribute for the previous two weekends, may need reassurance before he begins to harbour a niggling grudge. It is your job to nurse these players through their difficult times and get the best out of them.

In 1973 I captained the Rugby Meteors side that won the Cricketer Cup; my players came from as far apart as Newcastle and Ramsgate. We did our planning over the telephone with the senior players. Before each match all the players had a letter containing details of our side, the opposition, the ground, the contribution I was expecting from each of them individually, aspects I sought to improve upon over our previous performance, and likely areas of pressure. We kept the 'fringe' players fully informed and made it quite clear to them that their contribution was every bit as vital as that of those who played in every round. In short, we worked hard at becoming an integrated team and made full use of our resources.

In contrast, I know of one England cricketer in the past whose first intimation that he had been picked for his first-ever Test was to read the team in a newspaper. I doubt if he was alone in receiving this treatment, and I have heard of several others who found they had been dropped via the same source; it seems incredible, doesn't it? Yet it lends a certain point to a remark which John Inverarity, that charming captain of Western Australia, once made to me. He said that, in his experience, English and Australian Test sides were technically similar in strength, but that every member of an Australian side was always giving 100 per cent. Consider the MCC's 1974–5 tour to Australia. The omission of John Snow, then unquestionably the best fast bowler in England, was manifestly due to a failure of communication. The moral is obvious. It may take time and trouble to sort out a certain player's problems with him, but the alternative is not only that of having less than the best side playing, but also a lowering of morale. That might do for England, but not for a good club.

The summer of 1986 found David Gower's shell-shocked England side, back from the West Indies, faced with three

Tests each against India and New Zealand. England players had no chance in a late, wet spring to restore their confidence by spending long hours piling up the runs in the County Championships, yet there was no indication from the selectors that they understood the problem. They could have quietly let it be known that they would make no changes for two or three Tests while the side settled down again. Alternatively, they could have done the opposite, put some senior players out to graze while they 'blooded' some youngsters with a view to establishing a suitable blend for Australia the following winter. In the event the poor performances of the various England sides that summer were less the fault of the players than of the selectors: again a failure of communication. Messrs Bedser, Elliott, Barrington and Murray, one of the best Test selection panels of recent years, rated much more highly for sanity.

If I were a captain of England for a home series I should want the whole pool of players under consideration notified. I should also want the players who were not picked to know why, e.g. that the required complement of close catchers would be weaker, or that we expected to need an extra bowler if our all-rounders failed. (Again, if the no. 1 wicket-keeper was injured at some stage the choice between x and y as replacements might depend on several factors: x is a better bat than y, but the batting line-up looks strong; meanwhile y plays for the same county as A and B who are expected to be the match-winning bowlers. If the batting suddenly looked vulnerable and/or injury to A and B changed the balance of the side, then the choice between x and y might be reversed.) I should wish that any players left out should know whether we are juggling with the balance of the side and that they would almost certainly be required again; or whether they were just not good enough. In a club side one has the opportunity and should make the most of it.

Through this process of thorough preparation you will now have done everything possible to ensure that the cards are stacked as strongly as can be in your favour. The coming battle will be fought on your own terms and conditions. You can be flexible without being weak and have the confidence to pursue victory determinedly without being, or appearing, reckless.

5

Captain's duties

Make sure that you arrive on the ground with plenty of time to spare.

If you are playing away from home take a careful look at the wicket well before it is time to toss for innings. Walk around the ground. Get the feel of the place. Notice such things as odd slopes, differences in the distance of boundaries, the axis of alignment of the pitch in relation to the sun and the prevailing wind.

For example, my own club's ground at Limpsfield is wooded on one side and wide open on the other. The land slopes up towards the trees and the pavilion, and quite steeply down on the other side. The effect of this is that the trees appear to be much closer than they are, while the open-side boundary looks miles away. Over the years we have taken hundreds of catches on the tree-side boundary. Similarly, there have been very many run-outs from down the slope. Also the wickets themselves tend to be greener, in suitable conditions, the nearer they are to the trees.

When we go to a ground that is surrounded by houses, I am always conscious of the difference in light. I have even been quite blinded by the glare off the sight-screens at certain times of the day. Often I have decided to field first simply in order to give our own batsmen time to get acclimatised to these differences.

The groundsman can be a useful ally. A professional groundsman will always tell you his troubles with the weather or that his predecessor made a mistake which is still affecting his wickets. So, if your hosts have one, always take the trouble to find him and have a chat. He will appreciate your interest in his job and may reinforce your visual impression of the wicket with such gems as, 'It was a bit green last week, so I've taken off a bit more grass this time,' or, 'I haven't watered this so much: I'm trying to get more bounce into them as they have been so dead recently.'

The most honest groundsman I ever came across said, 'We put the wrong sort of loam on last autumn and it hasn't bound in properly, I'm afraid. It looks all right now, but the top will go later. Can't do anything about it, so if you win the toss, bat.'

I lost the toss. He was quite right!

Even when visiting less well-endowed clubs you can glean some information. Ask who does the wickets. It may be a local council operation (lots of grass, little rolling) or one of the players. He might give you a hint such as, 'We made 250 on it last week,' or, 'It doesn't help the spinners much,' depending on his particular forte.

When you are playing at home you should arrive early enough to welcome your visitors. Show them to a clean dressing-room. Point out where the bar, showers and tea-room are. Also you will want to ensure that everything is ready for the match: clock, score-board, umpires' coats, bails, and new ball. You will then have the opportunity to introduce any new player and have a word with your own umpire and scorer. They should not feel that they are just part of the furniture.

The Laws say you should toss for innings 15 minutes before the start of play, on the field of play. It does not have to be on the pitch or the square, although that has a better feel about it. Traditionally, the home skipper tosses and the visitor calls. It is therefore quite important that all of your team are on the ground before then. This is not just pedantry on your part, and they should recognise that. You have enough factors to consider before deciding to put the other side in to bat, without the added burden of finding out afterwards that both your opening bowlers are going to arrive an hour late.

If you have players missing when you toss up, and their absence indeed would affect your decision, you can delay your choice until 10 minutes before the scheduled start (see page 230). This is not common practice, but it is perfectly legal. What is not allowed is to change your decision once it is announced. However, we are not yet quite ready for the toss.

Once you are out in the middle with the opposing skipper,

and before the coin goes up, you must agree with him the hours of play, length of intervals, which clock you are to follow, and how many new balls you are to use. As the home skipper you should also inform him about any idiosyncrasies of the ground, or local rules. For example, what the custom is about overhanging trees, sight-screens inside the boundary, or the fact that a ball has to clear a certain hedge to score 6 runs. Any of these special conditions will also have to be agreed with the umpires, the Laws (3.3) say, before the toss. This is pedantic and I cannot imagine an umpire refusing to abide by an agreement the captains have reached, although, obviously, in extremely unusual circumstances the captains will want to use the umpires' advice and experience before agreeing conditions. One example: the Hurlingham Club in London has an

What are the rules about the tree?

extremely small ground with a tree in the middle of it. The ground is often used by wandering clubs, so it is not unusual to find that neither captain has played there before. What happens about the tree? Ask the umpires.

If you do not have an umpire, or you have but he will be late or leave early, apologise to the other captain. Not many people realise that umpires have to be appointed before the toss and 'No umpire shall be changed during a match without the consent of both captains' (Laws 3.1 and 3.2).

Players do get cross when sides turn up without umpire or scorer, particularly when it happens several weeks running. So one could imagine a careless offhand attitude being countered by an insistence that one of the defaulting team officiates throughout the match, thereby reducing them to ten men.

The umpires are also involved in approving the ball(s) to be used, before the start of the match. The procedure I use, when playing at home, is to give the new ball(s) and a box of spares to our umpire. He then relieves me of a job by taking them to both his opposite number and to the visiting captain.

When we are away from home, at some moment between my telling our umpire of the playing arrangements and the start of play, I merely say to our umpire, 'The balls all right, Ron?' With a good umpire I can rely on his judgment to the extent that I do not need to look at them, and he will make sure that there are no halved kookaburras floating about for (in England) our batsmen's discomfiture. Kookaburra balls were developed specifically for Australian conditions and have proved extremely popular. In England their hardness and polish can make them almost uncontrollable in humid, green conditions. You are entitled to disapprove of any of the balls produced before the start of the match.

So much for quality: you may also agree not to use a new ball for either innings, or just one for the match, provided you do so before the toss. Once the coin has gone up and the subject has not been mentioned it is too late to do anything about it if your opponent insists on his rights and knows the Laws or can successfully manipulate the umpires to agree with him. 'Either captain MAY demand a new ball at the start of each innings' (Law 5.3). So do not neglect this, even if your particular grade of cricket has never seen a new ball before!

At the start of England's second innings in the final Sydney

Test of the 1978–9 tour, on a broken wicket and with England needing only a handful of runs for victory, Australia elected to continue bowling with the old ball that England had been using. It was an unusual decision, but perfectly correct.

Two other oddities I have encountered are:

1. We had agreed on one new ball for the match. I won the toss and put our opponents in, only to be handed a re-polished one. Because we had agreed upon it, I got my new ball after making a fuss. Otherwise the captain's idea had been to produce two re-polished balls, one for each of us, if he batted first, but only one brand-new one if we did.

2. We had again agreed on one new ball for the match. We batted second and luckily I faced the first ball – a new one. I always wonder if my other batsmen would have stopped the game, as I did, and ask for the original. So be warned!

The hours of play, time and length of intervals should be quite straightforward matters, but beware of the fixed tea interval in both full-day and half-day games, and, especially when playing away from home, try to be aware of the implications of your host's proposals in this respect.

Here is a day that went wrong: we agreed on tea between the innings, then we declared so early that it was not ready: a loss of ten precious minutes. When we did have tea it lasted for half an hour instead of twenty minutes because of sharing facilities with the Third XI on a neighbouring pitch with the loss of another ten minutes. A certain draw. The moral of this is, if you look like declaring early, tell the tea-ladies!

I have another mistake to expiate. One day we fielded first, bowled the opposition out and came off for tea – only to find I had failed to organise any! Naturally I apologised to the visiting skipper and suggested that we played on after a ten-minute interval and had tea 50 minutes later, while we raced round and found some. He refused, saying we had agreed to tea between the innings, which was correct. Amazingly the umpires permitted the 20-minute interval to be extended to an hour until we had physically had tea to eat and drink. It could only happen in league cricket!

It does not often happen in club cricket in England, but a drinks interval, happy event, should be arranged in advance, just like any other. I may say that no visitors of ours have ever complained when we have taken them out unscheduled refreshment in the session before tea. Obviously an unscheduled drinks interval during the innings of the second side is a completely different matter. It is highly likely to be against the interests of one, or even both, sides. In any event, drinks cannot be taken after the start of the last 20 overs.

Finally, before the time comes to go out and toss you will want to have decided on your opening bowlers, should you be about to field first, or, if you are batting, your batting order. I do not always have my order written out at this stage because often there is a personal preference to be discussed, but I try to do so. But there is the little matter of Law 1.2, the nomination of players: 'Before the toss for innings, the captain shall nominate his players who may not thereafter be changed without the consent of the opposing captain.' Did you know that? I had been running sides for twenty years before I discovered it.

Between honest sides who know and respect each other this Law is irrelevant, but there is a famous story of a Star Batsman who was out first ball, immediately after tea, in a London club match. His club's Third XI was playing at home, too, on the next-door ground, and also batting second. In the bar that evening *they* all seemed to think that Star Batsman had played a fine innings!

Of course, with knockout limited-over competitions, it is quite normal to have twelve players on the ground for the match in case someone gets injured. You may not know a single one of the opposing side's players, so there is an opportunity for sharp practice which nomination should prevent.

The more we consider the subject, the more it becomes clear that part of any captain's duties includes the reading and understanding of the Laws (see Appendix I). Better than that, your local branch of the Association of Cricket Umpires will hold instructional lectures every winter. The amount you learn about the game by attending such a course will stagger you. Be staggered early in life! I wish I had.

I heard of one occasion when a lack of knowledge of the Laws actually cost a match, and in a knockout competition at that. What apparently happened was that an opening bowler, having delivered half his allotted overs, and being a poor fielder, was replaced by the twelfth man who was an excellent fielder. When the bowler was required to bowl the rest of his overs he could not do so because he had not been back on the field for long enough.

This raises the question of what happens if you find that several members of your team are late. What do you do on winning the toss? The instant response is to bat first. I have done that myself for years, but I am sure that, much more often than not, it is a mistake.

Consider what happens. The batting order is all over the place. The batsmen are conscious that they must not get out until the others arrive, so they do not just play the bowling on its merits. Nor do they concentrate fully, but are for ever looking over their shoulders to see if the laggards have appeared. The most likely outcome is the loss of early wickets followed by the breathless arrival of the remainder at the crease without any chance of assessing the conditions or getting the feel of the game. Add to this the fact that top-order batsmen are not used to going in with the score at 50 for 5 (a very different sort of pressure from that of being 20 not out when the score has reached that low ebb) and you have a fair recipe for chaos.

On the other hand, if you field first, the situation can develop very differently, provided you have two bowlers who can bowl reasonably well with the new ball, even if they are not normally opening bowlers.

It is possible, in fact, to set an adequate field with only eight or nine men. Do away with a few slips or make do with two on the leg side. Forget mid-on or have one man patrolling the covers instead of two. Normally you have essentially three spare men, so it does not take a great deal of juggling to do without them for a while. If your bowlers bowl a good length and line, and the batsmen are kind enough to want to have a look at the ball for an over or so, those fielders would not have anything to do even if they were there.

In a curious way, too, the pressure is back on the batsmen again. They look around the field and see gaps all over the place. 'Gosh, we're in clover here,' they will think. They then get frustrated if they find that they are not bombing along at a merry rate. And they will not be; a straight, length ball, just doing a little bit, is not going to be hit anywhere even if there are only four of you playing, let alone eight or nine.

The bowlers, instead of experimenting with leg-cutters, or 'the other one', or 'my little floater', are, without any advice from you, going to concentrate like mad on keeping a good, tight line. The fielders will be conscious of having to be on their toes and having to work that little bit harder.

Then, finally, the recalcitrants arrive; suddenly the batsmen find themselves ringed with dragoons of fielders. Yet another bonus the fielding captain had hardly expected. Having successfully disposed of ten fielders, I invariably find myself standing in the middle of the pitch and having to say to the bowler, 'Now where would you like me to go?'

'Oh,' he says, looking round the field with a vexed air, slightly guilty almost, as though expecting to find a yawning gap he had overlooked. 'Oh well, let's have another slip then.'

All this makes a daunting list of points you as captain have to remember, especially if you are doing the job for the first time; but most of the hassle can be taken out of the job if the skipper sits down the evening before the match and writes out his batting order on a slip of paper (and I like to mark off my bowlers, too, to settle my mind). On the back of this slip, jot down a check list: coin, ball, no umpire, boundaries, tea, 20 overs, etc.

I suggest this because, as a visitor, I have so often found my host attempting to toss before any of the foregoing matters have been mentioned. That tells me of his inexperience, a useful tip later perhaps, and causes him to feel foolish when I stop him and ask. It is a great temptation to assume that all will be well. It will not. Never let him toss before you have all the information you require. You are not being unduly pernickety. You are not being rude. If anything, he is.

Since a sound knowledge of the Laws, regulations and arrangements for the day can be a very important factor in your success, make sure that the whole of your side knows about all the agreements for the match. Your batsmen are your representatives in the case of disputes about the weather, the light, or condition of the ball. I once actually played in a match when the batsmen denied their own side victory by shutting up shop when they seemed to be winning easily. It transpired that they thought stumps were to be drawn at 7.00 instead of 7.30!

Last, as ever, the umpires. The game cannot work properly without them. They wish to be a help to you. They want to be involved. If you give them the chance they will take a pride in doing their job well. So ask their advice about the various ways of organising a game. If you want a prompt start after tea and your declaration, you need them to be in their places on time. Put the onus on them. If you keep them fully informed and make friends with them you will be pleasantly surprised how active their co-operation can be.

Between the innings it is the umpires' duty to check the score-books and agree the total. In many games the players are umpiring, so it becomes the captain's job. Make sure that the total in the books is the total on the score-board.

The home captain has another job at the end of the first innings if his side has been batting – that is, to ask the fielding skipper what he would like done to the wicket. The side about to bat has the right to have the wicket swept and/or rolled for up to seven minutes, but not cut. In addition, the creases will often require re-marking and the bowlers' footholds may be repaired.

On grounds where there is a full-time groundsman permanently in attendance, he will go out and ask the fielding captain his preference at the fall of the ninth wicket. I hope you never find yourself in the position of N. H. Bennett, who was captaining Surrey at The Oval against the Indian touring team in 1946. He asked Bert Lock for a light roller at about tea-time on the first day. Sarwate and Bannerjee intervened to the tune of 249 runs, by which time what was wanted was not a roller but a plough!

At the end of the game, win or lose, it is always a pleasant gesture to shake your opposite number by the hand, in full view of both sides, as you or he is leaving the field. Immediately after that it does not take much trouble to thank both umpires and scorers for their efforts. Find the lunch- and/or tea-ladies and compliment them on their food, even if it was not great. Have a word with the groundsman; wandering sides usually club together to give him a tip.

More often than not the home side's elderly chairman or president will have been watching the game. He will be overjoyed to be told how much you have appreciated your visit to his lovely ground. Later he will mention to his counterparts from other clubs what a good game they had with you and what pleasant people you are.

You cannot begin to play cricket without the time, trouble and sheer hard work of these people. To acknowledge the fact will only enhance the reputation of your own club, and ensure that you are never short of good fixtures.

There will always be one or two members of the side who have to slide off quite soon after a game, for one reason or another. Home or away, they should find the opposing captain before they go, and thank him for the game. As members of the home side, of course, they should be aware that it is their duty if possible to stay and entertain their visitors. They should therefore apologise for not doing so.

6

Wickets

A good wicket, no matter whether it has been prepared for a half-day match or a five-day Test, should help the new ball a little at the start, become fairly plumb in the middle of the match, and take some spin at the end. In order to do so a wicket needs depth of firmness and the right amount of grass.

The reasons for this definition are important. First, the luck of the toss will not give either side an undue advantage. Second, all types of bowler should have an opportunity to offer something positive at some stage. Third, the batsmen will be confronted by a wide variety of problems. On the other hand, they will be able to deploy a wide repertoire of shots.

Pace and bounce in a wicket encourage both stroke-play and attacking bowling. Most wickets will differ from this perfection, however, in one way or another, and for a variety of reasons.

First, moisture: a wet wicket will be slower, in general terms, than the same strip when dry. Beware, though, the hard wicket that is wet on top – the flier (page 67). A match-stick will offer a good guide: if it can be pushed easily into the soil then the moisture has probably gone down far enough to be safe.

Second, grass: a wicket with a lot of grass on it will help the ball to 'seam', but it will prevent it turning for the spinners because it is too skiddy. This will apply whether the wicket is hard or soft. A hard grassy strip is the proverbial 'green top'.

Third, moss: differentiate between grass and moss. Moss has very shallow roots. When a ball pitches on a piece of moss, therefore, it rips it out and leaves bare earth and a dent. The result is that a wicket full of moss will become worse as the

Beware the hard wicket that is wet on top. A match stick will offer a good guide. . . .

game progresses, but such wickets (a) are usually slow and (b) they produce steep bounce, probably steepest when the ball is new. Moss, by the way, is generally pale in colour, but treatment turns it black.

Since wickets with too much grass help the seam bowlers overmuch, wickets devoid of grass must eventually help the spinners. Dry ones may well be good batting strips initially, but they will turn to dust as they wear. Mudheaps ought to be unplayable since the ball will both turn and stop. Once they start to dry out they vary in bounce, bits fly out, and of course they do everything quicker; they are then unplayable to all but genius. Melbourne in 1928–9 and The Oval in 1926 provided just such a strip. That explains what 'Hobbs-and-Sutcliffe' meant to England.

There was another infamous 'sticky' wicket at Melbourne in January 1937 when Walter Hammond proved once and for all that he was no ordinary batsman with an amazing innings of 32 (*sic*). This was the occasion on which the Australian bowler Sievers took 5 for 21 and provoked Hugh Trumble to say that he deserved to be dropped for bowling such rubbish. He was.

The fourth factor is the depth of firmness. A fast wicket with bounce cannot be created overnight; it has to be built up from below. In order to do this the right type of soil, the correct doses of water and sufficient heavy rolling are needed over long periods of time. The end-product will be akin to concrete underfoot and have a distinct sheen to it.

The indications of when they are as firm as that will be that the whole square is hard, the old wickets undamaged, and usually a pale-coloured soil on a well-drained site. It goes without saying that not many English club wickets can be like this, for the necessary staff and machinery are only available on county grounds and those of the major schools. Their whereabouts are therefore well advertised, but beware such events as a change of groundsman. Be sure that the evidence of your own eyes does not conflict with hearsay.

These examples are extremes, of course. Nearly all wickets, mercifully, will be what might be termed intermediate wickets, usually slightly over-grassed or moist rather than wet. In which case they are unlikely to affect your decision whether to bat first or second, or to help one class of bowler significantly more than another. Extreme conditions call for far more accuracy; a few wasted overs of spin on a green top, for example, could cost you the match if the opposition knows its cricket.

Ask yourself: 'Is this wicket likely to get easier or more difficult during the match? Why?' A green wicket will, if anything, get better; more certainly if the sun shines. Sun and maximum rolling both help to remove the sap that causes the problems. A dry and loose wicket, however, will become worse, although the looser it is the lower and slower will the bounce tend to be.

The type of wicket I always have most difficulty in reading is the one that is slightly damp. It is always a problem, even with the help of a matchstick, to know just how firm it is underneath. In addition, what looks superficially the same wicket will play quite differently in May compared to August. This is because a May wicket is built on a damp subsoil which by mid-summer will have dried out. In addition, a typical club strip will probably be played on four times a year with four periods of rolling and preparation. So it stands to reason that later-season wickets should be firmer than those that have had less rolling earlier in the year.

The result tends to be that early-season wickets are rather dead. Mid-season wickets with moisture in them can be lively early on, then become easier as they dry. Late-season wickets can actually behave in the opposite way sometimes, as early evening dew suddenly provides some juice.

These predictions will often be wrong, but that does not matter overmuch. If you ask yourself the question 'when is the wicket most likely to help the bowlers?' you will not be deceived too often.

For example, if you think that a certain wicket looks as though it might help the new ball at first – then field. If it does not help very much, at least you can bet that in the absence of rain it will not become more difficult, so you have lost nothing. The only way you might lose out would be to take a chance and bat first, only to find that it is more lively than expected.

Similarly, if you believe that a wicket is going to grow more difficult as the game goes on, and it does not, then you will have ample evidence of the fact during the later stages of the first innings.

The general prediction about soft wickets, however, is twofold. If they are soft all the way through they are more likely to become worse as the game progresses. This is because the ball, taking bits out first, leaves a surface that is not only corrugated but also part grass, part mud. In addition the drying process is uneven, a dry skin on top of damp subsoil. An under-prepared wicket (probably the majority of club wickets) will exhibit this more violently than a well-prepared one, and the key to this, in turn, is flatness.

A flat wicket can only be prepared by long rolling in the spring when the whole ground is in a plastic condition. So squat down and look for little undulations. If the wicket is flat it should feel firm even though it is wet. An under-prepared wicket will be more spongy.

A well-prepared wicket is likely to roll out easier as it dries. The subsoil is more compact and therefore there is less room for moisture between the soil particles. Hence, when the sun dries the surface the effect is far more uniform through the depth of the wicket.

The theory of rolling the wicket between innings (as opposed to groundsmanship) is simple. First, as a roller flattens out the "'umps and 'ollows" made on the pitch during the first innings, the heavier the roller the more effective it will be in doing so. So from that point of view, when you are offered a roller between innings, always ask for the heaviest roller available and for the full seven minutes allowed by the Laws.

The only danger here is that on a very dry wicket, showing signs of dusting, it is possible for a heavy roller to create more dust. Because such a wicket will not have dents in it anyhow, unless the top is loose and bitty, you will need only a very light once-over roll, if at all.

Second, however, as it squeezes the soil together tightly the roller forces moisture between the soil particles. The effect of this is twofold. In the first place it spreads the moisture more evenly throughout the depth of the wicket. In the second, since excess moisture can only escape upwards, the roller brings it to the surface whence it evaporates. So a freshly rolled wicket may, for a short while, be slightly damper on top than previously, but will then dry out more evenly. The heavier the roller the greater this effect will be.

Once again there can be a danger. It is possible to create a wicket, under certain circumstances, which is hard and dry underneath while all the moisture has been forced to the surface: the flier. However, in my experience, this only happens when a wicket has been 'doing a bit' anyhow and after quite a short time it dries out to a markedly more benign strip than it would have been without the roller.

Finally, the roller does have an effect upon the grass itself, bruising it and forcing moisture out. So a heavy roller will tend to quieten down a green wicket. In practice, however, most club grounds have only a light roller available between innings. Even if they do have a heavy roller, the chap to drive it or the horse to pull it are usually otherwise engaged. This does not really matter because most situations are intermediate, but if there is a heavy roller ask for it.

The important point above all is to recognise the conditions in which your side is likely to find itself in trouble, and to try to mitigate them. Conversely you may have to bide your time for a while, when you are fielding, until the effect of the roller has worn off.

7

Match drawn – boring cricket?

Everyone has played in games where the final scores are 240 for 5 declared: 160 for 6. Have you ever been so bored? Once my side was batting when we managed to persuade the fielding captain to let us all out of our misery and get into the pub half an hour early. That sort of situation can be read about in county cricket every week. Club results list them by the dozen every Sunday, not to mention the hours of mid-week purgatory when the victims have taken precious days off from their holidays and could even then be sand-castling or golfing.

A captain has absolutely no right to inflict such suffering on his players; and there is a real danger that boring cricket could

Have you ever been so bored?

drive players away from the game or to other clubs. Consistently positive, enjoyable cricket, on the other hand, will steadily attract good players and lead to a longer, stronger fixture list. At least the limited-over game has brought some change of attitude.

This is the nub of why this book came to be written, for every single one of those declaring captains, when nailed into a corner of the bar, will tell you honestly and sadly: that the other side were too bad; that he was terribly unlucky to get those four early wickets; that if Joe had not dropped that catch all would have been over; that he had to allow for Hurricane Henry who always makes a hundred in half an hour, except today. If he is a nice man, and nearly all of them are, he will even meekly, wonderingly, ask – 'Where did I go wrong?' And make no mistake about it, *he did go wrong somewhere*: that deadly-dull boring draw is not bad luck or the other side's fault. It does not creep up on you unexpectedly. It is eminently avoidable. And it is always the fault of the declaring or first-innings captain.

There are only two types of draw; one when your side is on a hiding to nothing and you manage to get away with it. Well done. The other is when you fail to win. You then get all your team together in your dressing-room and apologise profusely, for it is your fault.

To be fair, there is also a third type of draw, when you have had a cracking good, even contest all through. No one is going to complain at a draw when the batting side needs 4 runs to win, with 1 wicket left, off the last ball of the day, and gets only 3 of them. Yet, to me, that is still a failure. Having got so near I feel I really should have been able to take that one extra wicket.

I recall one game which ended with our opponents facing our fast bowler for the last ball of the day, needing 2 runs to win. I had two men saving singles, one on either side in front of the wicket, and everyone else close catching. We bowled the mandatory straight half-volley. He simply blocked it. Had the roles been reversed I believe any one of our side would have gone for glory.

Similarly, a highly-respected London club captain was once extolling the cunning of one of his bowlers. He had to get the tenth wicket with the last ball of the match while the batsman needed a six to win. The bowler in question was a spinner, but he bowled a flat, low full-toss, *very* wide of the off stump. No chance of being hit for six, admittedly, but how on earth could he win with a ball like that? The respected captain had evidently not considered the possibility.

'What, just give them the game on a plate? Don't be ridiculous.'

'No, sir. Just a good full half-volley preferably on leg stump. Then the batsman has to move his feet *and* play a proper shot . . . '

'And if he does?'

'Then he gets caught at long-on, doesn't he?'

'Hell of a risk, though. No.'

Is it not sad, though, to be so defensive when the odds are better than 50:50 in favour of the fielding side? The point, it seems to me, is that if you are going to play cricket you might just as well try to win. If you keep trying to win you will sometimes lose and you will have a few, but very few, draws. The draws you do have will be honest and (almost) never boring.

Unfortunately, this is not the case in most clubs. If your club has lots of draws it is a failure of attitude and a failure of technique on your part and your captain's part. Many people seem to assume that it is part of the natural order of things that many, or even most, games of cricket should end as draws. They are wrong.

However, before I examine such attitudes and techniques in detail, let me explain why I am dogmatic and arrogant about the way so many clubs, and so many players, approach their cricket.

In the Surrey Cricketers' League final tables in 1977, for example, 120 fixtures produced 45 draws plus 29 abandoned matches (16 clubs). In 1980, 153 fixtures produced 55 draws plus 27 abandoned matches (League increased to 18 clubs).

You may think these figures unremarkable, and I agree, just as with the club cricket results in the Sunday paper and the results in the County Championship, which always seem to produce a high proportion of draws. But is this the natural order of things? No! These results represent hours of boredom, an amazing lack of any desire to win and an appallingly low level of captaincy skills.

Look at those figures again:

1977:	45 draws	+ 29 no results	= 74	
	37.5%	+ 24.1%	= 61.6% of fixtures	
1980:	55 draws	+ 27 no results	= 82	
	35.9%	+ 17.7%	= 53.6% of fixtures	

Well over half the fixtures produced an inconclusive result. These years are taken at random – any others would reveal much the same situation.

Need this be so? During the seasons 1959 to 1976 my club, under various captains, including young trainees on many Sundays, produced very different results. These seasons are not, of course, random ones; they covered a period when the club adopted the attitudes and practised the techniques advocated in this book.

The full results of those 18 seasons (see Appendix II) are as follows:

Played 793	Drew 139 +	abandoned 52	= 191
As % of total	17.5% +	6.5%	= 24.0%

You will see immediately that the total percentage of drawn plus abandoned matches (24%) is approximately the same as just the abandoned matches for average clubs. In other words we had almost no draws at all except in matches where the weather curtailed play.

Some players might riposte: 'Anyone can achieve that, simply by giving up a match as lost when you cannot win it. I don't believe in that. You must always fight like mad not to be beaten.'

'Well,' I reply, 'we didn't have too many losses either – 160 in fact. About 20 per cent, just under.'

'In that case you must have had a ridiculously strong side.'

'Well, I suppose it wasn't a bad side, but, if so, how did we get such good players to turn out so regularly over such a long period?'

In fact we did have a fair number of good players, but they did not have to play regularly. Also, we made full use of all our players. Everyone had something to contribute. In addition, we made as sure as we could that the cricket we played was fun.

It can be done. Let us examine how.

I am not concerned here with the good draws, but with the bad ones. I repeat: they are avoidable. In order to avoid them we must examine the circumstances and attitude of mind, on both sides, which give rise to them.

To begin with, let us assume we have won the toss and elected to bat first. We shall take as our working model a standard one-day game. The hours of play are 11.30 to 6.30, lunch at 1.30 for 40 minutes, tea an hour after the end of the first innings for 20 minutes, 10 minutes between innings, two new balls and 20 overs from 5.30.

If the batting time were to be divided equally, half-time would fall at 3.05: 2 hours 55 minutes each side. In practice a convention has grown up over the years that the side batting first usually declares a little after half-time, so the fielding captain will probably be expecting a declaration at, say, 3.15. He may not be acutely aware that the game started 10 minutes late or that lunch lasted for 45 minutes. Similarly he may not have realised that the 20-overs regulation probably gives him a further 10 to 15 minutes' batting-time bonus.

(I say that the practice has grown up over the years, but probably the reverse is true. Prior to 1889 the side batting first in a one-day match could not declare. For a long while after that one may assume that a declaration was little more than a magnanimous sop to the fielding side. Later a 60:40 ratio became the norm. Even today a 50 : 50 declaration, let alone the heresy of 40 : 60, is looked upon by many in the same dismissive vein as voluntary income tax.)

These matters are important because the opposing captain's attitude to our declaration and his subsequent handling of events is vital to our success.

Even more important is the following. Suppose the batting side, instead of splitting the time down the middle and declaring at 3.05, takes 5 minutes longer (in this case making 3 hours) it leaves the other side 2 hours 50 minutes: not 5 minutes but *10 minutes less*. This point should be engraved on your heart. For every one minute you waste, adding surplus runs to your total, you lose two precious minutes in which to get that last, vital wicket at the end of the day.

Finally, while your batsmen are using those last minutes they will be giving the ball 'fearful welly', so that 220 runs and

3.00 easily becomes 240 at ten past three. That is an overall rate of 80 runs an hour: not bad. But what rate are you asking of the opposition? 80 an hour for 2 hours 50 minutes will only get them to 226. What are they supposed to be, supermen?

In chapter 4, on the captain's homework, I pointed out that it is his job to run the match. That means we are not going to give the opposing captain any chance to decide for himself what he is, or is not, going to do. He will only make a mess of it. Some sides admittedly will always chase whatever target they are set, even to the point of suicide. That is fine, but we cannot rely on that. We must not give them any option. It should never cross their minds that their task is anything other than straightforward and simple; they are going to knock off the runs without much trouble.

Obviously, it is going to be very difficult for us to win if we have declared at 3.30 for 270. Why? They are going to come off the field feeling a bit niggled and defensive-minded. 'OK if someone bats superbly, but otherwise we've no chance, so just play it as it comes, chaps.' If a couple of wickets fall early, and on a good pitch, it is a certain draw with two whole hours before close of play.

On the other hand, if we declare at 2.50, leaving them half an hour longer than we had to get 200, what will their response be? 'Well we should get these runs all right, boys; ridiculous declaration really, no hurry, take your time and let's win by 10 wickets.'

Two early wickets fall again, but they are not in the least worried. Close the game up, then, so that they are not scoring runs. Still not concerned, bags of time. Tea is taken with the score at 20 for 2. Your asking rate has suddenly shot up to 80 an hour. Chat from their captain to his side to keep it ticking along, look for the singles, etc. Tea, a great change bowler, obligingly does his stuff again. The new man is still instructed to play himself in.

Their captain next changes the batting order: 'Better to have a bit of a wing now, we don't want too many to get in the last 20 overs.'

Lo and behold, at 5.30 they still need 80 runs with only four wickets in hand. Just one mistake now and you are home and dry: the tail simply has to keep whacking at your inviting spinners and none of them has more than one shot. 'I don't quite know how we managed to lose that, just chucked it away, really. Of course, Charlie didn't help running himself out like that just as he was beginning to go well.'

We have all heard variations on that inquest many times.

As an added bonus, does it ever occur to you who is likely to win next year's game as well? They will come back so thirsting for revenge that a much tighter declaration should make suicide inevitable.

Naturally I am chancing my arm in this example, although nothing like so much as it might seem. However, you will often want to play your cards much closer to your chest. Even so, there is no excuse for the so-called professional attitude of getting into a position where you cannot lose before you try to win. The adjective 'professional' should be the highest possible accolade, not a term of abuse, as it is in 'professional foul'.

If you analyse the facts available and decide what the other side is thinking, it is amazing the risks you can run. But are they really risks? What are the available facts?

The first fact that emerges from this example is that our bowlers must have bowled well. Your bowlers *always* bowl better when they start off by thinking that they have to bowl well or lose you the match. This is precisely the opposite psychology to that operating on the minds of the batting side. Notice that, however easy the task in numerical terms, someone has to get his head down and play an innings. A generous declaration has made it that much more difficult for this to happen. The batsmen tend to leave the graft to someone else.

Second, you set your fields properly. Third, I assume that numbers nine, ten and eleven cannot bat. One can actually do better than that. Apart from prior information, what were you thinking about while lolling in your deckchair watching your batsmen smashing the ball all around the park?

Look at the fielding side. You can tell the cricketers by the way they move, their clothes. Look at them seriously one by one: their ages, shapes, kit, the whizzers, the slobs, and the bowlers. You can even tell by the way their captain sets his fields all day. If they are sloppy you are not playing against as good a side as if they are tight and accurate. They will certainly be less used to winning.

You know already the wicket and the outfield and you know what bowlers you have at your own disposal. Write down on a piece of paper how many runs you think each man could reasonably expect to score off you under those conditions on that particular day. Allow for the fact that not all of their good bats with '50' against their names are going to come off together; allow for some cross-batted bunny at the end who might hit a couple of sixes before you can get him out. Nevertheless, if you go through this exercise properly every match, it will amaze you how accurate you can become. Make a game of it with one or two friends – hand over sealed envelopes, if you like. Give yourself a margin of ten runs or so if you must; then declare. The effect can be shattering.

Having worked it out and looked at the clock you then have to inform your batsmen. You will have thought, 'another ten minutes' or 'as soon as we get to 190'. Do not on any account signal your intentions to the batsmen. They know perfectly well that the declaration is imminent and are progressing with appropriate haste, so the signal, two more overs, will not change their method. What it will do, though, is warn the fielding side. They were tired and hot, but will be rejuvenated by the unexpectedly early approach of the end to their labours.

Nor do you have to wait to the finish of an over to declare. Very often, for example, your 190 target will arrive with a four off the first ball of an over. Stand up, clap your hands and beckon them in.

(Incidentally, as you applaud the fielding side off the park, remember, if you are at home, to ask their skipper what he wants done to the wicket. The answer may be 'just a sweep' or 'once over with a light roller', but always ensure that the popping crease is re-marked for the benefit of the umpires.)

One of the captains I most enjoyed playing under *always* declared in mid-over. He said it displayed his intellectual control. But I have a blunder to confess: my 'Old Boys' side was once playing the school in front of a large crowd of doting parents. It so happened that as my target loomed, John Cuthbertson, a prolific scorer in club cricket and an Oxford Blue, was on the verge of yet another 100. His partner was batting very sensibly and was about 30 not out. 'OK chaps, I'm afraid you can take your pads off. We'll go as soon as John gets his ton.' John got to 99. His partner was bowled trying to engineer him the strike, and I had nobody ready to go in. So I had to declare. John, bless him, said, 'Don't worry, I have made a hundred before.' But many of the onlookers thought rather differently.

Sir Donald Bradman, having once been in a minutely close draw after a stirring match, is reputed to have remarked that he did not enjoy it overmuch. Asked what his idea of a good game of cricket was, came the instant reply, 'When I make 200 and we win by an innings and 300.' It is an apocryphal story which suggests that a real cracker would replace the quoted figures by 300 and 400 respectively!

So declarations are not about letting anyone reach their slow hundreds first, or not being able to get the last man out: 350 for 1 against 27 for 9 is still a draw. Rather, it is good, aggressive, positive batting that should set the scene.

Admittedly, we are bound to have games when we are bowled out for small scores or bat slowly, badly, or both. Nevertheless, it must be right to impart a feeling of urgency to our own batsmen. They should always strive to get on top and stay there, keeping the pressure on all the time. That does not mean everyone having a mad bang from the word 'go', but it does mean all your batsmen looking for runs, including always looking for two runs to third man to induce the misfield. It entails a high work-rate from all the batsmen all the time – not just for a final fling in the last few overs. It never hurts to let them know the sort of target you have in mind (which will often have to be changed); nor the fact that 201 for 9 is better than 200 for 3 in the same time.

If good batting puts you in the driving seat, however, it also creates the whole of the problem of making sure that you win. Let me try to encapsulate the facts.

First, you have to overcome the temptation to go on too long and amass a huge score that ensures only safety from defeat. Not easy.

Second, you have to analyse the wicket and your bowling strength. Are you absolutely sure that this wicket provides enough pace, bounce and movement for your bowlers to prise out batsmen committed only to defence? I repeat: are you absolutely sure? Consider the real facts. After declaring, you attacked and immediately took three quick wickets; a long hop hit down cover's throat, a wild slash marvellously caught at gully and a childish run-out.

Third, you are now so far ahead it is ridiculous, yet there is no indication whatever that you could ever bowl a side out on this wicket without their help. Your own batsmen found conditions easy enough, didn't they?

Do not be misled. The vast majority of wickets in England are easy-paced. Certainly they may take some cut or spin, but this is only important when batsmen are playing shots. They usually do not have enough bounce or pace for the ball to carry to the fielders from a defensive shot. It is not difficult to stay in on them. In these conditions club bowlers seldom do enough with the ball to prise out batsmen wholly committed to defence. If you doubt this, watch your own side batting. Count up over a season the number of batsmen who are out (a) playing defensively, (b) attacking and, to be fair, (c) something between the two. It is not the quality of the shot that counts but the intent.

The answer never ceases to surprise me. I have been a reasonably successful club opening batsman (with the admitted advantage of being a left-hander) playing in excess of forty innings per year, and with a career average, I should guess, in the mid-30s. For twenty-five years the number of times I have actually been 'done' by a bowler when playing a purely defensive shot has varied between once and three times per season. That is all, and it is no exaggeration.

This means that for at least three-quarters of my innings I have been out to bad shots or playing attacking shots to balls that I misjudged in either length or movement. In other words, the fielding side *almost always* needed some help from me.

This is the crux of the problem. Early wickets and a lack of self-confidence are the parents of deadly draws. It is precisely now, when your opponents have lost these quick wickets and you are winning so easily, that you are in danger of ending up with a draw – *unless you get them back into the game*. And that takes a lot of courage.

Finally, what do you say to your opening bowlers who have done just what you wanted? They want to bowl, and see a rich harvest opening up before their eyes. After all, if you do not want wickets, why ask them to play in the first place?

If they fully understand that what you want is to WIN they will love you dearly. They will have plenty of chances, when you field first, to go ploughing on for long spells to win you other matches. You can further demonstrate your faith and honesty on days when you know you could make lots of runs and win easily. Put the opposition in once for a while; let your quickies enjoy themselves. Why should the batsmen have all the plums? The batsmen may then be disappointed, but they can hardly complain when you have just gained an eight-wicket win.

'That is all very well,' I hear you say, 'but it can't always be that simple.' Indeed it is not. Every now and again you are going to get beaten, but when it happens it will be well worth watching.

The first game I ever played for my school XI was against the Butterflies C.C. We made 228 for 8 declared. They were 54 for 7 when a little, frail, fair-haired man, one Aveling Pickard, who had shaken, poked, prodded, missed (often) and yet survived, suddenly produced a number of choice shots. When the Butterflies had won, with time to spare, he was 160 not out. I never heard of anyone else ever declaring when he was playing, and he was forced to retire through lack of practice and ruining every match in which he appeared!

On the first-class level, in 1948 at Leeds, Australia were set 404 to win, a task never remotely achieved previously in England. Arthur Morris and Don Bradman managed it virtually on their own. If declarations always went according to plan, what a loss to cricket! We should all have missed one of the great emotional moments of cricket history when that elderly Yorkshireman, sitting by the gangway of the pavilion, stood, and with tears streaming down his face, stopped the triumphant Bradman for a moment as he left the arena with the only totally apt phrase in his vocabulary: 'Yer boogger!'

What higher compliment has any game to offer? What do you do about such chaps in the context of declarations? Nothing: if you happen to be beaten by such an innings, sit back, marvel at it, and thank God you were privileged to be present.

There will be times, however, when you simply cannot afford to lose. There is a lot of misunderstanding about this.

Remember Gary Sobers' declaration in the West Indies that gave England the match and the series? Once you let players of the calibre of Boycott or Cowdrey get 'in' they seldom make mistakes. But this is a problem rarely met with in club cricket.

Not only that, but a Test series is 5 × 5 days: go one down in the first match and you have months of uphill struggle on your hands. Similarly, at two-all in the series and 'even Stephen' on the last day, it takes a lot of guts to lay the whole of that season's work on the line – and probably your job as well. One has to be charitable.

At club level the pressures are less intense. OK, you do not want to lose your local Derby – but, in the end, will your relationship not be better if you both always try to win? It is only one match or two in a season of forty matches.

In league cricket it is slightly different; the points structure is geared to winning. One does hear occasional horrific tales of the last match of the season, though, when one side needs only to draw in order to finish top. Well, if you are in a league you might as well win it. Personally I should go flat out for that draw, then win if I could.

As I have said, if two sides are determined to beat each other until the last gasp, or when one of them cannot win and it battles to the death for a draw, they will always have a good, honest game. If you need points or limited-overs to make you play properly you have to pay the price.

Finally, however, having now spent some time examining declarations and how they ought to work, I offer one example of many that do not. There was nothing special about it, even though I think of it as 'the worst possible game'.

Framework: they are a village side, typical in that their bowling is always passable, their fielding keen, the field-placing slipshod and batting fallible.

In the past we have beaten them by wide margins for several years, so for them a draw would be a success. However, they have neither the temperament nor the expertise to pursue that line wholeheartedly. They enjoy the fixture and are pleasant people. There is no needle. On this occasion they are reinforced by the presence of one of their two local stars, who is a young county no. 3 bat (destined to play for England).

The wicket is typical of early September, slow, with enough grass for the ball to seam and for it not to stop. However it will turn gently and is of even pace and bounce: in a word, benign.

They win the toss and put us in. We make 178 for 6 off 43 overs and declare at half-time.

We open with one fast and one medium-fast bowler. The wickets fall at 1 for 1, 17 for 2, 30 for 3, in 14 overs and 50 minutes. That is also the end of the county no. 3 – and the contest. With 1 hour 20 minutes to go they need 148.

Our fast-medium man has taken all three wickets and the target, with the departure of no. 3, is already beyond them. We also have available a slow-medium seamer and three spinners. However the fast man takes a wicket in each of his next two overs and one over later the last 20 overs/hour begins. We have already bowled 19 overs. The score is 49 for 5.

In the last hour the fast man bowls 8 overs and a left-arm spinner 4 overs from that end. The slow medium bowls 5 overs and an off-spinner 7 from the other end. We bowl 43 overs in all and the score at the close of play is 98 for 6. The other spinner does not bowl.

The sixth wicket falls at 81 with 6 overs to go. This was as boring a draw as I can ever remember playing in, yet it was entirely avoidable, and for the following reasons:

1. Red light: their putting us in was clearly defensive.
2. We in fact batted slowly. After 50 for 1 in 37 minutes (11 overs) a schoolboy at no. 3 allowed them to bowl six maidens and it took us a further 30 minutes to reach 60. Red light again: not easy to get the ball away. Through having the batting order wrong we declared 10 minutes late.
3. Keep the target in sight. All the time the county no. 3 was there, it was just in sight. The minute he was out it went with him.
4. The moment he was out the gentlest spinners should have been on both ends with suitable gaps in the field. The requirement even then was to take two wickets for 70 in 5 overs. The 'last 20' would then start with them needing 80 for 5 wickets.
5. A confident captain would have started the score going earlier still – with no. 3 in, certain that his presence would keep the others committing suicide and that he would not have enough of the strike to win.
6. Tea took more than 20 minutes.
7. The pitch was too mild for the fast men to beat a

defensive shot but, being slow, made it more likely for the spinners to be hit in the air.

8. The asking rate was, as it transpired, 178 runs in 43 overs = 4 runs per over – the same as ours. We knew they were not a strong batting side (apart from no. 3). After 12 overs the asking rate was 5 runs per over.

This match contained almost as many mistakes as it is possible to make in a half-day game; including our losing the toss.

If there is a famous player against you it is much better for him to bat first where he can do the least harm. Both sides want to watch him make runs, and if he does it first then the declaration comes at 180 instead of 170: so what? If he bats second he will set problems (that is why he is famous), but you can have great fun trying to put the pressure on the other batsmen instead. You need the wholehearted support of all the fielders in this because of the amount of moving they will have to do.

You must not on any account be overawed by the famous player, as this captain was.

Our batting order: there is nothing wrong with putting a good schoolboy in high up the order. But it is important that he (a) knows the intended declaration total (in common with the rest of the side) and (b) gives all the strike possible to the more experienced player the other end. 'Message from the skipper, Bill, you're to take all the strike. So I'll give you all I can.'

The softer, hairy outfields so often encountered in May and September change a total of, say, 175 from being easily attainable to as much as 50 runs beyond the possible. On this particular day 150 was a good score in the absence of the famous no. 3. Since no. 3's contribution was minimal, 178 became impossible. Careful analysis of conditions and playing strengths was needed.

Having made a mess of it (as we all do from time to time), the only way out was full attack: as many slips and short-legs as possible; keep ringing the changes with different angles and lines; make the batsman continuously aware of being attacked, and, see that the fielders concentrate.

All our skipper did was to let the game drift out of his control, into oblivion. I would rather be beaten in the way

Australia beat England at Leeds in 1948 than settle for a sterile draw like that one.

Two-innings matches

Cricket is fundamentally designed as a two-innings contest. In the context of minor, as opposed to first-class, cricket this means a two-day match and there is no doubt that the opportunities offered by the longer form are attractive. There is a greater possibility of recovery from disaster, batsmen have a second chance, the lower order can contribute more, bowlers have to be more resourceful and there is a greater opportunity to give them all a chance. Strengths and weaknesses in every department are more clearly exposed.

Two-day matches are virtually unheard of in ordinary club cricket simply because of the problems of availability of players. Although the minor counties, clubs on tour, the services and some schools can still afford the luxury, one of the problems is that, because two-day matches are rare, captains have little experience of running them and therefore go wrong. And when a two-innings match goes wrong it does so twice as badly as a one-innings match. The extra scope is a two-edged sword.

Bear in mind that the fulcrum of an ordinary, one-innings match is the declaration and the concomitant perversity that the side with an apparent advantage has to give it away. Translate this problem into a two-innings match and any misapprehension on the part of the captains of the nature of 'advantage' is brutally exposed.

As an example, take a two-innings match, scheduled for two, 6-hour days, played in fine weather on a flat, hard wicket. Imagine you are the captain of side A. You win the toss and bat. After 3 hours the score is 220 for 4: when should you declare?

The answer appears obvious. It may be easier to score runs now, with an established platform, than in the second innings. Besides, everyone on your side is enjoying the day. So keep going for another half-hour to 260 for 7. At the close of play side B is 200 for 6. All your team will be quite pleased with themselves and with you: but they will be wrong.

Put yourself in the shoes of the captain of side B at the start of the second day. It is his turn to decide when to declare. He has two options; declare now and give you a 60-run bonus at the start of your second innings which will involve side B's scoring, say, 300 runs in 4 hours to win. Alternatively he can bat on for an hour and declare when the scores are level. You then effectively have a one-innings match to be played over only 5 hours. (Do not be side-tracked by side B's scoring 40 in half an hour before declaring or being bowled out: that does not affect the argument.) Now, as captain of side A, and given that you have to bowl out side B in its second innings in order for you to win, are you more likely to do so in 5 hours or 6 hours? That is right: the shorter the time side B have to bat the more likely they are to win and the less likely it will be for side A to win.

At 6.15 on the second evening, when the captain of side A is striving desperately to rescue a draw from a match he should have won, his players wonder what went wrong. The mistake was made at ten past three the previous day when he should have declared. The lesson is quite clear: the arithmetic and thinking that define the timing of a declaration in a one-innings match have to be applied just as rigorously in the first innings of a two-innings match.

The captain of side B is perfectly entitled not to declare overnight even though the scores are level. If he chooses to bat on the following morning he again will shorten the length of side B's second innings and load the result in his own favour, provided of course that side A makes another even-handed declaration. Side A will then be extremely conscious that they are making all the positive contributions. It does not require a notably fertile imagination to sense a deterioration in relationships threatening the future of the fixture thereafter.

So be prepared: in a longer match the responsibilities become much greater on the captain, and the penalties for failure more horrendous.

8

Running the side in the field – fielding second

Having made your brilliant early declaration you are now committed. Everything is going to depend on the handling of your bowlers and on the field-placing; how do you set about it?

First, you must attack. You must attack all out, whether with a new ball or the old one. Place as many close catchers as possible. Do not waste men at long-leg and third man, for you can well afford to give away a few boundaries in return for an early wicket. Besides, if you do place third man and long-leg, the batting captain will think you are being defensive and negative.

If you succeed in taking early wickets you have to make an *immediate* decision, and a vital one at that. You have a choice of either (a) going on as you are, in which case your opponents will have no chance of winning, and your bowlers will have to be good enough to bowl them out, in those particular conditions, in the face of a defensive action; or (b) changing the bowling, giving the batsmen enough rope to get back into the game and hang themselves later.

If you choose course (a) it will be a disaster should you fail, and boring for the fielders even if you succeed. Its only merit is that you cannot lose.

Choice (b), on the other hand, will enable you to get all your bowlers into the action, give the fielders the exercise they want and so make for a much more entertaining game, and a more certain win. Why *more certain*? Simply because it is much easier to get batsmen out when they are playing shots. Think of the trouble you have often seen sides having when trying to remove nos. 9, 10 and 11 when they are bent solely on defence; do you really fancy that sort of exercise against goodish batsmen for a couple of hours? The odds must surely be all in favour of determined batsmen. For example, I remember one game when the spinners had worked steadily through the opposition batting on a slow wicket until, with half an hour to go, the batting side had only 2 wickets left. Our captain brought back the two opening bowlers, both quite brisk. The apprehensive batsmen had no option but to concentrate. No more runs were scored. No further wicket fell.

The earlier batsmen had got out because they liked hitting the ball and the bowling was 'easy'. The slow wicket helped the ball to be hit in the air. The same slow wicket and old ball reduced the fast bowlers to their least effective. The tail-end batsmen had no opportunity or alternative to do other than defend.

Opt for choice (b), therefore, whenever you have an excuse to do so, i.e. 99 per cent of the time, and let people enjoy playing for you. You will want a side next week as well, remember! It is not enough to win; cricket should be fun.

If you delay making a decision you are effectively left with choice (a) since the batting side knows that victory is no longer on for them and therefore will not accept any runs proffered later with the required recklessness.

If you opt for choice (b), however, you must from then on *keep the target always within the opponents' reach*. This means you have to work out your runs-against-time equation all the while and you will be using your spinners to win the match.

The failure to take early wickets may or may not be serious. The opening bowlers may just be providing a pleasant 'framework' to lull the batsmen into a false sense of security before the disaster that is to follow, but they are using up time; and time is precious. There is never enough time to spare for bowlers who are not making things happen. As Andrew Marvell put it:

> At my back I always hear
> Time's wingèd chariot hurrying near.

This is not to say, however, that your opening 'framework' bowlers have no place. Your match-winning spinner cannot bowl effectively through the whole innings. His fingers get tired. But, just as it can be wrong to allow a good bowler to continue when he is not taking wickets (see next page), it is an even more common mistake to let a trundler go on and on just because he took a wicket towards the end of his natural stint. At the end of the day the score-book will reveal the truth: he bowled 20 overs for 1 wicket leaving the potential match-winner time for only 12 overs for his 4 wickets. No wonder you did not get the last man out.

Nor, on the other hand, does it mean that a bowler has to get wickets himself to win the match. The classic combination is that of generous leg-spin at one end with a mean little medium-paced 'dot' man at the other. Their analyses will read respectively 5 for 70 and 0 for 18 in their 12 overs each, but you rightly buy the latter a pint for winning you the match just as surely as did the leg-spinner.

Should you fail to take early wickets and find that you are giving away runs too fast, then you have to batten down the hatches. Keep changing the bowling, one end at a time, as frequently as you decently can and with as much variety as you can muster, until something happens. Then, with any luck, the arrival of a new batsman will enable you to bottle him up really tight and regain control. After a large and flourishing stand it is curious how often you can dispose of the next man quickly by keeping him quiet. After watching runs being gathered with ease he tends to panic if you squeeze him.

Just as it is extremely hard to persuade a batting side to change over from defence to attack, so it is equally difficult to change from flowing attack to caution. This change of tempo and pressure, and the feeling after a big stand that batting is easy, can be used to win the match for the fielding side. You need only to be aware of the possibilities, and keep the game slower and tight, in order to turn a match dramatically.

The need to take off a good bowler when he is not taking wickets was brought home to me one afternoon when, in fact, we were fielding first. We were lucky enough to have one Nicholas Héroys playing for us for a number of seasons. (He went on to captain the Old Tonbridgians to innumerable Cricketer Cup victories, and he is the only player who has done 'the double' for Limpsfield.) He was a superb medium-paced bowler, very tight and with immaculate control of the angle of the seam. This particular day the new ball was 'doing quite a bit' and we had a phalanx of slips and gulleys. Yet after about half an hour no catch had been offered and there were

50 runs on the board, mostly from leg-byes and thick-edged slashes high over fourth slip. In between, the batsmen played at, and missed, four balls per over.

When I took Nick off he was justifiably cross: 'It's still moving about, you know,' he said. It was, too, and some comparatively innocuous 'dobber' gratefully nipped in to bowl them out.

We worked out later what had happened. I thought Nick had been bowling very well, but had taken him off *because he was not producing chances*. I was wrong in the former sense, right in the latter. Normally Nick's success was founded on the admirable precept of 'if they miss I hit': a very straight bowler. The abnormal amount of movement that day meant that he was bowling off line, mostly outside the off stump, or outside the leg stump (and four leg-byes) when he strove to correct it. We also suspected, in retrospect, that he was bowling just a shade too short; the more the ball is moving the farther up it has to be pitched to take the edge of the bat. We both learnt much that day.

Whichever side is winning, and in general over a whole season of matches, try to be aware of the following:

1. You want your two spinners to be bowling at their best at the end of the match. So you do not put them on too early in case they flag with half a dozen overs and the last 2 wickets to go.
2. You have started with your most venomous pair of bowlers, but you do not want them on too long either. So, in a half-day match, you will have ten or a dozen overs in between. Use these overs in a positive way. Give your younger, less experienced bowlers a go. Maybe you have someone who is an erratic slinger, or a zoomy little swinger who cannot always be relied upon to bowl a consistent line. Yet, by a regular policy of giving these men a bowl they will gain confidence and rhythm and gradually develop. Give them defensive fields and constant encouragement: and you may well have found two extra bowlers you did not have at the start of the season.
3. If you put the spinners on too early, not only do you lose this valuable opportunity of widening the scope of the game and enriching your team, but there can also be an immediate problem. You may well need to have a few

overs nearer the end when the score is mounting too fast and you need to close up the game. For those few vital overs you are not trying to win, you are just trying to stop your opponents winning. You cannot afford that waste of time. Success will only bring a draw, not victory.

It will sometimes happen that your side has been bowled out and the opposition is left with ample time to make the runs. This gives rise to three distinct types of situation: (a) their batting resources, and the conditions, are such, relative to your bowling strength, that they really can win easily; (b) your bowling, helped by the conditions, will enable you to win easily; (c) a low-scoring but exciting match will ensue with the balance of power fairly even.

In the first situation (a) where it seems the other side can win easily, you have to do everything in your power to slow down the scoring rate, with luck until the clock catches up with events and comes to your aid. You should not, except as a last resort, set genuine 'limited-over' fields. If you do so, the batting side is apt to consider the proposition in the same terms, i.e. 2 runs per over or whatever. They then consciously look for those 2 runs per over. What you want is both to put enough pressure on them to induce a succession of maidens, and also for them to remember that they have plenty of time. That way they do not try to break out of your grip by, say, taking short singles. They will just take the runs as they come. To induce this you require a good length and line from your bowlers, enabling you to post three or four close catchers as well as a defensive framework.

In the second situation (b), where you can win easily, you must attack and bowl them out as described in the section on fielding first (page 109). Here you give maximum scope to the bowlers whom you judge most likely to be effective. You have no margin, or need, to give away runs. You have plenty of time and, one assumes, a helpful wicket. No problem.

The third alternative (c) is the most fun, of course. Low-scoring games of cricket are intellectually just as enjoyable as high-scoring ones (except for batsmen). You are back to the declaration situation, but with one difference; you do not have to keep the target within reach. It already is. Similarly, the margin of victory, by definition, will be small in conventional terms, so you cannot afford to get excited. The disciplines are much as in the first case. Do your utmost to keep each batsman struggling; even one expensive over can be disastrous. Remember, in both cases, that you will probably have to get through a host of overs, so your bowlers will need to be nursed more than usual. You have to concentrate.

This concentration when running a fielding side is hard work. Often I come off the field, after any match that is remotely taxing, feeling that I have been picked up like a wet rag and wrung out through a mangle. Most captains, though, do not concentrate enough, nor do they concentrate on the right things, such as keeping the fielders where they were put for every ball, not just the first ball of each over; or anticipating where an air-shot would have sent the ball and doing something about it.

In spite of everything there will, alas, be times when even your side is bowled out and the runs knocked off without ceremony. Although you just have to grin and bear it, a feeling always remains that you could and should have done better. During the inevitable inquest, how can the captain be sure that he at least did everything possible to prevent defeat?

Obviously, tight field-placing and a competitive attitude to the bitter end are the first requisites. That is easy. However, there is one vital concept which is extremely difficult to put into practice when defending a low score: for any bowler worth his salt believes that, given the chance, he will bowl them out for less than you scored. Should you fail to bowl the opposition out and have a genuine bowler you have not used, he is quite fairly going to say, if only to himself, 'Of course you didn't bowl them out. I was the best bowler you had for the conditions and you didn't use me.'

If you win, your selection of bowlers was correct. If you lose, you must be sure that you used all of your bowlers, and that each of them got on early enough to have a chance of winning you the match. For you can never be positive that X might not have done the trick. Make no mistake: this is one of the most difficult technical problems that faces a captain.

Two interesting and contrasting games come to my mind.

The first was a limited-over match on a two-paced, unevenly grassed, damp wicket, on which we were bowled out for 146. We had two bowlers considerably quicker than any of theirs, but both were hit about unceremoniously. Our next fastest bowler seamed the ball considerably. We also had two slow-medium seamers who did not bowl at all, and a spinner who turned the ball a lot but slowly in his one over. We lost by six wickets. It could be that the slower bowlers would have had no effect, but I for one would have been intrigued to see how the batsmen coped with the different problems they would have set. But I was not half so worried about losing the game as I was about the captain's mind. If he was aware of the possibilities he should surely have been itching to see whether he could exploit them. If not . . .

The second match was one I heard about at a dinner of one of the country's better-known wandering clubs. The visitors were out for about 90 and their hosts had reached about 50 for 1 in reply. The fifth bowler used then took 7 for 11 and the match was plucked from the fire. 'Never despair' is the moral of this. My father possessed a mounted cricket ball, presented to him to celebrate a hat trick; it was not just any hat trick, but one that he took when the opponents needed 2 runs to win with 3 wickets in hand! He bowled leg-spinners, so there is courage for you!

Perhaps so far I have rather glossed over the idea that your observation of the state of the wicket and outfield, your opponents' strengths and your knowledge of your own bowling resources, could give you a good indication of where the crunch is most likely to come. You will surely have a reasonable idea as to which bowlers are more likely to win you this match, and why. From this it follows that your other bowlers are providing the framework to this end. Your field-placing, too, will be geared to the same set of objectives.

An example might be that you have a fascinating but erratic spinner whom you expect could do the major damage for you. I have already suggested a more parsimonious performer for the opposite end while he is operating. It would be even more foolish to give away runs heedlessly before he comes on, so that, at worst, you cannot afford to bowl him at all, or have to take him off later because the equation is becoming too tight.

So keep relating what is actually happening to what you want to happen. Are they scoring too fast or too slowly? Are you winning or losing? Cricket may sometimes appear to be a slow game, but situations change with alarming rapidity. You have to learn to change your own attitude with corresponding alacrity. This means both that you have to be constantly analysing the situation and have your possible lines of reaction already in the back of your mind. The first essential, however, is to see and know accurately what is happening.

I remember once playing for a friend and being utterly unable to follow the reason for anything he did. At the start of the last 20 overs our opponents needed about 100 runs to win with 8 wickets in hand, and he asked my advice.

'Are you winning or losing?' I asked.

As he did not seem to know, I told him that it was impossible to get those 8 wickets, therefore he was on a hiding to nothing. I may say I was fairly blunt with the poor fellow, who thereupon posted me to the boundary to keep me quiet: and rightly so. There were four run-outs and the match ended in a tie, amid great excitement. But I still have no idea how he did it!

If you do have a sound idea of what you expect to happen you will not easily be misled by your framework bowlers unexpectedly taking wickets. OK, so there may be occasions when they also go on and win the match. It is far more important to recognise, however, the more frequent times when they take a wicket but are not winning the match. How do you go about it?

Watch the batsmen intently for signs of difficulty, or signs of ease. Tot up in your mind the half-chances, the near-misses. Was that sudden shot over the top desperation or growing authority? You are the feline predator stalking its prey, every sense, every muscle, every nerve-end tingling. However, just as a cat feigns complete unconcern from time to time, give yourself a rest when you can. Have a quiet joke with your neighbour. I find it helps me that my sides are usually only too willing to make fun of me. Then I turn the concentration back on.

Part of this concentration on batsmen will enable you to make accurate analyses of their abilities. This is an aspect of running a game that is seldom even considered by most captains, yet it is one half of the reason for all draws.

Consider this argument: a draw comes about because (a) the batting side thinks it cannot get the runs; or (b) the fielding side believes the batting side will get the runs.

As the fielding side, why is it that we think we are going to lose? We know the state of the wicket and have watched its behaviour closely during our innings. We knew about our bowling strength before the match started. We arrived at our declaration in the light of these factors (and, in addition, what we could glean about their batsmen during our innings). So what has changed? All that has changed is that the batsman (or batsmen) in residence has, for a while, been scoring faster than anticipated. This can change in two ways.

First, the range of shots at the disposal of most players – even quite good ones – is much more limited than one might expect. For example, I have seen a man make a hundred, of which 92 runs were scored on the leg side and while there were never less than five fielders on the off all afternoon. A more pragmatic approach to field-placing would surely have stopped him in his tracks. Do not be afraid of setting a 7/2 field if the batsman's style suggests it.

Again, I played in a match once which we lost because of several mistakes by an inexperienced captain, but all of them would have been discounted if he had watched one batsman who made 50. This fellow was strong, moved his feet well and ran fast between the wickets. He scored all of his runs, however, in a narrow arc between mid-wicket and wide mid-on and he always got into position to hit the ball there.

I cannot understand how the captain, however green he may have been, managed to let him score more than, say, 10 or 20. Yet this batsman provided an unusually exaggerated example of what one often sees in club cricket. You must, even if you are only 15 or 16, be aware of players, perhaps in your own team, who only cut and pull and cannot even hit a half-volley off the square. Or the opposite.

Do not ignore these signs. Exploit them. Analyse each batsman and make a positive reaction to him. You have to decide what you are going to do with the front-foot player; pitch the ball up and attack him, or keep it short and deny him. If you bowl short at the persistent cutter you are in for trouble – unless you face him with three third men and a square cover. What you must not do, however, is compromise by setting the square field and asking the bowlers to pitch the ball farther up.

Sooner or later the constant changes of emphasis, of tempo,

of speed and of contrast will work and the batsman will get out. (If your declaration was designed to enable your side to win and the batsmen continue scoring too fast, you lose: QED.) This is the second change in the rate of scoring. All right, while the good player was in residence and going well you were losing. Now he is out, you are winning. So cash in: attack the next batsman and get another wicket or so quickly. The good player has been helping you by keeping his side well up with the asking rate. If you take another wicket now they will fall behind the clock. Do not let them do this, nor be afraid of keeping them moving. This requires a certain amount of mental agility: the good player was giving you a problem slowing him down, now all of a sudden you have to turn right round and help them keep going.

So what has changed compared with 15 minutes earlier? It still *looks* as though the batting side is winning ('Fine innings by good player wins match,' it says in the reporter's mind), yet what is *really* happening is that the fielding side is winning. But since it is important that the batting side continues to believe that they are winning, is it any wonder that cricket is so often misinterpreted or captains underrated?

It has never mattered to me that my own side also thinks the batting side is winning at this stage, so long as they keep catching all the catches, and have faith. The problem in this situation comes when one is trying to help and advise a young or inexperienced skipper.

The key is control. With a good player going well the fielding side does not have control. As soon as he is out, the tail-enders' limited range of shots, coupled with precise field-placing, gives control back to the fielding captain. If he does not realise that he is in control again he will allow the rate of scoring to drop so low that the batting side cannot catch up again and a draw ensues. (See 'The Worst Possible Game', page 79.)

Time and again one sees this equation:

Overs to go:	10
Runs required:	50
Score:	120 for 5
Batsman no. 3:	not out 67
Batsman no. 7:	not out 6
Prognosis:	batting side winning easily.

An over later this becomes:

Overs to go: 9
Runs required: 49
Score 121 for 6
Batsman no. 7: not out 6
Batsman no. 8: not out 0
Prognosis: draw, or fielding side winning.

Equally, time and again one sees exactly the same defensive field-placing, the same bowlers in both cases. Yet in order for the fielding side to win, the positive requirements of the two situations on the fielding captain are totally, comprehensively, different: different bowlers, different field-placing, and new vital catching positions for the best fielders.

Note: If it is not necessary to change the bowling this is sheer coincidence. In the battening-down-the-hatches situation, the bowling has been changed frequently until a wicket falls, remember? So it is pure chance that the wicket falls when the 'generous' bowlers are on. It *can* be an indication that the conditions favour those bowlers, in which case the captain can appear to be even more generous than usual in the second stage. This is the stage (or, more precisely, one of the stages) in the game that calls for unswerving faith and imagination. Do you recognise, once again, that Old Trafford Test of 1961?

This dual requirement – of recognition of the facts and the use of the imagination – prompts some more memories for discussion, this time with a closer eye on the bowler than on the batsman.

On page 87 I pointed out that one has to recognise when a bowler is *not* winning you the match. Suppose someone has had, say, four overs somewhere in the middle of their innings. During those overs what actually has happened? Have any wickets fallen at the other end? Have any positive chances been offered? (You cannot say that a bowler is not doing well if he has taken 0 for 40 and seen six easy catches go down off his bowling, can you?) At what rate has the score been moving? How does this spell of play fit in with your requirements? I have played in many matches which our side has failed to win because the captain did not face up to this difficult problem. He did not ask himself those questions, let alone answer them. There is nearly always the opportunity to give Fred three or four or even five overs in mid-innings, *providing something is happening*. We are talking of the better part of half an hour, remember, during which time it is feasible for two pleasant up-and-down bowlers and two not very good batsmen to do absolutely nothing. When stumps are drawn with the score at 115 for 9 it is that half-hour which has deprived you of victory, not the failure to accept a half-chance in the last over of the day.

One of cricket's equivalents to the jam side of a slice of bread always landing face down on the floor is that Fred, having had his 4 overs, or 3.5 of them, which is all you can afford, then takes a wicket.

Schoolboys are usually taught to give a bowler another over if he has just taken a wicket. He will certainly want one. If you are fielding first it is undoubtedly right. It may be just as wrong, however, if you are fielding second. You have to be tactful and acutely aware of what is going on at the other end. With experience you can probably squeeze in one more over from Fred, but one only.

As captain you will find that you develop a sense about your bowlers: the ball losing its nip off the pitch or hitting the middle of the bat a few times when previously it was never quite there. You sense a bowler is tiring even before he knows it himself, or that this, for whatever reason, is 'not his day'. Take him off. Do not give him that one over more and let the batsmen have the satisfaction of hitting a couple of fours or the feeling of confidence that they have seen him off.

9

Think like a bowler

As a captain, or a potential captain, you cannot study batsmen or batsmanship too closely. Even if you are a batsman yourself, you will now have to think like a bowler. It is not by chance that most of the best coaches are, in fact, bowlers: they have spent a lifetime probing for weaknesses. Again it is quite remarkable how much a batsman advertises about himself even before he has played a ball: big man, small man, heavy on his feet or sprightly. Does he have an easy stance, or a cramped one?

Enter a new batsman. In which hand does he carry his bat as he walks in? If he holds it in his top hand he is likely to be a very different sort of player from one who holds it in his bottom hand. How does he hold his bat at the crease: hands together or apart, top or bottom of the handle? Is the face closed or open? Watch him take guard. It will cost you nothing in the light of what you have seen to call up a short-leg or a gulley. Should you be right you may have a wicket at once and you are a genius. What an effect on the morale of your side! Even if you put the man in the wrong position, never mind. The important thing is to keep thinking and trying. Contrast the excruciating pain of the little dolly catch lobbed into nowhere while you were thinking about it. No good moving the fielder there afterwards.

One caveat: you cannot do any of this if you yourself are too far away from the action. 'The closer the better' is no bad maxim. (See pages 123–24.)

Needless to say, this process of juggling with the bait, pouncing at the right moment and the pursuit of total victory is not usually a simple one. Some sides will fail to accept runs even when they are dished out on a silver salver. Sophisticated sides will not commit suicide with the relish you might hope for. You may have to feed them runs in a fairly subtle way. With a 'military medium' man on, for instance, you could bring up long-leg and/or third man, ostensibly to save the single, but just a little too square: every shot behind the wicket then goes for four. With a slow off-spinner you could have a straight long-on on the boundary, but leave the slog to mid-wicket or square-leg open. Similarly with a left-arm spinner, it only requires the odd delivery off line to keep the batting side rolling along smoothly enough.

If your opening bowlers are above the ordinary (in the eyes of the batting side) you will have a more difficult problem. As you have taken them off early, the batting side is likely to assume that you are keeping them fresh to finish off the tail. The trouble then is that they also think there is no point in chasing after the gentle stuff you feed them, the implication being that, should they get close to the target, you will merely block them out of it by bringing back the fast men. You may have to get one of your fast bowlers to 'go in the leg' and (while he is off for repairs) let them know he won't be able to bowl again!

The regulation of 20 overs in the last hour has, of course, helped to overcome such negative attitudes. No longer can one avoid defeat by simply refusing to bowl. The equation at this stage becomes much more precise. With an hour to go the umpires signal to the scorers, and all the players look at the score and divide by 20: 'Four an over. That's well on.' They are doing some of your work for you.

Day in, day out in club cricket, however, 100 runs off the last 20 overs is a much taller order than it sounds. What makes it so is the number of wickets in hand. In reasonable conditions the fielding side is going to be hard put to it to obtain 6 or more wickets in the 20 overs. On the other hand, 4 wickets (since they are the last 4) should be quite easy, so long as the batsmen have not 'put the shutters up'.

How often does your own side put on 100 runs for the last 4 wickets? Not often. It follows that an average 80 runs for 5 wickets will produce a fairly even contest, but one which I should nearly always back myself to win from the field.

Consider the arithmetic for the average half-day match: playing time 2.00 to 7.30 = 5½ hours; less tea interval = 5 hours 10 minutes. For the sake of simplicity let us assume this is 2½ hours' batting per side at, say, 18 overs per hour = 45 overs each.

If the sides bat at a constant rate, 100 runs in the last 20 overs grosses up to 225 for the whole innings; 80 in 20 overs is equivalent to a total of 180. On your ground, in your standard of cricket, which is more normal?

You can make an analysis of each of the clubs you play to build up a picture of their individual 'norm' against you in the past. It is your figure that matters, not mine, but I should be prepared to bet on the answer being nearer to 160 than 180, let alone 225. Do not forget, though, that it will change with the time of year.

There is one further problem. The rate of strike of the various bowlers at your disposal will be widely different. As an example, my own club's leading bowlers in one typical year was as follows:

	Overs/ Wicket	Wickets	Runs/ Wicket
A. Left-arm fast	3.7	48	8.8
B. Slow medium	4.7	12	9.9
C. Off-spin	4.4	33	10.1
D. Fast	5.3	11	11.8
E. Slow medium	3.6	24	12.0
F. Left-arm spin	4.5	69	13.6
G. Off-spin	4.0	47	15.6
H. Fast	5.3	18	16.6
I. Left-arm spin	5.8	37	16.6
J. Fast medium	7.8	17	23.0

Take note of the best two fast bowlers in the averages, A + D: 3.7 + 5.3 = 9 overs for 2 wickets. Similarly, the rate of the best two slow bowlers, B + C: 4.7 + 4.4 = 9.1 overs for 2 wickets.

Now consider the last 20 overs situation: A + D operating together will on average bowl 20 overs and take 4 wickets. Will they, though? One can assume that their striking rate is higher with the new ball than the old; and against batsmen concerned only with defence their striking rate must be lower still. So one could reasonably expect only 3 wickets from the pair in the last 20 overs.

B + C bowl their overs fast enough to get through 25 overs in the last hour, which gives them, on average, the chance of taking over 5 wickets. Given the situation of an attainable target and the batsmen therefore playing shots, my own experience of backing the fielding side to get 4 or 5 wickets for 80 is amply borne out. These are the optimum conditions in which the slow bowlers can operate.

Unfortunately, these figures are historical and are averaged, so they will not be the same next season or in the next match. None the less it is worth being aware that a standard half-day match innings is about 45 overs. The side fielding second has to take wickets at the rate of 1 : 4.5 overs in order to win. If bowlers B, D, H, I and J only on my list were used a win would be unlikely.

There is one other significant point that arises out of these mathematical musings. You will frequently reach a situation when, having had spinners on at both ends for the last 20 overs, nos. 10 and 11 are suddenly in together with 15 minutes and 4 or 5 overs to go. Should you now follow the precepts of the first-class game and bring back the fast men, to whom we always refer as the BHQs ('big, hairy quicks')?

Consider the following: in general, first-class wickets and first-class bowlers are quicker than their club counterparts. Bearing in mind the slowness of the wicket, accentuated by a soft, old ball, and the comparative slowness of your fast

'I always wanted to be captain but I didn't get A level maths'
WICKETS
RUNS

bowlers, are they really going to get through? And there is a further point; if you use your quick bowlers, according to the table above, you will manage to bowl only the 4 overs, not 5. If you persist with the slow ones you might even fit in 6 overs before the close.

Finally there is the attitude of the batsmen. Dedicated self-control is not the most notable attribute of tail-enders. They like making runs. They like hitting the ball. Once they have discovered how simple it is just to stop slow bowling on a slow pitch they soon gain confidence. It is not my experience that many of them can resist the temptation to help themselves to easy runs, and certainly not for 6 whole overs.

There is a strange corollary to this with the field-placing. In order to reinforce the tail-enders' aggressive frame of mind, do not necessarily pressure them with close fielders. If they have seen your slow bowlers hit around the park, and above all hit for a few sixes, you can encourage them to try and do the same. The odd thing is that you do this, not by having lots of close catchers, and, therefore, gaps in the deep field, since this disposition proclaims 'this is a good bowler' – no, you do it by setting your field for the 'slog'.

If, for an off-spinner, you have deep square-leg, deep mid-wicket and long-on, this advertises a poor bowler. If you also have the inner-ring mid-wicket and mid-on you have catchers exactly where the ball will be hit! The same applies to the left-arm spinner. The tail-end cowboy will try to slog him over mid-wicket, too. The one difference then is that the catch will probably go to short third man.

If you and your bowlers are going to pursue this line of thought, the bowling must be slow enough to allow the batsman plenty of time to wonder and, while the ball is in the air, to overcome his captain's instructions, revert to his natural inclination, and accept the proffered invitation.

The system also works best if one of the pair of spinners looks (or even actually is) better than the other. I have found the most pleasant combination to be the very slow off-spinner, harnessed with a standard left-arm spinner. The disparity in ability is further emphasised by slip, gulley, silly point and short extra for the latter. (None of these fielders is in danger: I do not believe in short square-leg for off-spinners in club cricket. If players in suits of armour are prepared to die for MCC and country that is their affair, and they are being paid for it!)

The net result of this particular combination is perfect. You get through the overs quickly. The ball is moving in opposite directions at each end, thereby threatening exposure of any technical shortcomings of the batsmen. One end is advertised as being very much easier than the other (which may, or may not, be true).

The problems presented at the difficult end are balanced by a lack of concentration at the easy end. There is a bonus in run-outs through either (a) a better player trying to shield a poorer player from the difficult end, or (b) every batsman trying to get down the easy end.

When a batsman gets out at the easy end you often see the next man in roll his sleeves up a little higher. The unspoken thought is clear enough: 'Bloody idiot, Harry. Let me show them.' Sometimes he will even fall down the pavilion steps in his eagerness!

You had only 15 minutes to spare when this situation started, so you have no time to change your mind. If you doubt whether it works, how about the following even tighter example?

One year against City of London College we declared at 240 for 7. Their bowling was not in the same class as ours over-all but, thanks to a superb innings by their skipper, Brian Capstick, they reached 235 for 8 with two overs to go. No. 10 faced our slow, slow off-spinner for the penultimate over. He scored 2 runs and was then caught off the fourth ball. Enter no. 11. Brian met him half-way from the pavilion. His instructions were obvious, 'Just play out the next two balls. I'll score the runs next over.'

My reading of the situation was exactly the same. Brian was 127 not out and going so well that I could see no way of stopping him. However, no. 11 played his first ball with deliberate ease. The thought crossed his mind that he could have hit it anywhere. The next ball was equally slow and inviting. It seemed ridiculous to waste such an obvious opportunity of winning the match, and the leg boundary was quite close. The only problem with that particular delivery was that it was on a length. It also happened to be straight. In the bar afterwards nobody believed that no. 11 could have been so stupid. More interestingly, nor did he.

One major pitfall arises out of the 20-overs-in-the-last-hour regulation. If you have spinners on at both ends, I assume you will get through your overs at the rate of 25 per hour. This is a useful bonus to remember when selecting the right bowlers to prise out the last couple of wickets. On the other hand, it can prove disastrous if you have a close contest. There you are, gaily doing your sums in terms of proportions of 20, and suddenly you find you have given the batting side a 25 per cent bonus. Very embarrassing.

Sometimes, of course, the technical ability of the batsman and the state of the wicket will put the odds heavily in his favour. In such circumstances one has to think farther than normal in the hope that the batsman can be persuaded to overreach himself. If the bowler cannot get him out, maybe he will manage it himself.

Here are some other thoughts, but without, as it happens, any definite conclusion.

We played a match on a good wicket in which our opponents, thanks to our respectable new-ball bowling and one hundred per cent catching, found themselves 40 for 5 after an hour's play. The next man in made a fierce drive at a half-volley first ball and was dropped at slip. The next ball he slogged hard at mid-on and was let off again. He looked a real flashy rabbit. However, within a few overs he settled down and then made a beautiful century with shots through a wide arc. Clearly he was a player of no mean ability.

The next time we came across him he was playing as a guest for another club. We had been bowled out for only 140 on a two-paced wicket which dried out easier and easier as the day went on. Our opponents ground on very stolidly with their limited batting line-up, after losing a wicket in the first over. Nos. 2 and 4 made 40 each before they were both out at 90. Enter our hero and another wicket fell before he had faced: 90 for 4. There was suddenly tension in the air and a feeling that we could win after all, provided we could dispose of him. With an old ball and a flat wicket and little room to manoeuvre, how to do it?

Having watched him before, I saw him as arrogant, impetuous, and clearly looking to win the match in a flurry of sumptuous strokes and a blaze of glory. But, being a guest player, he was not quite as concerned with beating us as the rest of his side. Temperamentally he seemed hardly the man to do a safe, solid, steady job.

I saw two ways of attacking him, which might even be interlocked. The first that struck me was simply to keep him away from the strike and try to bowl out the others. But with few runs to play with he could still be lethal if we slipped up even for one over. My second thought was to put pressure on him with a suicide squad close enough for him to take his eye and mind off the ball.

Then the two lines merged: if we could deny him the strike for a few overs and then use the suicide squad, the mental challenge would be even greater. The only question, then, would be whether one of our bowlers could serve up a nice, juicy yorker early enough to complete the job.

Sadly, neither you nor I will ever know whether the plan would have worked. Our captain that day had never seen the fellow before, so he could not possibly have been thinking along these lines. No matter: positive, imaginative thinking is more important to the side than winning every single match. Brain power is more important than ability.

There are, finally, three other techniques, or gambits, that should be mentioned:

1. *Opening the bowling with a spinner.* One sees from time to time the tactic of opening the bowling with a spinner from one end. This is a valid gambit, but has flaws of which one should be aware. Fair enough, opening batsmen would mostly prefer to start off against a seamer, especially with an old ball, but the spinner should not be left on for very long. Not only do his fingers get tired, but it is more important that he should be at his best later. Also it spoils the shape of the innings in that you may be left with the problem of having to give away runs when using a seamer; technically quite easy, as we have seen, but the batsmen will probably think you are being defensive when that is the last impression you wish to give. Nor will the bowler like it!

In Chapter 3, on Key Objectives, I described a match which we lost when we used only four of our seven bowlers. One of our youthful captain's problems then was that, on a slow turner of a wicket, he had opened with an off-spinner at one end. This induced tangled thinking with repercussions that filtered on into the rest of the tour, affecting the captain's self-confidence and that of the spinner. The tragedy was that he had almost got it right. What occurred is worth studying further.

The correct part was his thought: 'slow turner, therefore use the spinners'. However, by opening with a spinner he denied a goodish swing bowler a spell with the new ball, which might well have yielded a wicket (the seam bowler at the other end took 2).

Then, the spinner he chose liked to see the ball turn, which it did. So he pushed it through and inevitably bowled a fraction short all the time. It looked good, but did not achieve anything: he operated throughout but took only two wickets. As a rider to this, of course, the opposing batsmen all had a good look at him before they had to face him, and when we came towards the tail he was tired.

In the middle of their innings our young captain, who had started fielding at mid-off, found himself going deeper and deeper, at both ends, eventually arriving on the boundary. As the fielders drifted slightly out of position, as fielders always will, there were easy runs to be had, because he could no longer see the angles and gaps. This was exploited to the full by the limited batsman mentioned on page 92.

Thus, when the crunch came, although he had on a slow left-armer who collected 4 wickets in his 6 overs (the last of the match) the skipper no longer had the confidence to put on slow, instead of flat, spin at both ends. Nor was he able to exercise the control to have both run-savers or catchers in the right places. He thought their free scoring was due to bad bowling, when it was entirely caused by inept field-placing.

This was exemplified, not only by the 'wide mid-on player' but by the treatment meted out to the slow left-armer. First, he was walloped through mid-wicket, exactly down the line where that fielder should normally be. In this case he was almost at square-leg, instead of in line with the bowler's stumps: four runs each time instead of none.

Then, long-off was on the boundary by the sight-screen even though the bowler had been scooped a couple of times over extra cover. It was only after an old pro had felt compelled to interfere that long-off was moved to deep extra with immediate effect. On a slow turner the easy shot is over extra cover. It is difficult to play the ball to long-off when it is turning.

You can readily see how the worms of doubt and lack of confidence eat their way into ensuing matches after an innings like this.

2. *Manipulating the strike.* The tactic of trying to keep the better player away from the strike has uses apart from the usual ones, i.e., to slow down the scoring rate and increase the chance of disposing of the weaker player.

Almost every match produces certain moments when the fielding side would rather bowl at one batsman in a partnership rather than the other. Most of the time the preference is marginal and the importance of achieving that preference insignificant. The relative abilities of the incumbents and the state of the match are of course the principal factors; they can be self-balancing or both work in the same direction.

In one match we had made about 230 and then immediately removed two of our opponents' best batsmen for single figures. No. 3 made 150 and we won by 20 runs. It was crucial to our chance of success that he had plenty of the strike in order to keep the target within reach. Many times in mid-innings it happens that one batsman is going well, say 40 or 60 not out, and there is a new player at the other end. Clearly it is preferable to bowl at the new batsman. The object is not just to get him out, but also to frustrate the other into an indiscretion by upsetting his rhythm and tempo; still more, to take advantage of an opportunity to stem a brisk flow of runs so that the batting side's strong position degenerates.

In these circumstances there is clearly a requirement for plenty of close catchers, but also for a strong saving-one cordon to prevent any worthwhile contribution from the new batsman before he develops any fluency. Against the established player a strong saving-four cordon is vital, but it is more effective not to make the strike manipulation too obvious. Part of the object is to make the established player annoyed with his partner for not giving him the strike.

This is a completely different ploy from the end-of-the-match situation when you are winkling out the last few batsmen, but one established player is in the way. For one of two things has happened: either both the batsmen initiate the tactics by trying hard to protect the tail-ender, or the fielding side wants them to do that, as a means of taking their minds off dedicated defence. Either way the fielding captain can be suitably flamboyant in dictating to the batsmen the game he wishes them to play.

The trouble is that (a) it is extremely tiring on the fielders; (b) the bowlers press too hard when they get the 'rabbit' in their sights; and (c) you, the captain, get so distracted with working the ploy that you forget to keep trying to get both of the batsmen out.

You must not therefore do it for very long. You must change the bowling type to keep control: the edged squeeze for one to short third man off a medium-pacer will simply not be possible when a left-arm spinner comes on.

Never lose sight of the twin objectives: wickets and control. With these in mind, the techniques are simple enough. If the better player is facing, you try to deny him a single at the end of the over, thus exposing the tail-ender for the next one. If the better player is facing at the start of an over you try to deny him fours or twos while attacking him if you can. On the other hand, if the poor player is facing at the start of an over, then clearly you attack him as much as possible, but try also to deny him the chance of a single.

The batsmen, of course, will attempt to wrest control for themselves, as follows:

First, apart from the absolute no-hopers, it is well within the capabilities of many tail-enders to play two balls per over (knowing the pressure is on the bowler), thereby allowing the better player to take a single off the fourth ball of the over without trouble.

Second, as the pair develops confidence, the better player can look for fours at the end of the over, when the field is in. Tail-enders fail, more often than otherwise, because of lack of concentration, determination, discipline and confidence. Strike manipulation develops a strong bond between the batsmen: the better player provides the poorer with these talents.

Third, the better player should try to upset the field-placing, in particular to remove close catchers. Slip fielders do not catch so well when they have run down to third man and back a few times.

Fourth, the pair should, as soon as possible, take every run offered: the bowlers hate it. And fifth, the ultimate achievement is for the tail-ender, faced with the bowling at the start of an over, to score runs and escape.

The most remarkable demonstration of how not to conduct this ploy was given by Bob Willis at Melbourne in 1982. (Nothing against Willis: fast bowlers seldom make good captains. The bowler needs to be consumed by an unquenchable fire of controlled fury; the captain should be as ice-cold and calculating as a chess grandmaster.)

England allowed Border and Thomson to put on 70 runs for the last wicket, when they needed 73 runs for victory; and England only just scraped home. The key to this situation is to attack *both* batsmen, but in different ways. Border was hardly attacked at all: he even faced the second new ball without a single close catcher! The far-flung field allowed twos to be run. No change from pace to spin was tried to break the pattern. The batsmen were allowed to take control when, at the start of the partnership, they should have been simply screwed into the ground and destroyed. But all credit to them.

3. *Use of intervals.* I have mentioned that the tea interval is a great change bowler. It does not always take a wicket, of course, but just before an interval (lunch as well, or even at close of play in a two- or three-day match) the batsmen tend to shut up shop for a few overs out of deference to the next man in. This takes the pressure off the fielding side, so make use of it. If they are not going to attack you, you attack them.

If you have good bowlers on, then really cluster the fieldsmen around the batsman and put the pressure on him. There is an alternative strategy. I do not always carry it out, but I have it in my mind that an interval provides a good opportunity to use one's less good bowlers for a few overs, without their being hit all over the ground. While batsmen tend to be less aggressive just before an interval, so also, immediately afterwards, they will usually take a little care before getting back into their stride; and by then the better bowlers will be on again. So it is often wise not to change the bowling immediately for the restart. And the less good bowler does often take a wicket; why?

For the lesser bowler you cannot cluster the fieldsmen around the bat; even so the batsman is often still primarily

'I think hes appealing for the light'

Cluster around the batsman . . .

concerned with defence. Looser bowling may make him change his mind and half-hearted shots tend to be fatal. As an extreme example, a slow chest-high full toss last ball before lunch comes as a bit of a surprise. Providing it is straight it is very difficult to hit it downwards.

The other side of the coin is that your own batsmen should only be 'playing for lunch' if they are being put under pressure. The fielding side is at its most vulnerable after two hours in the field, so your batsmen should be taking every opportunity to cash in if the bowling is less than good. When all is said and done, however, if they do get out in those circumstances it does not greatly matter. The new batsman will admittedly have to start his innings twice in quick succession, but he will be also under less pressure, because he is facing a less good bowler, at least before the interval.

10

Running the side in the field – fielding first

There are very few problems about fielding first, although there are several pitfalls. The one golden rule is: always bowl your opponents out for as few runs as possible. This means *never* letting them off the hook when they are, for example, 20 for 5. *Never* relax when the last pair is together and *never* let them add those precious extra runs so that they feel they have just enough to bowl at.

This sounds simple and obvious: but the problem is essentially psychological. On a fine day and on a benign wicket your batsmen are looking for a chance to play a long innings. Your side has all been looking forward to a good close match, not a 10-wicket victory at tea-time. You also have three other bowlers itching to perform. But if you give in to these thoughts, you will lose only one such game in your career. Thereafter you will just work out better systems for beer matches!

The techniques of fielding first, or batting second, involve, initially, attack without giving away runs. So your fast bowler can have a long-leg if that makes him happier, and a third man as soon as runs start coming. If the opponents do get off to a good start, change to defence with just two or three close catchers and, most of all, keep changing the bowling, one end at a time, to set the batsmen constant new problems. Do not lose heart. We have all seen games where 120 for 2 at lunch has dissolved into 150 all out.

However, if you do lose the initiative, put the pressure back on as soon as you get the chance. I well remember one match where the opposition took 40 runs off the first 4 overs of the day. Our captain rightly put out a long-leg, a third man and extra cover. One run-out and one hat trick later they were 50 for 4, with a real 'rabbit' in at no. 6. Yet we still had cover, extra, mid-off, mid-on and mid-wicket as well as long-leg and third man! We could have had four close catchers at least without giving away any easy runs.

The one real problem in fielding first is to recognise when you have reached the point at which you are unlikely to bowl them out and are going to be faced with a declaration. Most captains do not then change to all-out defence – the limited-over field. How many times have you seen a declaration made with two slips and a gulley still posted?

But if you are half-hearted at that stage it becomes very difficult to keep the fielders keen and interested. All-out defence reveals your tactics clearly. It will mean that you spend a few minutes longer fielding, but the smaller the total you are chasing, and the shorter the time, the better. This is the obverse of your own declaration policy. If they do not leave themselves time to bowl you out then only you can win; a pleasant position to be in when you have been losing all the time until then.

A final thought: when your fast bowlers have won you the match with the new ball and your batsmen have not needed to play long innings, remind them in the bar afterwards of the parts they have to play. There will be other days. For one of the constant pressures on a club captain is this conflict between the simultaneous desires of winning and at the same time of getting as many players as possible into the game.

Although the prime requirement when fielding first is to bowl the opposition out for the lowest possible score as quickly as can be, there are temptations. Hence the pitfalls.

In one match, some sound but not exceptional opening bowling and a couple of slack shots found our opponents 36 for 4 on a good wicket after 18 overs. They were a strong side, at that time top of the Sussex league.

A bowling change at one end (to slow-medium, left-arm in-swing) brought another wicket quickly: 49 for 5. Then came a crucial mistake. The bowling was changed at the other end as well and various negative factors began to operate:

(a) the opening bowler was still going well;
(b) the new batsman was left-handed; and
(c) the new, fourth, bowler was a left-arm spinner.

In this instance there was no justification for taking off the opener, other than to give another bowler a turn. We all knew that left-handed batsmen tended to deal better with the left-arm swinger in question. His chief virtue was a very tight in-swing line that kept the right-handers 'tucked-up'. Since he was slowish, left-handed batsmen had room to bang him through or over the off-side whenever he drifted outside the off stump. Knowing this, the alternatives were to change the bowling again or set a defensive field. As it was we persevered with a 6/3 field: slip, gulley and a line of four saving the single.

The point is that, when a batting side is in trouble, it is vital to keep up the pressure on them. This bowler did not do enough to justify the gulley, so one slip, a line of 4 and deep extra cover – or even 7/2 with long-off as well and a tighter line of covers – would have offered a better field.

Similarly with the left-arm spinner; if he does not drop it on the spot immediately he should come off, and in any case the same double-ring tactics should be employed. Ours did not bowl a length, did not have a double ring, and bowled 10 overs.

Again left-arm spinners have a lot of latitude when bowling to right-handers. So long as they put it up on the off stump or outside they tend not to get hammered. To left-handers they have to bowl *at* the off stump, a tighter discipline.

Thus a series of small mistakes, all born of equivocal thinking, allowed a partnership of 33: 82 for 6. No. 8 did not offer: 94 for 7.

No. 9 had a violent swing whenever possible and he was allowed to get away with it: so the innings ended at 171 for 8 declared.

The match was lost long before the final partnership; for once sloppy thinking creeps in, the edge goes off everyone's concentration and it is difficult, mentally, to get back on top and in control. This continued to show when we batted; they bowled straight and well pitched up. We played a series of aimless shots and missed, got into a hole and no longer possessed the application to climb out and force a draw.

The result of the match hinged not on the ability of the players, but on the mental approach and attitudes of the two sides. One has to think clearly about one's objectives and create a unified sense of purpose to win. It is hard work.

In another instance, we fielded first on a really beautiful

wicket against a good strong batting side. The opening bowlers used the new ball splendidly and took the first 4 wickets for 30 in the first hour. Once the shine was off we took only one more wicket and they declared around the 200 mark (half-day match; one new ball for the match). It took only one good innings on our side for us to cruise home with plenty of time to spare.

We won because our opening bowlers did so well for the first hour. Thereafter we bowled a couple of overs of spin just to see if anything unexpected would happen. When it did not, we just plugged away with our three seam-up bowlers, keeping everything as tight as possible until the declaration.

Not very exciting, perhaps, but a good team effort. First, it was a fine response by the fast bowlers who, instead of having, say, half a dozen overs each when we fielded second, bowled seventeen overs apiece and won us the match. Second, the other seamer, with no real prospect of taking a wicket, played a vital role by keeping the batsmen on a tight rein when they were looking to break out of our stranglehold and make up for the slow rate at the start. We could not have won without him. Third, we were obviously going to spend a long hot day in the field and it would have been very easy for the fielders to get tired and lose concentration towards the end of their stint. The last half-hour of the innings, with wickets in hand, would have been just the time for the batsmen to clock up another 60 or so vital runs. Disciplined, dedicated fielding stopped them.

In the final analysis we won not by bowling them out, but because we slowed their rate of scoring so much (by taking early wickets, i.e., by offensive, not defensive, methods) that even though they declared 15 minutes after half-time, the total was well within our reach. In considering the timing of their declaration, they were of course on the spot. Had they gone on any longer they would have had no chance of winning as they simply would not have had time to bowl us out.

In fact I do not believe they knew they were on to a hiding when they declared. In my time I have done exactly the same and been beaten by 8 or 9 wickets. My point here is that the seam bowlers *won* us the match. It always appears that the batsmen who make 70 or 80 not out did so. Yet the space for them to knock off the runs was created by a fine performance with the new ball.

Look in the score-book. The bowlers' analyses read 2 for 60, 2 for 70, 1 for 40 and the spinner 0 for 15. Those do not appear to be match-winning performances, do they? But they were.

11

Field-placing, fielding, and the 'Big A'

Field-placing is built up of three essentials. These comprise: a basic framework, the bone structure as it were; then comes the more flexible portion, the muscles and fibres; finally there is a cosmetic element, an intellectual skin.

The basic bone structure is founded upon the premise that, in order to hit the stumps, any bowler must pitch the ball fairly well up to the batsman and bowl straight. If a bowler does that consistently then the ball has to be played straight or in the general direction of mid-on and mid-off. Of course, some deliveries will not hit the middle of the bat and will fly off the edge towards third man or long-leg. Similarly, the batsmen will not hit every ball straight and hard, so two more fielders are needed to stop him taking a single by just pushing forward instead: extra cover and mid-wicket. Thus in a perfect world, and to save runs, one could manage adequately with six fielders plus bowler and wicket-keeper. I call this the 'Big A' (see diagram 1). This is because it is the shape of the pattern of the field-placing, with the 'cross bar' of the A at the bowler's stumps. What, then, should we do with the other three fielders?

Three things tend to happen. First, bowlers, being human, do not always bowl a perfect length or line. Second, batsmen develop shots other than the straight drive. Third, to make life more complicated, bowlers produce lateral movement, swing and spin. These factors one can regard as the musculature firmly joined to the bone structure. This flexibility also takes account of the variations in pace, both of pitch and bowler.

Study the same essentials from the batsman's point of view.

If you speak to any good player he will tell you that his method is to play all the straight balls straight, into the 'V' between mid-on and mid-off – the 'V' which is the mirror

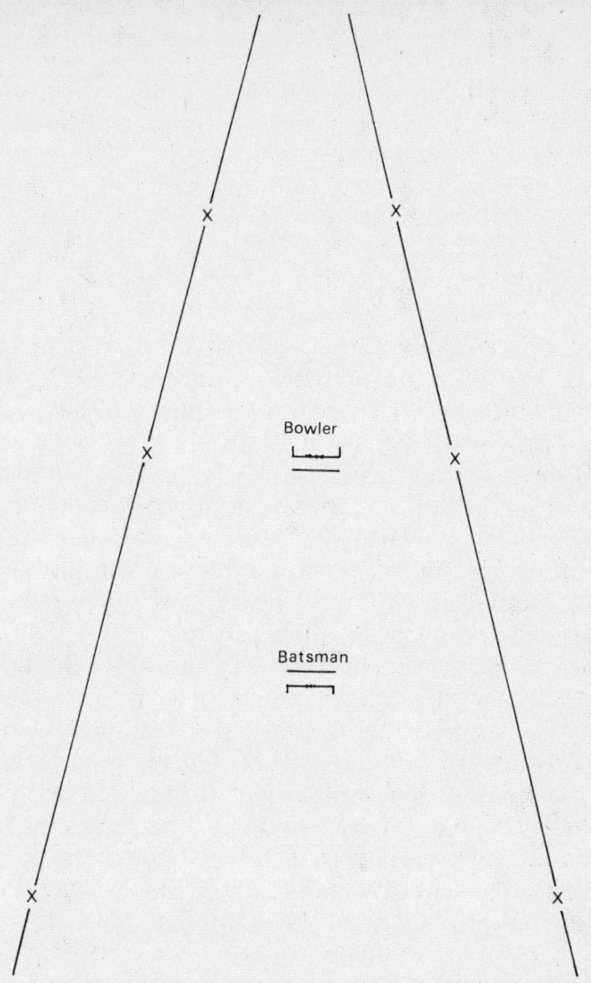

Diagram 1 – The 'Big A'

image of the 'Big A'. Gradually, as he grows more confident and the ball moves less, he widens the arc to take in mid-wicket and extra cover.

Any ball on his legs he will work away in complete safety, helped by both the lbw Law and the limitations on leg-side fielders behind square-leg. Around off stump, however, things are different. He can be caught in the slips or lbw. So he has to treat anything pitched fairly well up with some respect. Short balls outside the off stump, on the other hand, he can hammer away off the back foot.

So pitch the ball well up at off stump, day in day out, and the bowler must be in business. Strokes played into the 'V' are countered by the 'Big A'.

Alternatively, watch Broad, Tim Robinson, Athey, Gatting or Viv Richards, or even Metcalfe and Hick. Look at the photographs of Bradman and Boycott scoring the hundredth run of their hundredth hundred. What these good batsmen have to teach us is that line is much more important than length. This is vital to understand because you will constantly see improbable shots played, so the ball goes off in unexpected directions. Just as significantly, you will see batsmen aiming rustic blows to distant parts of the field without making contact. What you then need to know is whether the bowler is bowling well or badly. Is the batsman taking a chance out of frustration or is he merely dealing justly with rubbish? Is that huge desperate heave exactly what you were hoping for or is it a terrifying prospect?

It all depends on line. This is why bowlers like Dennis Lillee and Richard Hadlee are a constant torment. They vary their pace, they move the ball a little either way in the air, they consistently hit the seam and they probe ceaselessly at off stump. No relief, no escape.

A straight full toss will take a wicket if it is missed, so it still has to be played with a degree of care. A ball that is off line can be hit or missed with equal safety. The worst of sins is bowling that is off length *and* off line. You cannot set a field for it since, wherever you put the fielders, the batsman can pick a spot between them. So do not try: change the bowling.

Frank Booth used to relate how the first time he played for Lancashire was against Middlesex at Lord's in 1927. Lancashire were a bowler short and, after the captain, Major L. Green, had lost the toss, another bowler pulled a hamstring in the first half-hour of the match. At about one o'clock Frank bowled a long hop.

'Another one of those and you're off,' said the skipper. There was no one else to bowl, but at about 5.30, having kept going all day, Frank let another ball slip.

'Enough of that rubbish. I could do better myself.' Frank

duly came off, and he was not asked to perform again, not even in the second innings. He played in the next match but did not get on to bowl then either! A hard school.

Once you know about your bowlers you know about the batsmen. You can answer the perpetual question: 'Was that a great shot or a risky one?' Then you can safely post fielders to block a batsman's favourite shots without unduly disturbing the basic pattern.

Batsmen, as I have already commented, reveal much about themselves before they have played a single shot. Extreme examples are, of course, the tall man holding his long handle right at the top who is likely to be a strong driver, and conversely, the short fellow with his open stance and hands low down, and top hand behind the handle. It costs you nothing to push mid-on and mid-off back for the former or pull them in and square up third man and long-leg for the latter, denying them the chance of a confidence-building 4 early on. Similarly if you can deny an excitable West Indian, for example, any singles to get him off the mark, he might well attempt something flamboyant 'over the top' before he is set.

Good players are able to drive strongly into the 'V'. Poor players cannot. Therefore at the start of an innings, when you need have only two men in the covers, mid-off can be closer and squarer, virtually at extra cover. The same goes for mid-on. There are thus no easy singles to be collected by pushing the ball squarer either side of the wicket and you will find precious few players who can exploit the gap between mid-on and mid-off. Remember, though, one snag. There is now nobody backing up behind the bowler's stumps should cover or square leg shy at that end. Mid-on and mid-off have to work harder.

Most batsmen tend to play their favourite shots first. If you adjust the field on to the lines each batsman goes for at the start of his innings, you can be reasonably sure that he is going to be forced thereafter into playing the shots he finds less easy. Since most club batsmen have only a small range of shots, bottle those up and they have little left to offer. The danger in this is that you might find yourself following the ball about, putting fielders 'where that one went' after every shot. The golden rule, as always, is to think about what you are doing and why.

For example, a new batsman goes for the sweep early on, and misses. You had a square-leg on the boundary. The likelihood is that (a) the batsman likes the shot and will play it again; (b) since he was late on it last time, he will still hit it fine (i.e. latish) when he does connect because (c) the square shot is more difficult anyhow. So move square-leg round to 45°, or even finer, then leave him. Do not compromise by leaving him just a little bit finer than he was originally; he will still be wrong. Nor should you move him back squarer if the ball is swept there instead of fine; the batsman is obviously then placing the shot and will put the next one finer again. Result: he is setting the field (as he is trying to do) instead of you.

Notice one other point from this example: the fielder was moved *before* the batsman connected with the ball. Hundreds of times you see shots aimed and miscued or just plain missed. Almost as many times you see the whole episode ignored. OK, so it might have gone anywhere. Never mind: have a stab at it, you can only win. (Do not forget, though, that the edged shot would have gone in the opposite direction to one from the middle of the bat: the 'whang' to mid-wicket could be caught at short third man.) What if you get it wrong, as you will sometimes if you are trying? Just laugh, apologise loudly to all concerned, and go back to where you started.

Bradman says that he tried sometimes to play his *least* favourite shots first, so as to deceive. I suppose, then, you deliberately do not set the field where he is hitting the ball, but it becomes complicated after that. Bowling against Bradman usually was!

So far we are assuming that all bowling, as well as being pitched well up, is straight. It never is! This may come as a surprise, but, quite apart from swing or spin, a ball delivered right-arm over-the-wicket would bounce back off an imaginary wall at the batsman's stumps towards the leg side. Delivered from left-arm round-the-wicket the angle of rebound would be even greater. This reveals interesting developments in relation to swing or spin.

The classic angles are: right-arm over-the-wicket, outswing; left-arm over, in-swing; and their spin counterparts right-arm off-spin, round the wicket; and left-arm round, turning from leg to off. The greatest joy of all is leg-spin, right-arm over-the-wicket. These methods all depend on the ball's starting at an angle across the wicket and then moving to straight. They impose, therefore, the greatest discipline on the batsman.

This is because once the ball has swung or spun to straight it has to be played straight, almost regardless of length. It is difficult and dangerous to work it away to one side of the wicket or the other.

Having said that, of course, one thinks immediately of Les Jackson, of Derbyshire, who used to bowl from very, very close to the stumps, thereby delivering the ball almost from middle stump to middle stump and then cutting it off the wicket. Not much room for batsman's errors there, either!

Similarly the off-spinners John Emburey and Ray Illingworth bowl from very close to the stumps, bowling at 'all three'. Hence, too, Fred Trueman's constant plea for the bowler to get in close to the stumps: apart from increased lbw chances, the ball has only to move half a bat's width. The reason is that off-spin and in-swing delivered over-the-wicket merely accentuate the natural angle and really have to pitch outside the off stump in order to hit the wicket.

While it is not difficult to work out the general directions in which each type of bowling is most likely to be hit, constant alertness is needed to relate to what happens in practice. Let me give a couple of examples.

A left-arm bowler is swinging the ball back into the batsman from over-the-wicket: he can either be bowling a very tight line so that all the runs are having to be pushed square-ish on the leg side from around the leg stump; on the other hand, if, when the ball stops swinging, he lets his line stray outside the off stump, he presents the batsman with free hits in directions where fielders were not even needed before.

Again, there is often a fascinating problem with the left-arm spinner. He ought to be hit with the spin into the well-packed covers, but frequently he will be up against club batsmen who attempt to mow him to leg. Depending on the success of this tactic, captain and bowler will have to decide whether or not to move fielders from off to leg. If they do this, it is no good if the bowler continues to bowl the off-side line and is hit through the resulting gaps there.

You need to be acutely aware of the position of release of the ball for all of your bowlers. Not only how much they swing it or spin it, but whether they bowl from the return crease or near the stumps. You will find that, because of these differences, the field has to be varied surprisingly between two bowlers of the same basic type.

I have captained two very different types of left-arm spinners. One used to deliver all the time with his front foot close to his stumps to outside off stump and was consistently played on the offside. The leg hits off him always went in the air to somewhere between a straight mid-wicket and wide long-on. The other bowled with his front foot outside the return crease with the result that he was almost never hit square on the off side but usually needed five fielders on the leg side. The men on either side of the umpire had plenty of work to do, whereas there were no fielders there at all for the close-to-the-stumps bowler. Yet they were both classed as 'left-arm round'.

It hardly needs adding that the various speeds of bowlers and wickets will modify these angles. It is often overlooked, however, that a left-handed batsman has the same effect. Often one sees slips and short legs relatively out of position because of the change in angle.

If we relate the effects of the angles of swing or spin now to the limitations of individual batsmen we should be well on the way to complete control of the majority of club batsmen. There are three factors to be considered:

1. the arcs in which that particular bowler should be hit;
2. the strongest shots in the range of the individual batsman; and
3. the selection of the most appropriate bowlers (though this is also influenced by the state of the match and the wicket).

Finally, do not hesitate to adjust the field for each batsman. And never settle for half measures, any more than you would if one of the batsmen was a left-hander; compromise is not control.

For example, in one match I had a right-arm, medium-pacer bowling to a left-hander with the old ball. I wanted only two men in front of the wicket on the off side because of the state of the match. A left-handed batsman tends to strike the ball squarer on the off side than does a right-hander, because of the difference in angle. (The same applies with a left-arm bowler to a right-handed batsman.) Therefore, I positioned a cover point and an extra cover instead of a mid-off.

However, I had not allowed for the stiffish breeze blowing from the direction of third man, which caused the ball to swing in. This made the extra-cover drive a more dangerous shot, but the straight drive that much easier. When the bowler was twice driven through mid-off, I moved extra cover there instead.

This was a small incident, but it shows the thought processes involved. First, the field was set according to my experience of that particular bowler, that type of batsman and the state of the match. Second, the field was changed according to what was actually happening.

Third, it is important to realise that other alternatives were open. I could have taken out one of the close catchers and put in a mid-off as well as extra cover. I could have taken the bowler off because he was bowling badly. But I did not consider he was bowling badly, and I needed the close catchers to take wickets for me.

The justification of my action would have been for the left-hander to have been bowled off the inside edge trying to drive through the resulting extra-cover gap. But what actually happened was that he was immediately out the other end! As it turned out, that was useful as well; we had two slips and two gulleys on a slowish wicket which was taking a little 'cut' from time to time. First he had steered a ball between second slip and first gulley; then he missed a dab shot aimed in the same direction. So I moved the squarer gulley to the other side of the finer one and at once he took a brilliant catch above his head. It does not often work as simply as that, however!

We should also consider the subject of angles from the batsman's point of view. The following diagram (see next page) shows how important are the straight edges of the 'Big A' in relation to the size of the gaps between fielders.

Since we wish to encourage our bowlers to bowl straight, to pitch the ball up and be hit straight or perish, consider the difference between the two halves of this diagram. The two halves are not, however, off side and leg side, but simply geometric illustrations which apply to both sides, left- or right-hand batsmen, left- or right-arm bowlers.

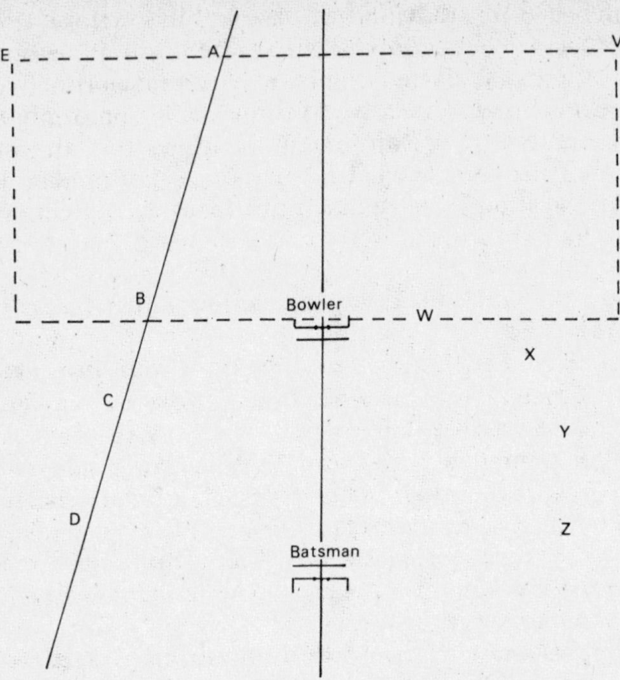

Diagram 2 – Fielding angles from the batsman's viewpoint

First, the ABC half: A is well back, with B able to cut off the pushed single towards A. In addition the bowler, if he is delivering from the same side of the wicket, acts as a further short-single fielder in the same arc. At the moment of impact, A–D is a straight line.

Compare this with the WXYZ half where W has come in much closer and W–Z is a semicircle. It is now easier to hit a ball between W and X than between A and B. It is also easier to push a single between W and X because W is in X's way, preventing a throw at the bowler's stumps. X and Y have billowed out a yard or so compared to B and C, while Z is closer to the bat than D.

If we now look at the dotted rectangle, A is covering most of the ground that E cannot reach, whereas the drive over W's head is perfectly safe. Any mishit in the A–E area is bound to be caught.

All these problems have arisen on the WXYZ side of the

diagram because of one fault: W has crept in too close, thereby forcing X and Y out of position. In fact the situation is worse than that. Because the batsmen can drive the overpitched ball successfully through or over W, the bowler naturally stops pitching the ball so far up, and thus invites the cut and the pull. This can have serious repercusssions. Not only has it possibly lost the present match, but that bowler will go into the next match with a lack of confidence arising from the feeling that he has been bowling badly. He may well have done, but the fault was his captain's for failing to set his field properly.

There were two instances when the captain of our side made this mistake. In the first we were playing on a ground with a very short boundary on one side. Cover and extra were placed on the boundary – only a few yards deeper than normal, but too deep to save the single. The result was that the bowler felt he was off target, giving away singles every time he pitched well up. So he bowled short and was hit square. On a ground of this shape, of course, it is more vital than ever for the bowlers to be played straight.

On the second occasion our young captain, a marvellous fielder, was at mid-off with the field set correctly. His problem arose because extra cover was not very mobile. The batsmen then started taking pushed singles towards mid-off, who naturally came closer and closer in to save them, only to have two successive fours then hit past him just out of his reach. Of course, the captain ought to have gone to extra cover and the slow mover to mid-off. Extra cover could then have cut off the firm straight push, while mid-off would still have been deep enough to stop the fours.

In passing, it is worth nothing that the short straight boundary presents very few problems. Mid-on and mid-off can go back on the edge, mid-wicket or deep extra will tend to be straighter than normal. The batsmen will be looking to hit over the field bowler's head and there will be no empty spaces in which the mishit can evade the fieldsmen.

The easiest way of noticing gaps in the field, of seeing that the angles are as tight as possible, and that the 'saving-one' fielders are at the right depth, is to look at it as nearly as possible from the batsman's position. Where then should the captain field?

The major influence must be the individual captain's personal skills and preference. He has enough to do without having to worry about his own ability to field adequately in his chosen spot. Confidence here goes hand in hand with confidence in handling the rest of the side. So field where you are happiest to field.

There is a tradition among schoolboys that the captain should field at mid-off so that he can talk to his bowlers. Personally I do not agree with this; the bowler has enough to concentrate on without you butting in after every ball. Plenty of time for a quick word between overs or when wickets fall, or during the intervals and even after the game.

Of one thing I am certain, however; it is impossible to control the game from the boundary. As part of the 'Big A' (and the left half of diag. 2 on page 122), mid-off is apt to find himself there from time to time, like it or not. Moreover, it will be apt to occur simultaneously at both ends. Wearing yourself out running from end to end of the ground is not the best preconditioning for cool, calm and collected control.

At the age of 13, I received the biggest 'rocket' of my life, bellowed across a dozen other games, for allowing myself to end up in just that situation. It still rankles! If you are on the boundary, the bowler inevitably takes over as captain and you end up with a sort of *ad hoc* committee. You should be in control. You set the field. If a bowler wants a fielder moved, he asks you, he does not do it himself. If you do not agree, you say so. Argue about it afterwards by all means, but it is you who carry the can or the kudos for losing or winning, not he.

All in all, if possible, I favour the close-catching positions for captains. There are several other advantages. The fielders are all looking at the batsman. Therefore, since they will be looking in your general direction, too, it is comparatively easy to move them about silently, with just a gesture. You are also easily able to consult your wicket-keeper as to how much the ball is moving in the air or off the pitch, or where did the batsman fetch that one from which went over mid-wicket? His line of view can be vital. Finally, the batsman should be aware of you controlling the match, dominating him. Anyone who has watched Brian Close at work, or worse, played against him, can subscribe to the power of that particular influence.

The captain's position on the field is not the only one to

consider. It is equally important to use everyone to the maximum advantage or minimum disadvantage.

Since you want and expect the ball to be hit to particular positions for particular bowlers, one or two of these positions are vital. Whatever else you do, make sure that those are filled by the appropriate experts. First slip and cover point are normally regarded as specialist positions; but consider also extra cover to the off-spinner. A grandfather there can make it impossible for the spinner to bowl at all, whereas a good man can virtually win you the match. The difference is that great. Consider mid-wicket, too: a man on the fence who is confident of catching anything within his orbit which does not carry for six, will probably be happy to run from end to end of the ground between overs (at least for a while) rather than see a gobbler go begging. Make full use of the men who know they are good in certain positions. They will repay your open faith by giving you one-hundred-per-cent effort. Bill Athey virtually won the various one-day series for England in Australia during the 1986–87 season by making mid-wicket a no-go area for batsmen: a perfect example of this concept.

I might add that you will, with luck, come across one or two bowlers who expect to do enough with the ball to make every fieldsman vital. Alec Bedser was once reputedly asked his advice by a small boy who was having trouble getting any wickets at all.

'What field do *you* have, sir?' asked the youngster.

'I have four short legs one side, three slips and a gulley the other. If it swings in, he's caught in the short legs. If it goes the other way he's caught in the slips. Anything that goes straight on just knocks all three down.'

The opposite to this splendid notion will be encountered in every single match. I started this chapter by blithely suggesting, in the 'Big A', that one could set an adequate field with six men plus bowler and wicket-keeper. Let us hope you never find yourself in quite such straits. On the other hand, you will often have three men who offer very little in the field. What can you best do with them?

In the first place, clearly, you must hide them; but you can also use them for extra garnish. For example, if we return to the ideas of likely arcs and vital positions, the largely decorative positions become clear for the different styles of attack:

In-swing:	cover point; third man
Out-swing:	mid-on; mid-wicket; long-leg
Off-spin:	short third man; cover point (!); backward of square on the leg side, saving one
Left-arm spin:	mid-wicket; behind on the leg side, saving one; also, very often and oddly enough, cover point.

There are, however, more sophisticated uses of the spare men, the most common of which is when you have batted first on a slowish wicket and declared, and are using only one new ball for the match.

Whenever you place a long-leg and a third man for the opening overs, it gives the batting side an impression of defensiveness on your part which you want to avoid. Since the ball now is unlikely to move about, the slips are equally unlikely to be called upon to catch anything; but they do give a sense of attack. Hide your buffoons there for a while; if a ball strikes one of them, someone else may even catch the rebound; at worst 4 runs will be saved.

When you are anxious for the opposition to keep their score ticking along without making it too obvious, a poor fielder in a vital position can work wonders for you. (But do tell the long-suffering bowler what you are doing!)

Also make use of any left-handers in the field. They are often especially good at mid-wicket, or in the covers for left-handed batsmen, where they can pick up and throw at the bowler's end much better than can a right-hander.

My first lesson on garnish, which could well have utilised several non-fielders, blossoms in my mind as the years go by. We had been bowled out at school against Oundle on a flat, fast wicket (by one Richard Boggon, round-arm but distinctly brisk) for 60 runs before lunch. Not the most enjoyable of feasts followed.

However, we had in our ranks a very high-class off-spinner, M. J. S. Preece, whom our captain quickly introduced into the attack. Nothing turned, or suggested the remotest possibility of turn, that day. Nevertheless, the four short legs we posted persuaded a sufficient number of batsmen that something was happening. And it was. First slip was taking catching practice as the ball kept clipping the off stump while all the batsmen played for the turn. We squeezed

Make use of any left-handers in the field

home by one run. For all they had to do those short legs could have been halt and blind!

Let us look at the ways in which the 'Big A' concept might be applied in practice to the various demands imposed by match situations.

Consider the first morning of a Test match with that tense expectant buzz filling the ground. How much will the new ball move about and bounce? The stage is set, the opening batsman looks lonely and vulnerable. What a field! Only one man away from the bat, in the covers, three short-legs and a great hungry arc of slips and gulleys. Any mistake now and he will be out. What an incentive to a bowler!

At first sight this does not seem to relate to the 'Big A'. What has happened? First, the ball is likely to move about considerably and the batsmen are not going to take chances driving. Mid-on and mid-off are therefore not needed. They can go into the slips.

Second, wickets are everything at this moment so long-leg and third man can come up to catch instead of staying back to save fours.

Third, mid-wicket joins the short-legs for a bat-pad catch as the batsman, striving to avoid giving a catch to those hungry slips, overdoes it, or receives one that nips back off the seam.

Fourth, extra cover guards against the off-side push, the only viable shot left. He is the only one of the original six who has not moved. Fifth, the three 'spare' men are slotted into the slips as well, but now doing a vital job. Everything is logical.

Later in the morning, once the batsmen are safely through the early barrage and the ball is behaving more predictably, the field has to be modified to keep on the pressure. The three seamers change about and try different ends. Long-leg and third man drop back, mid-on and mid-off reappear. The 'spare' men probably remain in the slips or are used to reinforce various ploys: an extra man for the mishit hook or a deep gulley for the airy cut. The attack may be varied from off stump to leg, or holes left to tempt an indiscretion. The three 'spare' men put on the squeeze wherever is appropriate.

The development of the spinner's role is the opposite to that of the fast men. It is mid-afternoon now, the score going along steadily, say 120 for 1, the shine gone from a softening ball and the pitch plumb. It will be two or three days yet before the ball can be expected to turn (quite a thought to one who can expect ten overs maximum in a half-day match!). So the spinner has to start by bowling defensively and hope for greater rewards later.

For the off-spinner one might expect mid-on and mid-off to be well back, extra cover and mid-wicket level with the bowler's stumps, third man up to save the single, but long-leg up for the catch at backward short-leg. Those, again, are the basic six of the 'Big A'. One slip will be needed for the floater, while there are various options open as to the employment of the other two 'spare' men. If the bowler keeps to a marked off-side line, including many floaters, he could have a cover point and a man just behind the umpire, saving the single; five on the off and four on the leg.

Conversely he could bowl a tighter line, dispense with cover point, have a deep square-leg on the boundary and bring the saving-one man in front of square or even to forward short-leg. It depends on just what type and speed of off-spinner he is, but it will be unlikely for him to need a wide long-on out on the fence at this stage: the batsmen will be looking to build a really big score and will not be hitting over the top until tomorrow. However, there is a spare man square or short on the leg side to go out when needed. The basic six is not disturbed.

The classic left-arm spinner has the same basic six fieldsmen, but the man previously at long-leg or short-leg is now saving the single. The bowler can afford to have all his three 'spare' men on the off side, giving him a very strong hand unless the batsman is going to hit him against the spin. The extremely accurate bowler of the type of Derek Underwood can afford to bowl varied lines to split fields, but, again, the 'Big A' with its basic six remains.

By the fifth day of the match, with the spinners in control on a turning wicket, the permutations should be fairly obvious. The off-spinner's three 'spare' men can go into the short-legs, while the left-armer has his vultures in on the off side. Incidentally, that famous photograph of Underwood claiming the final Australian wicket at The Oval, with every fielder in the picture, *should* be strictly for the birds. Any stout mishit would have cleared the field. That possibility should always be catered for as well (see photograph 8).

However, you, too, will encounter strange circumstances. First, there will be the times when you have only ten or even nine men. Second, there will be a bowler who has worked out some singular plan of his own with a corresponding extraordinary disposition of the field. Third, there will be occasions when you are under severe attack by well-set batsmen on good wickets. In all these cases the 'Big A' with its basic six-point configuration will stand you in good stead and not leave huge childish gaps to be exploited.

If you remember the original basic principles you can also afford to have fun at a batsman's expense. I remember a man from Essex who once visited us with a remarkable reputation as a run-machine. He certainly had an amazing eye; he only used half his bat, holding it so closed that every stroke shot off to square-leg. We moved more and more fielders over to the leg side, ending up with an 8:1 split! So the bowlers did not dare bowl outside his off stump, and he soon went off swearing never to grace our ground again.

Another perennial problem is the left-handed batsman. Most bowlers dislike bowling to them for two reasons: first, lack of practice; second, the field is so often poorly set, making the bowler less effective.

The main point to remember is that, in view of the ideas about arcs and angles discussed earlier (pp. 121–23), the balance of fielders on one side of the wicket or the other will mostly remain the same as it was for the right-hander.

For example, the off-spinner with three men on the off side (plus a slip) now has three on the leg side. Usually then it is a case of moving one man, or at most two, to the other side, and it makes life easier for all concerned if you keep the movement circular (i.e. mid-off to mid-on, mid-on to mid-wicket, etc.) rather than, say, extra cover going across to extra cover again.

It is worth stressing again that, just as you would change the field for a left-hander, so you should change it for each different type of right-hander in a partnership. If one man is trying to belt every ball out of sight, set the field accordingly for him. Never allow a batsman the freedom of benefiting from his partner's strengths. Never compromise by having a field that is not quite right for either. This applies also to close catchers. The hit to slip is very different from the prod (as my left knee can testify)!

It is important, especially when the side fielding second is winning fairly comfortably, not to allow the game to become too static. There are always several men who have nothing much to do, but there is no reason why they should not be involved from time to time. Here is an example.

In a whole day match we had batted first and made 238. Judging by their fielders, I felt that we had about 100 runs more than we strictly needed. By the middle of their innings they were going passably well, but the quality of the batting was such that wickets were bound to keep falling.

We had an off-spinner on at one end and a left-armer at the other. The left-arm spinner began with three men on the leg side saving the single; cover and extra cover; mid-off; slip, gulley and short extra. The first ball of an over turned and beat the forward prod easily, so we moved short extra to square gulley. Next over he got an inside edge on to the pad on the leg side, so we brought mid-wicket in to forward short-leg.

No further adjustments were strictly necessary, but mid-on had not fielded a ball all day so we brought him up as a second forward short-leg to let him concentrate for a while – and we got a wicket as a bonus with the batsman trying to hit through the mid-on gap. Also we brought extra cover in short for the new batsman which gave him a change and, at the same time, gave cover and mid-off a few balls to chase.

A left-hander came in and had a hearty slog for a while which helped both the score and the variety of the fielding positions.

The off-spinner had begun with forward and backward short legs, three saving the single on the leg side, slip, and three saving the single on the off side.

We swapped fielders about from time to time for him by bringing short third man up to gulley for a series of 'floaters'; by having two backward short-legs for a while, then two forward short-legs straight. None of these moves actually got a wicket or really looked like doing so. They might have helped, but at least they stopped the fielders getting bored.

Finally, because the sun was shining low and bright across rather than down the ground, we swapped three of the fielders over from one side to the other and vice versa, so that no one had to spend the afternoon looking into the sun.

This business of keeping players interested sounds superficial, but it is quite important and it stems right back to the team selection stage. A host of seam-up, military-medium bowlers can quickly become tedious, and this leads to a lack of concentration by the fielders, poorer groundwork and, worst of all, dropped catches. Have you noticed how much better your side performs when the situation is tight? The same applies to batting, for that matter. Some sides seem all to bat in the same vein, while others set constant problems with left-handers, grinders, sloggers or nippy runners alternating.

Who sets the field?

The question may seem naïve, yet it has to be asked because of attitudes in first-class cricket. Cricket history, especially Yorkshire cricket history, abounds with stories of senior professionals refusing to let the captain change the bowling, let alone mess about with the field.

Immediately following the appointment as England captain in 1980 of Ian Botham, I was discussing the wisdom of that choice with a retired professional. Some comment of mine elicited the response, 'You don't think Brearley used to set his field for him, do you?' My reply in the affirmative was met with some scorn.

The paid cricketer is by definition well versed in the technical skills of the game, but often he has surprisingly little idea of the values of organisation and motivation or of the nature of leadership.

The exploitation of the weaknesses of a particular batsman has always to be conducted within the confines of the overall tactical requirements. Any bowler has to understand this. There is no room for conflict. Similarly, the observations of captain and wicket-keeper should be of immense help in what ought to be a partnership. The bowler who wishes to set his own field is not helping himself, his captain or his side.

I believe that there are more good captains in club than in first-class cricket. The acerbic attitude so often evidenced by professional bowlers seems to endorse this view. Any experienced player who thinks captains are unimportant or even a nuisance has certainly had to play under a few bad ones. But if the player's view is jaundiced the fault almost certainly lies with his captain.

A criticism one frequently hears about captains is this: 'He just follows the ball about all day, putting fielders where it has just been hit.' However, once you know about line, the 'Big A', and the 'V' you will not find yourself chasing the ball.

Do not be surprised, though, if you find yourself sharing my experience in one respect. There always seems to be a period in a fielding session, when the batsmen begin to play their shots and I respond by moving some of the close catchers out into defensive positions, during which the runs keep on coming. The reason is that I simply cannot get the field right until the batsmen have shown me the pace of the pitch and the outfield, the weight and shape of their shots, and what they regard as an easy single. Once they have done this I can begin to squeeze out their favourite shots, cut off the fours, and manoeuvre them into risk-taking.

When you are fielding first this can be unnerving, but when you are fielding second it actually plays into your hands. The confidence of the batting side is greatly helped by seeing runs continuing to flow despite your efforts at containment; and when the supply dries up they still do not see the proposition as hopeless. They keep going; or at least they keep on trying and so give you a chance.

12

Field diagrams – fast and medium-pace bowlers

Field diagrams should never be taken too literally for they offer only the most basic information; but they are included here in the hope that the reader will enjoy picking holes in them. The trouble is that once the cross is marked on the paper, there the fielder is, stuck too deep or too square and nothing can be done about it. Also, anyone with experience of the game will immediately call to mind a particular bowler of the type shown who always feels quite naked without his deep square-leg or long-on, for example, even though he never gets hit there.

Nor do field diagrams make allowance for batsmen's individual idiosyncrasies, apart from my own two favourites, Larwood's 'My field for Bradman', from his book *Bodyline?*, and Laker's field for his nineteen Australian wickets in 1956. (How Tony Lock managed to take only one wicket at the other end I shall never understand.)

The sort of problem which a field diagram specifically does not cover is illustrated by my own club's left-arm fast bowler. When the ball is new he sends it down well outside off stump to give it room to swing back. Consequently, when a fair number of his deliveries do not swing enough, they get hammered away square on the off side. He needs, therefore, a very square third man. But if he follows this line of attack he palpably does not need a long-leg; yet because he is bowling in-swingers he feels that he cannot aim at the stumps without one! Once the shine is off, exactly the opposite happens; he bowls a much tighter line, leg-stumpish, and he does need a long-leg. However, he also says that because the ball is not swinging he needs a third man. In fact he does not, because his control is better and he hardly ever bowls wide of the off stump!

My basic advice is, stick with the 'Big A' and use your brain. Also you will not find long-stop in any of the diagrams! This may seem an inane statement, but consider the following situation:

We were fielding second against Southborough in Kent. Their picturesque village-green ground, a postage stamp cut into the side of a hill, has a fast outfield and only 30 yards from stumps to boundary. With 3 overs to go they needed 20 runs to win with a wicket left; close enough to be interesting, but comfortably within our control.

Two boundary leg-byes later the game suddenly looked like getting out of hand. Because of the shortness of that boundary, long-leg had no chance of cutting off anything fine of him, even though the bowling was barely medium-pace. So we had a long-stop. What I did not expect was a dividend: the batsman tried to sweep, got a top edge and was caught on the boundary, a yard in front of the sight-screen, by the long-stop!

So always remember that field diagrams are no more than points from which to depart – and perhaps to return to when the variants come unstuck.

It is not possible in diagrams to show the precise distance of various fielders from the bat because that will vary with the ruling conditions in every match. The important points, however, are these:

1. Close catchers have to be close enough for the normal chance to carry to them on the full. Provided that this overriding principle is followed, the deeper they are the more time they have to see the ball. Ian Botham, for example, stands very close at second slip in order to make sure that everything that comes in his direction is a catch. He holds on to chances that would be too hot for almost anyone else, and he starts with his hands on his knees. But he is a genius.
2. 'Saving one' fielders must be close enough to do just that. Their depth will depend on the length of the grass, damp or dry, the activity of the batsmen and their own agility. The deeper they can be and still save the single, the better, since they can then cut off more potential fours as well. They need constant attention.

The 'saving one' fielders behind square will, of course, be severely modified by the speed of the bowling. I remember watching Michael Holding bowling to Geoff Boycott on the first morning of the 1980 Lord's Test. My companion remarked, correctly, that his slips were so deep that, apart from short square-leg, there was no one close enough to save the single. Not likely to be your problem either.

3. The boundary fielders are out there to save fours and sixes, so they should use every yard of available space and stay as deep as possible. However, third man and long-leg may very often be so deep as to be giving away 2 runs instead of just one for each 4 they save. In which case they should come in enough to save 2 and 4.

Similarly, boundary fielders who may be expected to get catches will find life far easier if they start right on the edge, not 10 yards in, but there is nothing against having mid-wicket 15 or 20 yards in from the edge for the batsman who cannot hit any farther even at full power.

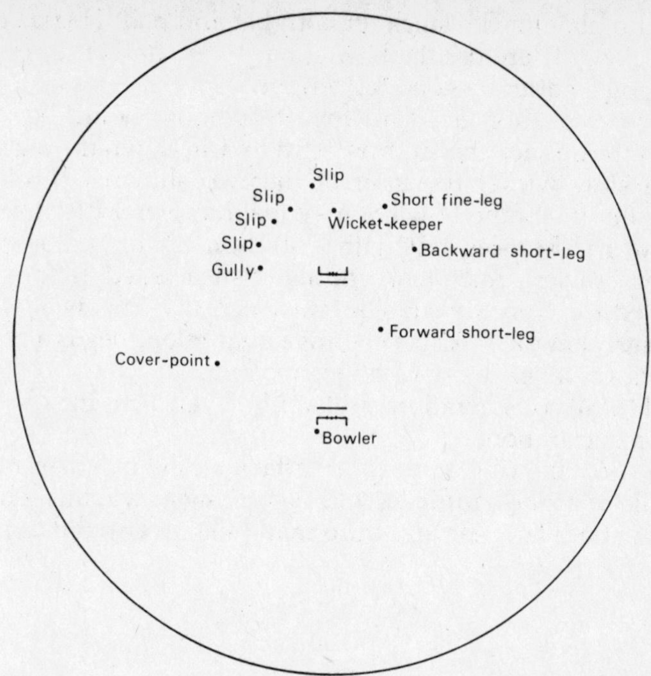

Diagram 3 – Fast out-swing bowler, right-arm; new ball, fast wicket

Fast out-swing bowler, right-arm- new ball, fast wicket: the field for all-out attack

Any variations will depend on pace, both of wicket and bowler, movement, both off the seam and in the air, length and line. They also depend on the personal preference of the bowler and on the confidence of the individual fieldsmen. To give two examples:

1. Mid-off: depends on pace, relative to the particular batsman, and swing. Also some bowlers tend to bowl a little short without a mid-off to avoid being driven. Others will relish the challenge as an opportunity to exploit the yorker.
2. Short-legs: depend on line and movement off the pitch. Forward short-leg is expected to take catches on a wicket that 'stops' or if there is variation in bounce, i.e., for the ball that billows off the splice. Short square-leg comes into his own when there is movement off the seam,

notably for the snick off both bat and pad. He has to be close. Therefore the bowler has to be confident of bowling a naturally good full length.

Backward short-legs are for deflections. Some bowlers, when they attack the stumps, tend to drift down the leg side. On a slow wicket the finer of the two shown is probably superfluous. Some bowlers may feel happier with only one backward short-leg but with a mid-on or mid-off instead. Other bowlers may feel unduly disheartened if they are snicked for 4 on the leg side, in which case it is well worth placing a long-leg. Also a slightly squarer long-leg is a potential wicket-taker against a reflex hooker.

All these considerations still apply, even with the old ball, after a declaration.

The 'double ring' concept to attack a new batsman in the middle of a side's innings, without giving away runs, entails placing both long-leg and third man plus cover point as three

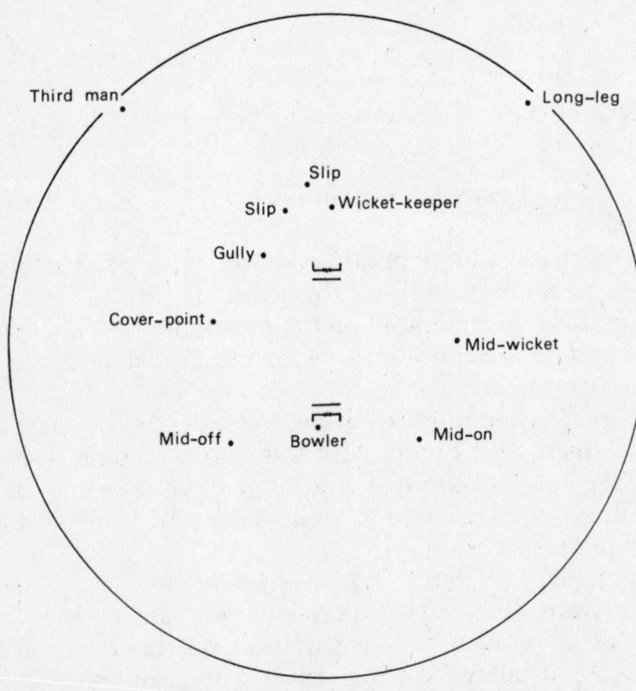

Diagram 4 – Fast bowler, right-arm (defence)

defenders, the remaining six as close catchers. Sometimes mid-off and/or mid-on may be needed as well.

Fast bowler, right-arm: the field for defence

Two slips and a gulley are the only remaining standard attackers. There is also the possibility of retaining mid-wicket as an attacker in a variety of ways:

(a) short forward square-leg;
(b) backward square-leg, with mid-on considerably wider; and
(c) third slip, with mid-on at mid-wicket. (It is easier to 'work' the ball rather than drive it through mid-on.)

In general, it is better to use these fields for a fast bowler in a defensive context in short bursts (2–3 overs) and to give the longer defensive role to medium-pacers.

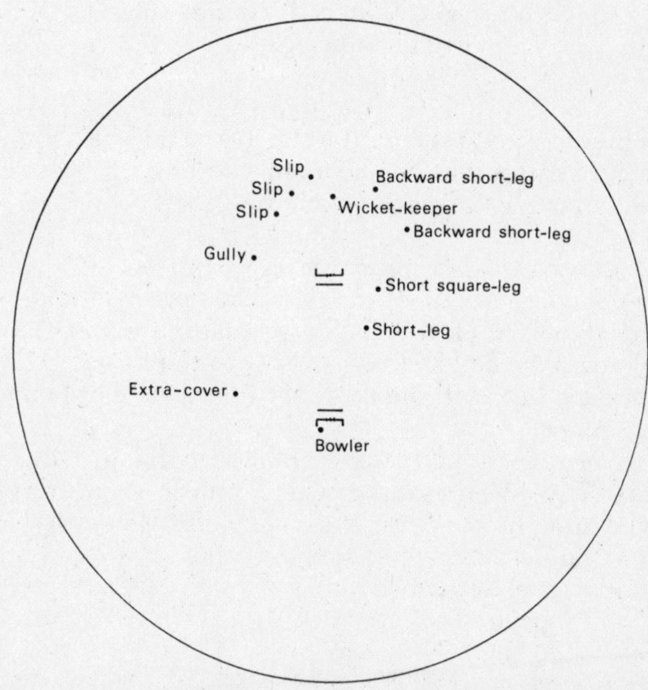

Diagram 5 – Fast in-swing bowler, right-arm; new ball, fast wicket

For the last few overs before a declaration see page 182 (Limited-overs).

Fast in-swing bowler, right-arm; new ball, fast wicket
Compared to the fast out-swing bowler (page 137):

(a) cover-point comes straighter at extra cover;
(b) fourth slip has moved over to make four short-legs;
(c) two gulleys may be preferable to three slips; and
(d) instead of a mid-off, when the occasion arises, mid-on will probably be more effective.

Having noted the considerations for out-swing bowling, the one other major factor is line. Some bowlers maintain an attack at and outside off stump, others leg stump and outside that. Clearly, for the former, it may pay to move one short-leg into the slips. In the latter case selection is much easier for the batsman, the strong slip cordon of three is superfluous and you end up with a negative leg-side configuration three men in, three out. A waste of the new ball.

In defence
Two of the slips go to square third man and mid-off, forward short-leg retreats to mid-on and fine-leg to long-leg. Two close catchers can remain on each side of the wicket.

Left-arm fast bowler, over the wicket
Left-arm bowlers are, in effect, a combination of both in- and out-swing bowlers. However, because of the angles involved (see page 122) the better close-catching configuration is as for out-swingers, but with the three short-legs all tending to be slightly squarer.

The cover-point area creates a problem in that the straight-on ball can easily be hit square, whereas the in-swinger has to be played straight. It is, therefore, difficult to get away with only one man in the covers. However, the on-drive is more difficult if the ball does not swing much. (See introduction to Field Placing, page 114.)

Medium-pace bowler, right-arm or left-arm
This conventional field-placing uses little initiative and covers

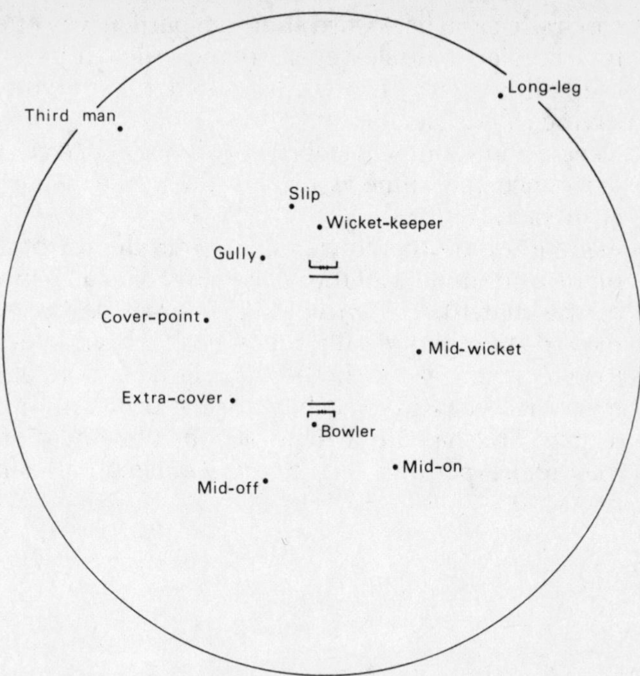

Diagram 6 – Medium-pace bowler, right-arm or left-arm

a multitude of sins. It assumes an oldish ball and a little movement in the air or off the pitch.

The variations on what is shown are usually as follows:

(a) For slower bowlers and/or conditions, third man and long-leg can come up, squarer, to save the single. On the off side this will create an extremely tight ring; and liberate one man: second slip, or short extra cover.
(b) On large grounds third man and long-leg often have to be several yards in from the boundary to save 2, as well as 4, runs.
(c) Consider second slip instead of extra cover for out-swingers.
(d) Consider also two short-legs instead of cover point, mid-wicket or gulley/third man for in-swingers.
(e) I have found that slip, short third man, cover point, extra cover, mid-off, mid-on, mid-wicket, backward

square-leg and backward short-leg particularly effective for a bowler at the slower end of the scale who is moving the ball both ways: two close catchers, everyone else saving the single.

(f) Keep a count of the number of gulley catches your club gets once the shine is off. Could he be better used elsewhere?

(g) Depending on the bowler's pace and degree of movement, and the state of the wicket (and of course the state of the match), the wicket-keeper may be better employed standing up rather than back. He and you have to take a view as to whether he might be more likely to miss the occasional catch, but pick up a stumping in return. This has the twin attractions of being more fun for the 'keeper and of giving the batsman a feeling of pressure.

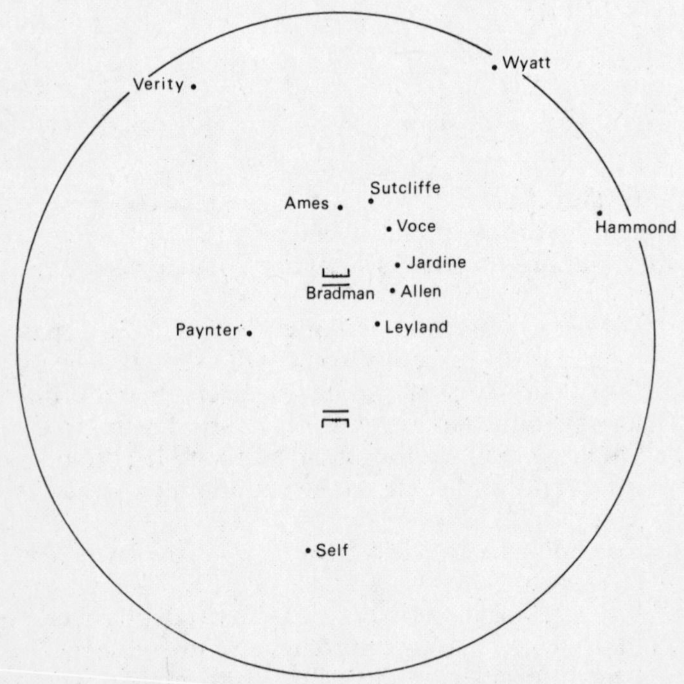

Diagram 7 – Larwood: My field for Bradman

Larwood: 'My field for Bradman'
Fast leg theory or 'bodyline'

By 1932 Bradman had become such a prolific run-maker that 'fast leg theory' was adopted to try to keep him quiet. This was dubbed 'bodyline' by the Australian press on the 1932–3 MCC tour there. It worked to the extent that Bradman's average was halved to 50, but at far too high a cost in terms of human relationships. The diagram is taken from Larwood's book of the tour called, simply, *Bodyline?*

13

Handling spinners

Arthur Mailey, the Australian leg-break and googly bowler, was fond of relating how, early in his Test career, he bowled three successive maiden overs, whereupon Warwick Armstrong took him off with the words, 'I've plenty of people in the side who can bowl maidens, thank you, your job is to take wickets.' It was a shrewd assessment of the nature and possibilities of spin bowling.

Off-spin

The most common form of slow bowling in club cricket is right-arm off-spin. It is, for this reason if for no other, the most widely mishandled, misunderstood and, of course, badly purveyed form of bowling.

The ordinary up-and-down medium-pacer on a poorish club wicket has only to keep sending the ball down, just short of a length and straight, for his dividend of 2 or 3 wickets per match. Variable bounce and a minimum of lateral movement will do most of his job for him, and there is little scope for a variety of field-placings. Precious little intelligence is called for. With slow bowling, however, both captain and bowler alike have to think hard.

Let us start at the top: Laker, Titmus, Allen and Illingworth; Lance Gibbs, Tayfield, Prasanna, Venkataraghavan; Emburey. The one quality these bowlers have in common is superb control of length and line, coupled with a rich skein of variations. Also, compared to club spinners, they spin the ball far more.

Spin is most important. The ability to spin the ball severely immediately provides the first range of variations: turn from zero to maximum. At the same time the highly-spun ball will fly differently from one that is simply rolled. It will dip more quickly at the end of its flight and tend to drift away to the off side before pitching. This underlies the classic tactic of several minimally-spun balls followed by one that is heavily spun. The batsman's foot goes down the same line as before, the ball drifts away 'dragging' the bat after it. Quicker dip in flight drops the ball shorter than the batsman anticipates and the sharper turn brings it through the opened 'gate' to hit the stumps.

The good player counters this by bending his front knee more and reaching farther with his top hand. Instead of bowling him, the ball then flies off the bat to short-leg. Hence Jim Laker's remarkable field of three, sometimes even four short-legs; but note that the degree of bounce and turn he could command allowed them to stand relatively deep.

When the good batsman moves on to the attack he will be looking to get down the pitch and drive the ball through mid-on and mid-off, forcing the fieldsmen back. His next move is to widen the arc, hitting through mid-wicket and extra cover. The bowler is then forced to vary length and line, presenting opportunities square with and behind, the wicket.

In his turn the bowler strives to force a mistake in timing, to produce a catch, by variations in flight, pace and angle of delivery. He will bowl over the wicket and round the wicket, use the whole width between the return creases, and the length between popping crease and bowling crease. He will float some deliveries from leg to off, hoping for a stumping, a slip catch or lbw through the sweep. By varying the height of his arm he can vary the height of bounce, and also affect the flight. By holding the ball in different positions in relation to the seam, he can produce lateral variations of float and turn, combined or singly. All the while he will be probing for weaknesses, or trying to counter strengths. It is a fascinating duel.

When we think of the great off-spinners of the last thirty years, we are struck by their differences rather than by their similarities. Compare the high, bounding, exuberant delivery of Lance Gibbs to the gliding stealthy approach of Prasanna or Illingworth. Titmus and Tayfield relied heavily on their 'arm-balls' or 'floaters' and built their repertoire around them.

Accuracy, I suppose, was the special hallmark of David Allen, Lance Gibbs and now John Emburey.

These differences are important and apply no less to club spinners. The flatter, accurate spinner can be treated day in, day out, as a stock bowler. The bowler with a slower, loopier flight is a buyer of wickets, to be used with a bank of runs behind him. The man who in fact uses more little out-swingers than anything else is apt to be hit through the off side on his bad days rather than to leg. The big spinner has to bowl a different line from someone who only rolls the ball. In other words the off-spinner is not a standard animal. The way he is used, the timing of his spells and, above all, his field-placing need careful thought. There is no other type of bowler in the game who destroys himself so regularly by poor field-placing as the off-spinner. (For field diagram, see p. 158.)

The point is that there has to be a bond of confidence between captain and bowler. The context of the game and the conditions may be just what one spinner likes best, yet next to impossible for another. One may expect to take the majority of his wickets through catches in the deep. Another may actively hate any sort of deep field and expect his catches to be close in. Get it wrong and neither will bowl successfully.

Captain and bowler have to plan together, watch what happens and make constant adjustments. The captain in particular has to be quite certain as to whether the bowler is bowling well but is giving away runs because the field is wrong; or whether he is bowling poorly to the correct field. He needs to decide (with the bowler's help) which side of the wicket he wants the ball to be hit. Is the bowler going to adjust his line to meet that criterion or is the captain going to move the field to accommodate the line being bowled? He can do one or the other, but not both.

Length, too, presents subtle problems. I remember one rather muddy September wicket when, after the initial skirmish with the new ball, I put our off-spinner on to bowl. As he gives the ball a generous tweak and has a pleasant loopy flight, he should have been unplayable. All that happened was that every ball turned and hit the batsman on the front pad. For three solid overs. Becoming bored with this, I suggested that we push mid-off and mid-on back, give the batsman a half-volley to drive, and have a bowl at the other man instead. Up came the half-volley, but instead of the expected single, the batsman drove over the top of it and was bowled. Thus encouraged, the bowler kept pitching much further up and duly got them all out.

What this reveals is that, when the ball is turning a lot, it is often a temptation to bowl slightly short. The bowler naturally likes to see the ball pitch, see it turn and see a defensive shot. (Incidentally, the out-swinger who consistently beats everything outside the off stump is often guilty of the same fault.)

Finally, there is the question of pace. The better batsmen see the ball earlier and decide on their shots sooner than indifferent ones. Therefore a spinner has to bowl within a slightly quicker range to the former than to the latter. I am not advocating bowling flat, but the bowler needs to have an awareness of differences in tempo, as it were, the idea that he should find a point on his scale around which he is more likely to deceive the better player.

It is no bad concept that, in the early part of his spell, a bowler should vary his pace as much as possible in order to discover which seems to be most effective against that particular batsman in those conditions. Thereafter it is generally the case, apart from the odd surprise ball, that subtle changes of pace are more successful than violent ones. I do remember, however, one bowler, previously a fast bowler, who changed to being a leg-spinner. He used to obtain many wickets with his fast ball, precisely because it was genuinely fast and carried real surprise.

There are plenty of opportunities for a bowler even before he comes on to bowl himself, to note batsmen's preferences. Initial variations of pace will help to confirm these. Is he quick to get on the back foot to anything remotely short and cut it? Does he seem anxious to charge down the wicket to a slower one? Or does he essay the sweep early on?

Depending on the state of the match, the spinner can opt either for feeding those shots and attempting to get the batsman out through his overdoing them, or for denial. Of the three examples mentioned, the cutter might be undone by a ball just short enough, but delivered from wide of the crease or made to turn or bounce more than usual. The charger, on the other hand, can be foiled by mixing up the line to provide a stumping. The bowler might deliver some balls from near the return crease, others from close to the stumps. A ball bowled with a low round-arm action will be on a slightly different line from that delivered with a high arm. A spell from around the wicket accentuates these changes of angle even more. Alternatively, the charger can be served continuous loopers, with a blanket defence on the straight drive, so that he has to hit harder and harder and eventually lofts one. Arm-balls on a leg stump line might defeat the sweep.

In carrying out these sorts of tactic, captain and bowler must understand and help each other. And especially in the case of bluffing the batsman.

We have all watched Test matches in which, as soon as a spinner comes on, the batsman is surrounded not only by slip and leg slip, but also by an armour-plated short square-leg and silly point. In club cricket no one in full employment stands at short square-leg. Silly point is a different matter. It is a perfectly safe position, given a bowler who can be relied upon to pitch the ball consistently well up.

In Test cricket silly point is there to catch the rebound as the ball is spun to hit bat then pad, or the left-armer's drifter, to the same effect. In club cricket he is not there for any such purpose. He is there to make the batsman feel crowded and to remove some of his concentration from ball to fielder. The ball does not get spun sharply enough to bounce anywhere. So, as the fielding captain, try not to fool yourself, and think along the following lines.

First, a bowler who is not used to having a silly point will find the innovation nearly as difficult to live with as the batsman. So warn him well in advance, and be prepared for him to bowl less well. Also, be selective about when you set a silly point. The most effective time is not likely to be as soon as that bowler starts his spell. Let him first settle into line and length. Better wait for a wicket to fall. Wait, again, for the new batsman to take guard. Adjust the field as you would normally and then, last of all, bring in your silly point. This ensures that the move has the batsman's full attention as close to the delivery of the first ball as possible. It is then as difficult as you can make it for him to switch his concentration, fully, on to the ball.

Do not persist with the position against the well-set player at the other end, nor for the new man, unless you can see it having some effect.

The players waiting to come in are watching the game. They may or may not be particularly conscious of your silly point. Subconsciously, though, they are all getting used to him, which defeats the object of the exercise. So chop and change, and remember: it is really just bullshit. The bowler may indeed get wickets for you, but not in the manner you see on television.

Against the tail-enders, the slower a spinner bowls the better. Several factors prompt this assertion. Tail-end batsmen like to hit the ball, preferably for 6. The more tempting the bowling, the harder they swing and the more across the line they will play. Providing the bowler keeps a full length – and this is vital – the chances of consistent contact being made are nil.

Furthermore, all the field bar two can then be on the leg side, thus packing the mid-wicket/long-on arc. The lack of pace on the ball and the full length make it very difficult to score in the arc between extra cover and the wicket-keeper on the off side without correct movement of the feet and top hand. Not only will tail-enders fail to do this, they will also find it difficult to watch the ball pitch. Having had to raise the head to follow the ball in flight they find it very difficult to get it down again.

At first sight it seems unlikely, but is in fact logical, that the slowest spinners are frequently the most effective of their species on very slow wickets, too. In theory, of course, the batsman should find it easy, because he has so much time. In practice, soft conditions call for considerable self-control on the batsman's part and it is difficult to hit an almost stationary ball consistently hard over a sluggish outfield. There is, therefore, a strong temptation to take the opportunity to speed up the scoring rate with a few sixes. To do so the ball has to be hit, not only cleanly, but very, very hard indeed.

Left-arm spin

Much of what I have said about off-spin bowling applies equally to left-arm spin, but, for a captain, handling left-arm spin can be even more enjoyable.

Most club batsmen (and others) score the majority of their

runs on the leg side. Indeed many, especially the most prolific, score all, or almost all, of their runs to leg. That, if you are bowling off-spinners, is fine. All the shots are being played 'with the tide', as it were, but five or six men on the leg can easily become seven, or even eight, to stifling effect.

If you then put on a left-arm spinner, the batsman, leopard-like, will almost certainly not change. But now most of your fielders are on the off side. Since the batsman will still want to score most of his runs to leg, this is where the fun starts.

Is the batsman going to be defeated by being made to play on the off side, which he is unable to do so well? Or is he going to be defeated by trying to work the ball to leg, precisely because of those tempting gaps? Or is he quite capable of scoring freely enough on the leg side in spite of the spin in the opposite direction? Mostly, of course, he will get away with it for a while, but for how long? How expensive can you allow your bowler to be?

You now have to analyse how good the batsman is: the arc and range of his shots, in the air or along the ground. His footwork will tell you. You also need to decide how well the bowler is performing, both as to length and line.

None of this is difficult. What is difficult is to decide what to do about it – and without compromising with a dangerous 5/4 split of the field, full of holes on both sides – before you have to remove the poor demoralised bowler from the firing line.

If you can anticipate these situations, you will find also that you look forward to dealing with them. Think again back to Richie Benaud and Peter May, and to Tony Lock at Sydney. I am sure Benaud was positively itching to find out what would happen if he pitched in Trueman's footmarks; but he needed the excuse of Ted Dexter's innings to give him the opportunity and, therefore, the courage to try.

So the next time someone keeps slogging your left-arm spinner to leg, have a try at solving the problem yourself. Ask him to bowl over the wicket, at leg stump, to a 7/2 leg-side field, and see what happens. You will have a tremendous evening in the bar if it works!

There is, though, something very serious about left-arm spinners as a breed which causes problems for their captains and prevents them from being as successful as they ought to be. This is because they nearly all bowl from the wrong place, for they place their front foot on the popping crease and not far from the line of the return crease.

The theory is that the ball can then be delivered to pitch on the off stump and turn to straight, but still hitting off stump: OK, fine. In practice, however, most such balls pitch outside the off stump – when they can be ignored, or they offer a free hit. Conversely any ball that pitches on the line of the stumps and fails to turn enough, can be tucked away on the leg side. Either way the batsman does not have to hit into the 'V'.

Consider, for example, the full toss. Outside the off stump the batsman can simply select his preferred slot, early or late, and take four runs. Straight full tosses are, because of the angle of delivery, effectively going down the leg side anyway, and we all know what happens to them! But what I am suggesting is that the wide angle of delivery is as great and basic an error for the left-arm bowler as for the right-arm one.

Throughout this book I have harked on the importance of line; and this reminds me of how Jim Sims, that delightful Middlesex leg-spinner between the wars, was once admonished for taking a hat trick, all bowled, with very poor deliveries. 'Ah,' he said, 'but they were *straight* bad balls.'

Fred Trueman measures the quality of a bowler as being, apart from the size of his posterior, that he delivers from very close to the stumps. The left-arm spinner has a physical problem in getting close to the stumps, of course, since his delivery stride takes him away from them. But there is a simple answer. He should bowl from further back. His front foot should be on the bowling crease or just in front of it, instead of on the popping crease. The back of his leg then can virtually be brushing the stumps.

Think of the different effect this has on the pattern of the game. Given a good high arm, we are almost back to wicket-to-wicket delivery: nothing wide of off stump, nothing drifting down the leg side. The ball hardly has to be spun at all. The bowler also has the bonus of being able to use the full width to the return crease, and length to the popping crease, as variety whenever he wants it.

The effect of this on field-placing is dramatic. The man behind square on the leg side becomes superfluous. The batsman has a much harder job to get the ball away on the leg side, because he is hitting against the tide while the ball is in the air, as well as off the pitch. But in any case, the bowler now has a spare man to put at straightish mid-wicket.

This extra fielder at mid-wicket is very helpful in another way: for the full toss. No, I am not talking about setting fields for bad bowling; just confidence. Let me explain. I like to bowl slow off-spinners myself, the sort that go up before they come down. I usually have six men on the leg side, usually four on the single and two out. I take lots of wickets with full tosses (my friends say, 'All'!). Why? Because, as Jim Sims said, they are straight, and because the lower-order batsmen hit them in the air. But what I truly do is bowl many half-volleys, some of which do not bounce!

The point of this is that the conventional left-arm spinner, with the conventional 6/3 field, cannot bowl slowly enough, because he cannot keep bowling half-volleys, because he dare not bowl full tosses, and because he has not got my army of men at mid-wicket to catch the results.

Plenty of food for discussion here, I hope. But while you are planning and experimenting together, be aware of two things: differences in method, and differences in technique.

Think, for example, of Phil Edmonds and John Emburey. Edmonds likes to have men clustered close and about the bat, very aggressive, expecting a wicket every ball. Emburey has a totally different, softly, softly, attitude; float one a little, spin one slightly, just like tickling a trout.

It is difficult for a bowler to bowl to close-set fields if he is not used to doing so; just as some spinners, expecting to take their wickets from edges, hate to be lofted into the outfield. Try to let them learn how to handle both approaches.

There are differences, too, in the physical shape of delivery patterns. I have mentioned it as being between different types of off-spinner, but bowling around the wicket produces a different pivot, a rounder swing of the bowling arm. It is surprising how many left-arm spinners have problems with their run-up and lose their rhythm. On occasions Edmonds' run-up not only varies with every ball, but he even gets into a state of being barely able to bowl. For some reason, this is far more common with left-arm than with right-arm spinners. So be tolerant.

One of our left-arm spinners once got himself into a muddle through running in too fast for limited-over matches and then effectively 'quitting' in his delivery stride when trying to bowl slowly again. Not surprisingly he suffered a crisis of confidence.

We went back to the basic techniques and got him bowling again, but then, of course, it was vital that he not be slaughtered. We talked through his field and the reasons for it. If he bowled properly on or around the line of the off stump he had four men in a line on the off side, as normal. But we also gave him plenty of cover against the inevitable full toss by having two men on the leg-side boundary. His field then looked like this:

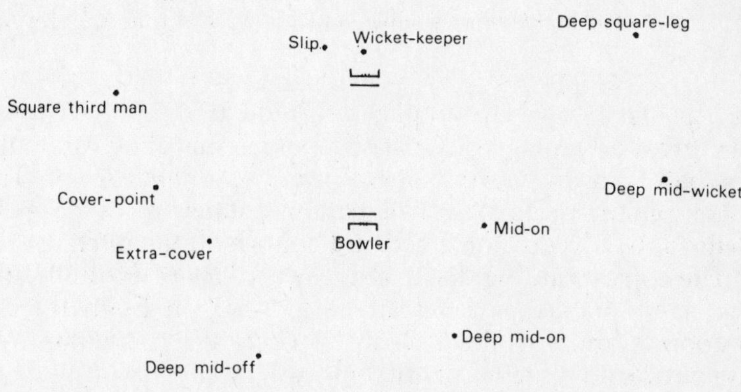

Diagram 8 – Defensive field for left-arm spinner, 5/4 off side

In the event he was naturally a bit diffident to begin with, and several full tosses were hit to the two men on the leg-side boundary: no fours, just singles and the occasional two. Maybe a dozen runs were scored off his first 2 overs.

This was just what we expected, but then the captain lost his nerve. Calamity!

He moved the field around to that shown in Diagram 9, i.e., one of the covers came over to near the square-leg umpire and he also allowed mid-wicket to sidle squarer as well. The batsman immediately responded by hitting a four at comfortable catching height straight through extra cover and another through the yawning gap wide of mid-on, as shown by the arrows. It is a cautionary tale.

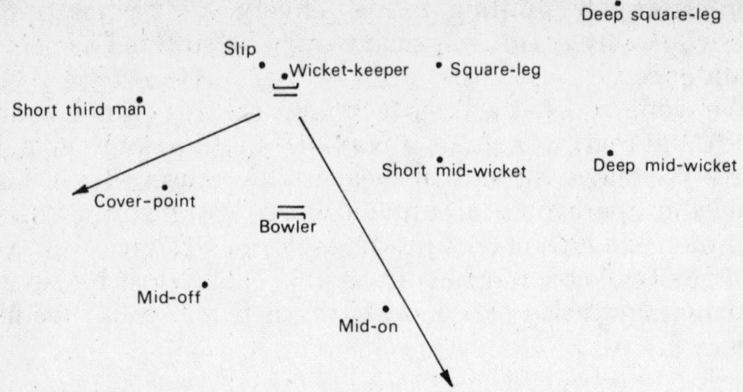

Diagram 9 – Field for left-arm spinner but without off-side line, 5/4 leg side

Leg-spin (see diagrams on pages 162 and 163)
The great advantage of wrist-spinners is that they can make the ball turn on wickets where finger-spinners cannot. The extra spin imparted to the ball that this entails causes more dip in its flight and greater speed and bounce off the pitch.

The corresponding disadvantages are lack of accuracy and the need to have a 5/4 split field. Also, in England, the preponderance of slow, damp wickets often nullifies the theoretical advantages on pitching.

Wrist-spinners need to practise hard, experiment widely, think about their art and above all make great efforts to win the confidence of their various captains. Their biggest problem is usually that they do not bowl often enough. However, they can help their own cause very often by developing a sound grasp of what they are trying to do and the appropriate field-placing.

I suppose the hallmark of the best of wrist-spinners is the possession of a 'googly' in their repertoire. This ball, invented by B. J. Bosanquet at the beginning of the twentieth century, creates confusion enough to defeat even the best of players. It does however add to the field-placing problems.

Whereas a left-arm round-the-wicket finger-spinner can usually bowl quite happily to a 6/3 off-side field, the mechanics of greater spin and less accuracy of the leg-spinner usually mean that he cannot and needs four fieldsmen on the leg. The standard result, if there is such a thing for these idiosyncratic creatures, is shown on page 162. Clearly, a frequently employed googly will tend to slide down backward of square on the leg side. If you fill this gap then the off side will look very sparse: can he bowl a tight enough line?

Do not bowl it too often is the simplest answer. Arthur Mailey in *10 for 66 and All That* describes how he became too accurate, enabling the batsman to pick his 'bosie' simply because it was always on a different line from the leg-spinner. Once he started to deliver a few bosies down the leg side and leg-spinners outside off stump he began to take wickets again!

For our purposes we can classify leg-spinners into three broad groups plus one special case. First, there is the type to which the standard diagram relates (p. 162). This is the roller, rather than the vicious spinner of the ball. He tends to be more accurate and often with a flatter, less loopy trajectory. He will be more reliable, and easier to handle with simple variations in his field. Short third man can come in to gulley: deep mid-wicket can advance to save the single, with the ordinary mid-wicket either closing in 'on the drive' between mid-wicket and mid-on or moving across to the off side.

Second are the 'loopers', bowlers with a generous loop and more spin. They are a breed apart: small men with strong fingers and great cricketing longevity. They just keep tossing it up, year after year, and watching the hilarious results. One marvellous old chap we sometimes play against has the field shown on page 163. This incorporates a deep gulley about ten yards from the bat: cover-point, rather too close, as is mid-on, and a chap who appears to have been forgotten and loafs about some fifteen yards away at square-leg. His 150 wickets per year include a huge proportion of spirally spinning mis-hits to these four men, who all appear to be in the conventionally wrong place.

Thus one's advice to all schoolboy leg-spinners is, 'Don't grow! Don't give up! Learn to bowl *slowly* and accurately.'

The third group of leg-spinners consists mainly of those who have ignored this advice. They are the ones who bowl faster and more aggressively. The more successful among them bowl brisk in-swingers and leg-spinners in harness, instead of attempting the googly which flies out too slowly. Given anything approaching helpful conditions they can be quite terrifying for batsmen and close catchers alike.

A rather different approach is to use the top-spinner as standard. This has a loop in flight and tends to bounce higher and faster than the batsman expects. It also has the advantage of being able to be bowled straight. The idea is that the bowler has only to impart the minimum of side-spin – half a bat's width – to achieve an effect.

This is also an effective approach for the left-arm wrist-spinner. He has the huge disadvantage that his standard delivery, the chinaman, is just an inaccurate off-break to right-hand batsmen. But if he can overcome that and bowl mostly top-spinners and googlies he becomes lethal.

Do not forget the use of a left-arm wrist-spinner against left-handed batsmen. I am one of the latter and was confronted with a left-arm wrist-spinner in a net when I was a schoolboy. I was helpless: the mirror-image effect did not help.

'Have you ever batted against one of these before?' asked the coach. 'Never!' 'Well, when you meet the next one he will get you out.' He was right; but mercifully about twenty years later.

In general, left-handed batsmen have far more confidence to move their feet against leg-spinners without the fear of being stranded. And they are so often helped by the most atrocious field-placing.

The bowler then has two options. Either he continues to bowl what are essentially now off-breaks, with a proper 6/3 leg-side field, and maintain a tight line of attack. Or he bowls googlies as his stock ball, at off stump and outside, to an off-side field.

14

Field diagrams – the spinners

Off-spin

The most extraordinary off-spin bowling performance of all time was surely that by Jim Laker against Australia at Old Trafford in 1956: altogether his analysis for the two innings was 68–27–90–19.

Bowling round the wicket, he hardly had to vary his field (see below) at all, except, one assumes, to juggle with the depth of mid-on and mid-wicket. This was, however, in the days before the restriction to no more than two fielders behind square on the leg side.

Mike Brearley carried this field-placing a daring step further, in a sense, for John Emburey and Geoff Miller in Australia in the winter of 1978–9 by having no short third man (they both bowled over the wicket). He could thus have a mid-wicket saving the single as well as one saving the fours. On a turning wicket, without footwork, there is no escape!

Few club off-spinners, however, are accurate enough to justify three short-legs: short square-leg is more likely (and

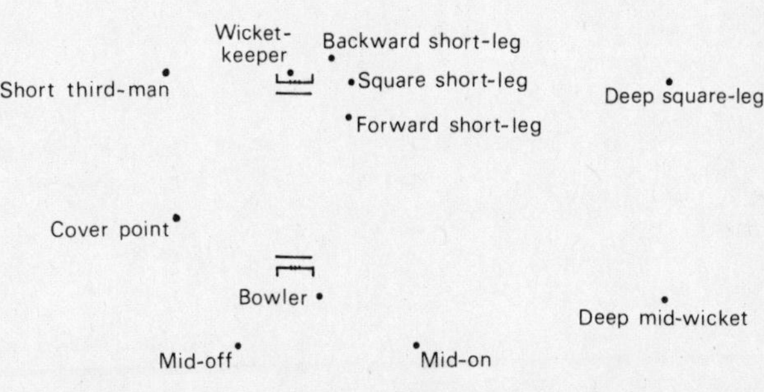

Diagram 10 – Jim Laker's field, Old Trafford, 1956

more sensibly) found at slip. There are still three close catchers and the double ring (see 'Left-arm spin: Attack', p. 160).

The most important man on the field is, extra-cover: but note that he is *not* cover point.

Square-leg can be placed to save the single, on the boundary, or even in 'no-man's-land' if there is reason to believe that a mishit will not carry to the boundary. He can also be either saving the single behind square or stay on the boundary for the sweep.

In defence the normal arrangement is the same as for left-arm spin leg-stump defence (p. 161). There may, however, be occasions when a cover-point is needed as well as extra-cover; in which case the soundest move is probably to do without one of the men behind square on the leg side.

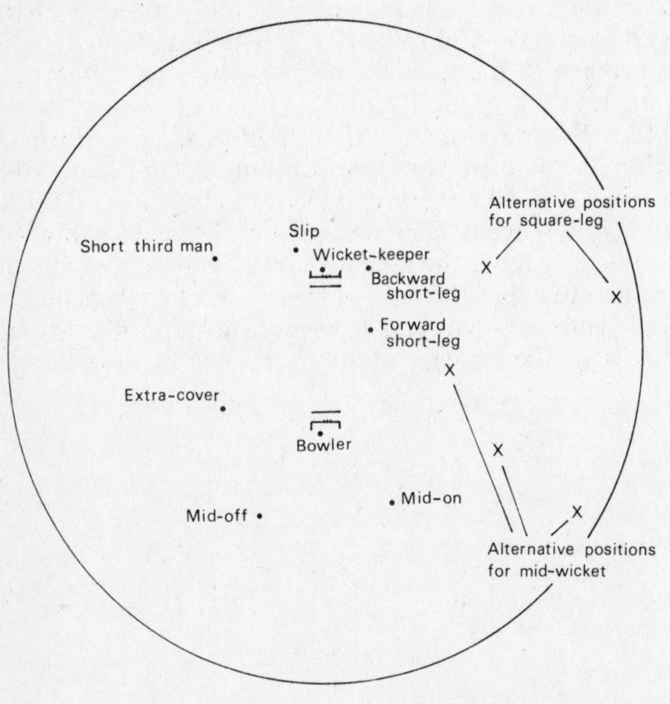

Diagram 11 – Off-spin – club standard field

M. A. Noble's field for right-hand, medium-pace spinner on a good wicket

A highly respected and successful captain of Australia in three series against England was M. A. Noble. Having lost at home in 1903–4, he won the Ashes, 4–1, in 1907–8 and retained them 2–1 in 1909. This diagram is taken from his book *The*

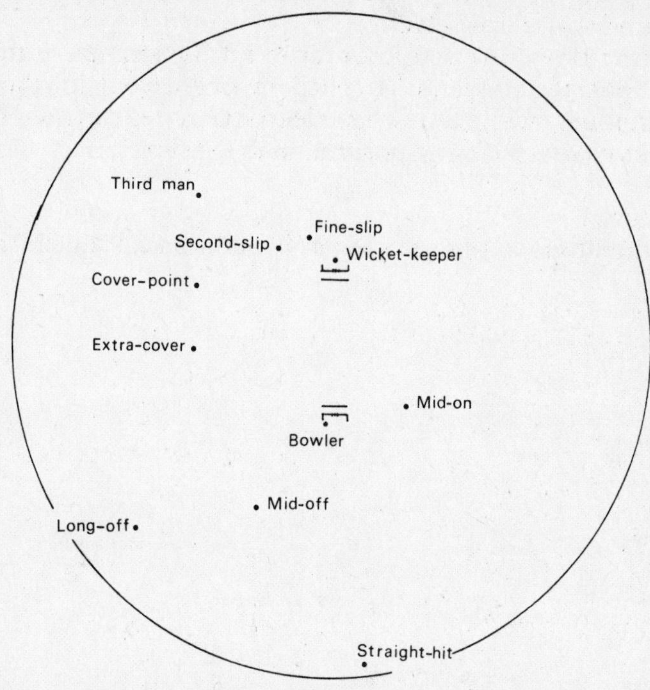

Diagram 12 – M. A. Noble's field for right-hand, medium-pace spinner

Game's the Thing (1926). I am not sure who the bowler was he had in mind, although he described him as 'right-hand, medium-pace spinner' and specified a 'good wicket'; but I have an uncharitable wish to see I. V. A. Richards bat against him!

Left-arm spin (basic)

This is the classic standard: good close pressure and double-ring cover. The batsman has to be competent and work hard to break out.

To attack

One of the covers, either cover or extra, can reinforce the close catchers on the off side. Mid-wicket can advance to forward short-leg; backward square-leg can move right in.

These moves naturally assume that there is plenty of turn. Forward short-leg is for the rebound as the batsman over-compensates for the turn. Backward short-leg is for the 'chinaman' or the arm-ball.

Notice, however, that in order to hit the stumps in these conditions, the bowler has to pitch on, or even outside the leg stump, thus inviting the sweep: deep square-leg can therefore be a better wicket-taking position than leg slip.

In defence

There are three basic strategies on a good wicket. The first is to

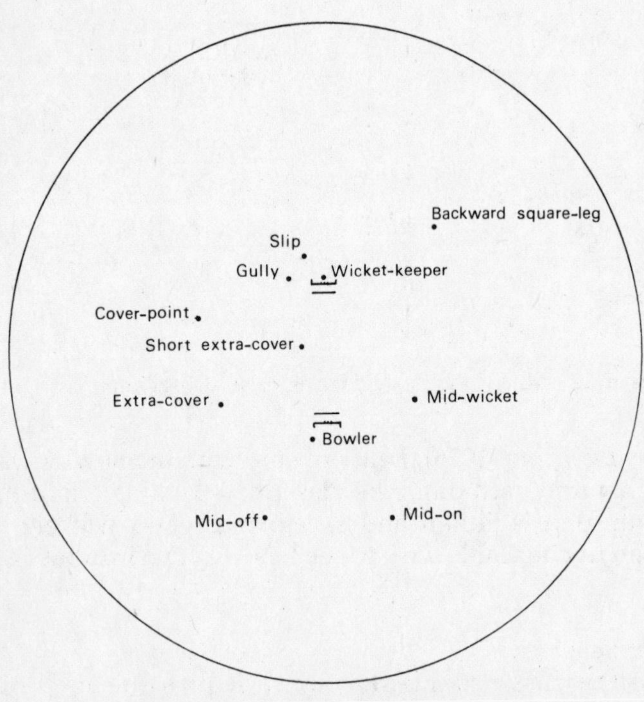

Diagram 13 – Left-arm spin, basic field

A captain's first duty is to win the toss! The author (*right*) and Nick Héroys toss for innings for Rugby v. Tonbridge in *The Cricketer* Cup final, 1973. On this occasion the author lost the toss but his side won. (*Patrick Eagar*)

Old Trafford Test, 1961. Benaud bowling round the wicket. (*Below*) he bowls Peter May first ball round his legs. (*The Photo Source*)

It takes courage to face the fast bowlers, whether you are a recognised batsman like Kim Hughes (*above*, fending off Willis), or a tailender/night-watchman such as Underwood, playing his jumping back shot against Holding. (*All Sport/Adrian Murrell*; and *Patrick Eagar*)

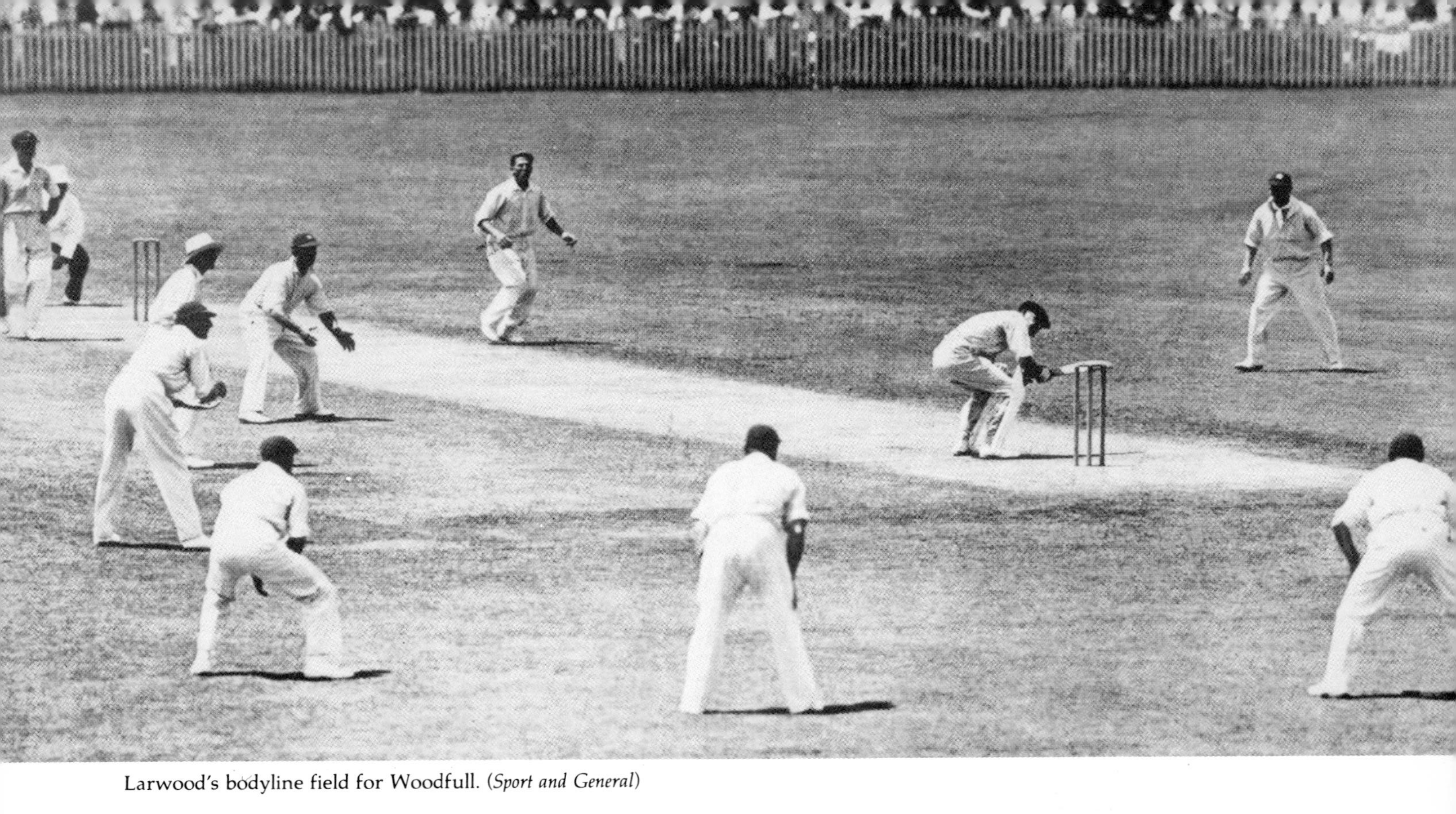

Larwood's bodyline field for Woodfull. (*Sport and General*)

It takes fitness and plenty of practice to field as brilliantly as Solomon here and achieve a famous tied Test. (*Brisbane Courier Mail*)

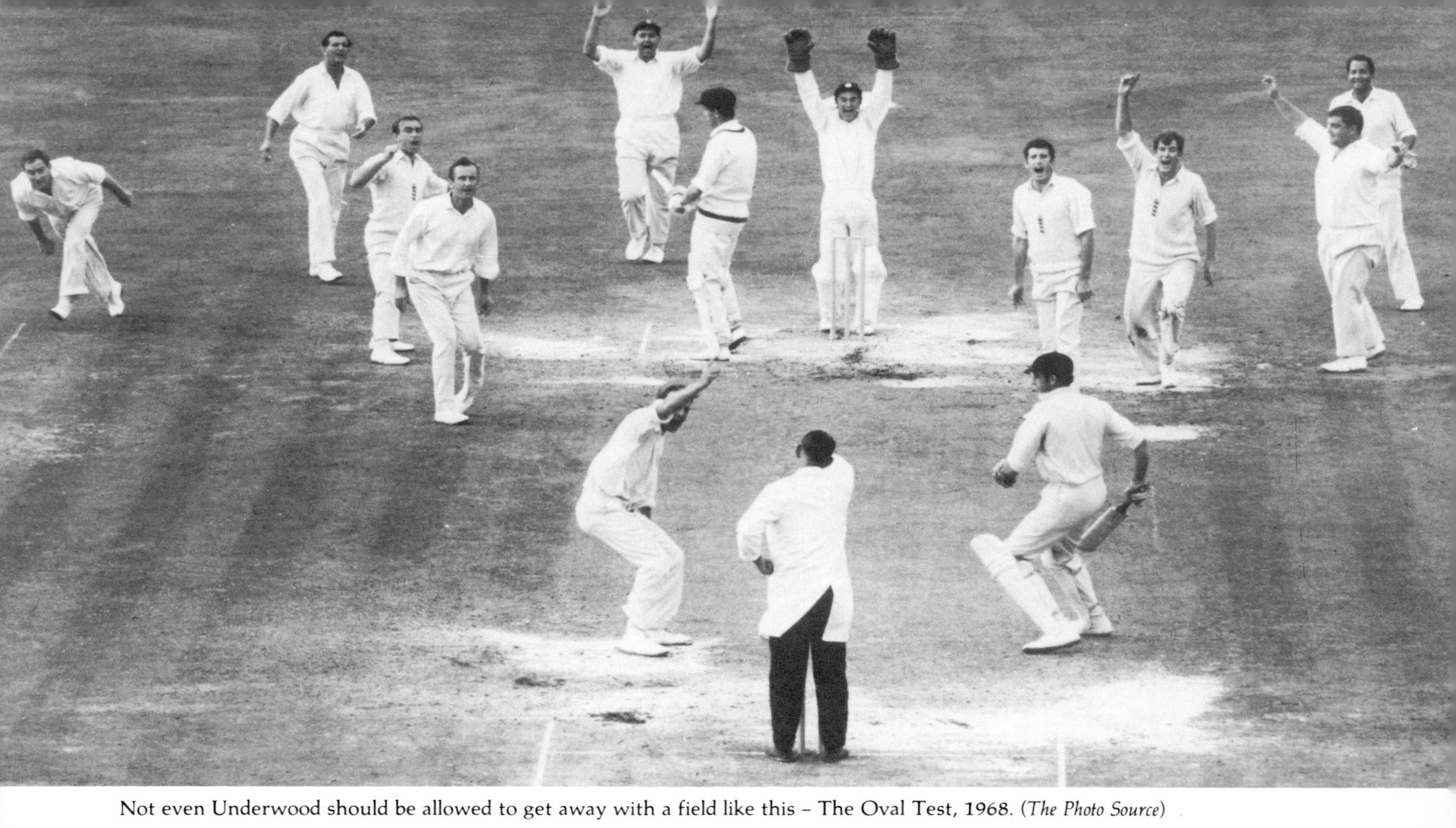

Not even Underwood should be allowed to get away with a field like this – The Oval Test, 1968. (*The Photo Source*)

Nor should Lillee, with his confidence-trick nine slips against New Zealand at Auckland, 1977. (*New Zealand Herald*)

Bradman's hundreth run of his hundreth hundred. Straight into the 'V'. (*MCC*)

The same can be said of Geoffrey Boycott's on-drive which brought up his hundreth hundred, against Australia at Headingley in 1977. (*Patrick Eagar*)

keep the original 6/3 split, by retaining a slip and a line of five men on the off side. Mid-off and mid-on can then be as deep as the boundary. In theory a deep square-leg should not be needed. He can, therefore, be moved round to a straightish mid-wicket on the boundary. This assumes, of course, that the bowler is going to continue to bowl *at* off stump.

The next alternative is to bowl *outside* off stump to a 7/2 split, with backward square-leg now on the extra-cover boundary.

The third alternative is really a limited-over ploy, but it has its place in proper cricket on occasions. It involves bowling over or round the wicket with a preponderance of arm-balls and attacking leg stump. The split is then three on the off, with no slip; and six on the leg side: square-leg, deep mid-wicket and long-on; and three men saving the single.

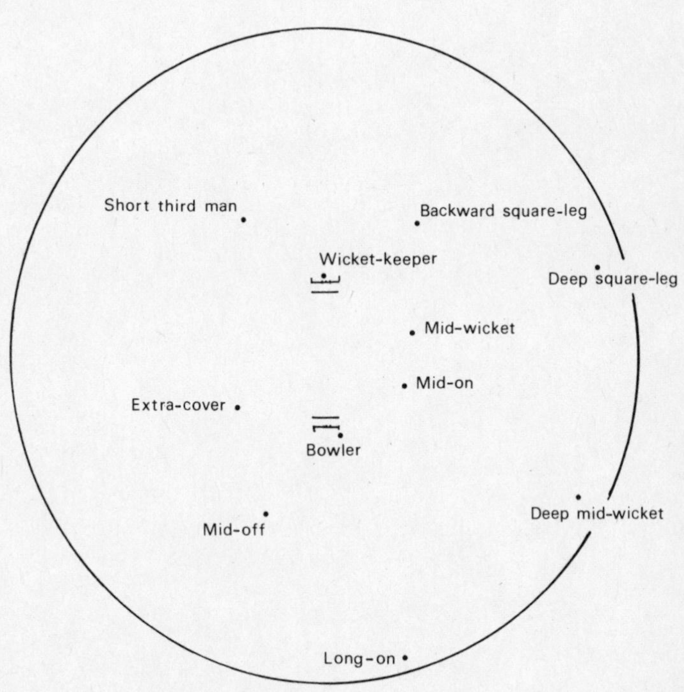

Diagram 14 – Left-arm spin – leg-stump defence

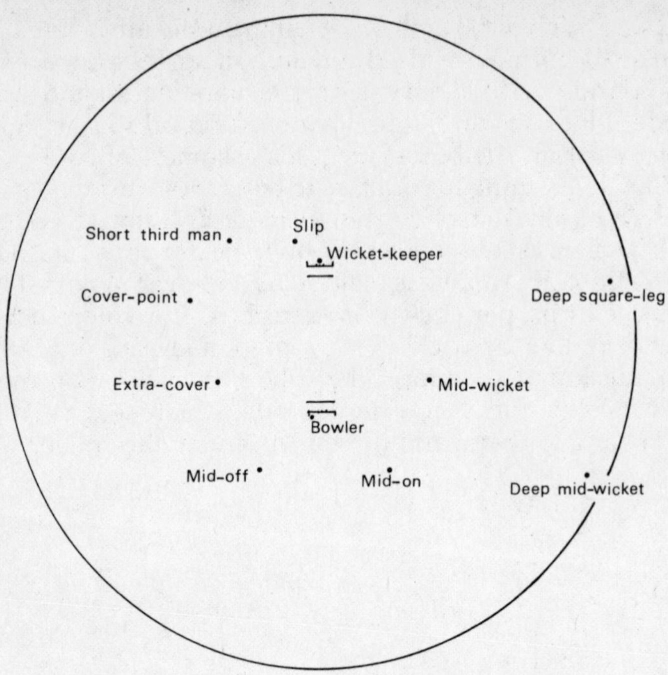

Diagram 15 – Leg-spin – standard field

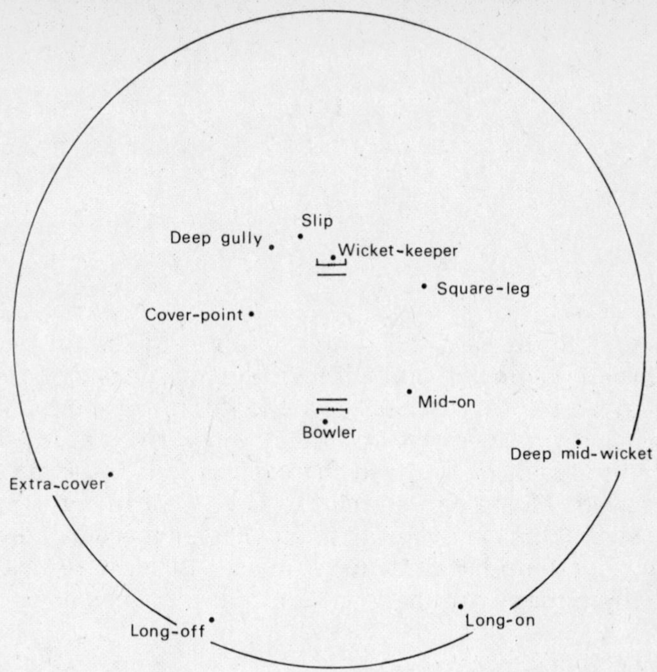

Diagram 16 – Leg-spin – field for 'looper'. See page 155.

15

Batting

At first sight the captain's duties, as far as the batting side is concerned, begin and end with writing out the batting order. It is indeed important that he should do this properly, at the team-selection stage. He will then have arrived at his 'best' order and still have scope to change it slightly if the match is going well. Most people prefer to have a fairly regular position, so that they know in advance what is expected of them. I have played under captains who use the lottery system, whereby a man who made a hundred one week at no. 5 is

Some captains prefer a lottery system for their batting order

quite likely to find himself at 6 the next, behind a chap who has been on holiday for a couple of weeks. It does not require much perception to find this less than reassuring for the players.

Suppose you have an opening bat who is going to miss a match. Most sides have a more senior player who used to open but now bats lower down. Do not expect results if you ask him to open 15 minutes before the start. Tell him a week in advance and let him have the chance of a net and the necessary mental retuning.

As the season progresses, a leading batsman may lose form and welcome a less onerous position for a game or two. Absentees may allow one of the middle order who has done well to be promoted. Again there will be opportunities if nos. 3, 4 or 5 have been having a glut of runs, to drop one of them down the order on a day when things are going well and keep one of the lesser lights in practice and confidence.

These adjustments come under the heading of man-management. There will also be technical changes. For example, no. 3, although a gifted stroke-player, may get out, too often for comfort, playing his shots too lavishly against the new ball and so have a more significant part to play a couple of places lower down the order.

One of the Second XI players might have a run of good scores and need promoting. There is then the vexed problem of playing him at, say, no. 6 or 7, where he may well not get an innings, or putting him at his usual position higher up, where he probably lacks the necessary experience or confidence to fill the role. There is no hard-and-fast answer. You need his help as to preference, and you both need the help and understanding of the rest of the side to get him through his initial ordeal.

If your side is batting first and is given a good start, there will be many occasions against the weaker fielding sides when the majority of the batting order is technically unimportant. Those are the times when you can experiment: you merely declare for 10 runs or so less. The actual total is not significant.

If you are batting second, however, it is vital to make the order as effective as possible. You do not want a hectic last-minute scamper. You want to get on top and stay on top and win at a canter. If you alter the order then you can end up with one of your best players stranded on 40 not out at one end while the tail-enders are demolished at the other. I speak from bitter experience.

The most important sections of the batting order are the top and the bottom. It makes an enormous difference if the team has a regular, reliable pair of openers to get most innings off to a sound start: it takes a great deal of clawing back into the game if you lose two quick wickets in every match.

Similarly, nos. 10 and 11, when you come to think about it, also have a vital role to fulfil. We used to have an excellent opening bowler – R. H. Neve, who took over 1,000 wickets for Limpsfield from 1956 to 68 – who refused to bat anywhere else but last, his beloved 'Jack' as he called it. He said that if he had to bat it was to do one of two jobs: he either had to defend like mad for quarter of an hour to save the match, or hit his only ball for 4 to win it. It gave him enormous pleasure to achieve either and he frequently displayed considerable courage and determination in so doing. Not a bad attitude.

I also recall another no. 11. I was running a wandering club side and was telephoned by a delightful Etonian, about three months before the game, who said he was qualifying for the club. He did not bowl, was an indifferent but keen fielder and batted no. 11, always. As it would save me a number of phone calls, I said that I was only too pleased for him to play.

On the great day we eventually found ourselves chasing a target of about 220 and we reached the final over of the day needing 6 runs to win with 2 wickets in hand. We got 2 off the first ball of the over and lost a wicket the next: 4 runs to win, four balls to go. The stage was set for the entry of our hero.

As he made his resplendent way down the pavilion steps, he stopped near me:

'What would you like me to do, Captain?'

'Just get 'em. Good luck.'

At the crease he took guard with great care, enquired of the umpire as to the number of balls remaining in the over, took an immense time imprinting on his memory the exact location of every fielder and after a few majestic twirls of his bat, stood ready to do battle.

Bat held aloft above his head, he greeted the first ball with outstretched pad. After checking his guard again and making a further detailed examination of the field-players, he did exactly the same with the next delivery – and the next two! Exeunt twelve other players dumbfounded.

In the pub later, amid considerable noise, we asked him what he would have done had I told him, 'Don't get out', instead?

'Oh, exactly the same thing.'

The prime contribution of batsmen in successful sides is self-discipline, rather than the scoring of runs *per se*. Both those nos. 11 had self-discipline but the first allowed his play to be subservient to the requirements of the side and the situation. Which is vital!

An instance requiring such self-discipline is when the opposition has been dismissed for, say, 130 runs on a wettish wicket with 2½ hours left to play. The fielding side will then try to bowl tight, have a strong ring field saving the singles, and hope to frustrate the batsmen into committing suicide. In those circumstances the only real scoring shots are off the full toss, or full half-volley, or a rank long hop.

Singles can still be steadily garnered with careful weight and placing, but there is to be no flamboyant cover driving, no wristy working of the ball through the leg side, no artistry, no glamour; just a steady workmanlike accumulation of runs to reach the target. It is not much fun, but satisfaction comes from a job well done.

One sees thousands of batsmen get out through trying to play shots that are not only not 'on', but in the circumstances not even needed. They are not prepared to subject themselves to the discipline and requirements of the side. It is all very well for them to go in, play a few exotic shots ('what a good player,' they will say) and get out. Somebody has still to get his head down and graft to win the match.

Nor is there any excuse either for batsmen who progress so slowly that they ruin the timing of your declaration, or cause their partners to commit suicide in an attempt to make up lost time in pursuit of a total.

One can be adamant about this on two counts; first it is the captain's duty to instil a sense of collective responsibility into his batsmen and give them as precise a target as possible. They should always be aiming at a specific total, even when batting first. There should usually also be a specific timescale involved. For example, if your side is batting first, you might aim at a total of 200, incorporating 50 runs in the first hour and a declaration time. Again, when batting second and chasing a similar target, your instructions might be that on no account is the score to be less than 120 at the start of the last 20 overs (i.e., 80 runs needed).

If the batsmen know what the target is they will do their best to achieve it. If they are left to work it out for themselves they are much more likely to work it out wrongly.

A remarkable example of this effect occurred in the 1978–9 tour of Australia, in the fourth Test. England had batted without conviction in the first innings to be all out for 152. By lunch on the second day Australia were 125 for 1. Thereafter, in the face of prodigious efforts by the England bowlers, Australia failed to carry the attack to the enemy and were dismissed for 294. Had the batsmen applied a little positive thought to their position on the second afternoon, when England were bowling without Willis and Hendrick, and Gooch trundled down 40 amiable balls for 14 runs, they could have perpetrated a massacre. As it was, Brearley's inspiring leadership in the field then continued into England's second innings where Randall's dedication to saving the match, and unfailing concentration, enabled the side to crawl slowly and painfully to a position of comparative safety by the close of the fourth day.

On the fifth day England calmly and adroitly settled down to exploit their hard-won advantage. Australia were now in a difficult situation psychologically. Having voiced their opinions in the press to the effect that the England second innings was boring, strokeless, negative and generally unworthy of the best standards of the game, their players were now faced with the most tantalising target: 205 runs in 266 minutes on a wearing wicket.

By shouting the odds at the end of the fourth day, the batsmen were in no proper frame of mind to approach their final target with the resolute sobriety needed. They had a long time in which to get the runs. What they needed was a long steady start; 60 to 80 runs in the first 2 hours without losing more than one wicket would have been perfect. By then they would have held the initiative and the later batsmen could have applied pressure and acceleration.

Instead of that they hit their way to 38 in no time at all, lost a couple of wickets, and did not know what best to do next. Brearley seized his chance. By setting 7/2 fields for his two off-spinners, Emburey and Miller, he was able to have close catchers and at the same time block all the scoring shots. But what he was really doing was capitalising on their frame of mind: 111 all out. A win by 93 runs. Thank you very much.

England were indeed lucky to find so able a captain as Brearley just at the time of Packer's incursion into cricket; for he is a strong contender for the award of best captain, *qua* captain, England has ever had. However even the best make mistakes, which is some comfort for the rest of us.

Incidentally, M. A. Noble won a very similar victory for Australia in the fifth Test of the 1907–8 series: Australia 137, England 287. Australia then set England 279 to win (Trumper 166) and won by 49 runs in the last over of the match. (See also p. 159.)

I have stressed the importance of mental discipline, the setting of targets and a side's collective psychology in achieving success, but it is just as instructive to give an example of deficiency in these respects. In making judgments of quality about such abstract subjects as leadership, it is easy to scoff at a side's being out-thought. Therefore it is doubly instructive to examine a situation in which a side, although it understands such matters, is still 'done'.

England's tour to Australia in the following winter of 1979–80 saw the return to Test cricket of the Packer players. There continued the barrage of publicity to the effect that all the best players had been with Packer: Roberts, Holding, Croft and Garner having provided West Indian substance to this allegation during the Prudential Cup in the summer of 1979.

For England the return to the fold of their Packer players posed more of a problem than for the other Test-playing countries. England had been through a highly successful period in terms of results, whatever the arguments as to playing standards. Several very young players had seized, with both hands, the opportunity to establish themselves. Meanwhile, there seemed to be doubts as to the continued high level of performance of Underwood, Woolmer and Knott, who had played with Packer. The close-knit team spirit (established by Tony Greig in India before he joined Packer), carefully nurtured by the selectors and the tour management, could be in danger of being undermined. On the other hand, the pressure to include Packer players, in order to demonstrate the end of schism, was considerable.

Australia, too, had a larger number of players to welcome back. They were hurt and angry at the events of the previous winter: 'Just you wait, Poms.' There were plenty of English batsmen whose careers and nerves had been shattered by 'Lillian Thomson', so there was no shortage of experience of the reality that could be expected to be awaiting those Poms. The publicity then was insistent: Dennis Lillee was waiting at the end of his run, with the wind at his back, on the fastest wicket in the world, his home ground, the WACA in Perth.

The message got through! Boycott and Randall were removed by Lillee without scoring, in reply to Australia's modest 244. From that moment, although Brearley made a determined 53, Australia were in command.

Injuries and those selection problems had meant that England no longer had the infallible catching and impenetrable fielding ability of recent seasons, so they had not been able to lift themselves mentally back into the game before setting off in pursuit of 350 in the final innings. Lack of application and of belief in themselves then allowed them to succumb to the awkward left-arm bowler Dymock.

Their mental approach to this match was coloured by another factor which should not be overlooked. Concurrent with the triangular Test series there was also a limited-over series, the opening salvoes of which had already been fired. England, in its three opening games, had beaten West Indies once and Australia twice. One would have thought this a helpful start, but not a bit of it! The Australian attitude was that limited-overs is a negative form of cricket of little value. 'Just you wait till we play you at real cricket.' Bad planning, the failure to agree playing conditions and bad publicity over the question of the Ashes all helped to put added pressure on the tour management. The ease of England's second one-day victory had been too good to be true: neither over-confidence nor self-doubt is a helpful prelude to a stern contest. So the first requirements in the avoidance of disaster are planning, the creation of a positive mental approach, and the setting of targets. The next is that the batsmen should talk to each other.

Batting is always a partnership. So it is vital to make it a successful and happy one. Each partner must be aware of the preferences, problems and requirements of his colleagues at the other end.

First, the openers have to decide who is going to face. If one is left-handed I believe he should always do so, because it tends straightaway to make the bowlers struggle to find a line. They then relax slightly when faced with the right-hander, so he has a bonus, too. Since I am, or was, a left-handed opener myself, for many years I had a bet with my partner that the first ball of the season would get me off the mark. I invariably won because it was always short of a length outside the off stump! Outside off stump, because I could see the bowler mentally adjusting his line: short, because soft May footholds do not give the same push as the floor of indoor nets.

After the first over from both ends, there should be a mid-wicket chat about such matters as swing, and movement off the seam. The non-striker can help by noting how close to the stumps or otherwise the bowler delivers.

As the innings progresses, one batsman will often find that he is out-scoring the other. The latter should say to him, 'Gosh you're going well today, I'll give you as much of the strike as I can.' Even if he does not literally do so, he will have helped enormously just by saying it.

Conversely one batsman may find one of the bowlers difficult to play. He should tell his partner, who will say, 'OK, I'll take him for you.' The batsman with the problem can then settle down and just play him: he does not have to worry about scoring off him any longer; that is now his partner's job. Again, his partner does not have to take any further action himself. The chat is enough.

The opening batsmen also have a duty to communicate with the rest of the batsmen. The latter are watching the initial overs with some trepidation and want every possible assurance that there are no insurmountable problems of pace or bounce. So the openers should consciously try to cultivate an attitude of composure and confidence – even if they do not feel it.

Of course, the bowlers will try to do the opposite. I remember Peter Loader, of Surrey and England, bowling me a bouncer one evening which ballooned way over my head off a

very slow, wet wicket. My partner had the temerity to rib him about it later after play. 'Oh,' said Peter, 'that wasn't for him, but if one of you had got out at least I'd have had the next batsmen thinking. He will have seen it all right.'

Also, when a wicket falls, it certainly helps the incoming batsman if the incumbent has a word with him before he faces his first ball: 'He's a little faster than he looks', or 'It's keeping a bit low that end', or 'He's bowled quite a lot of yorkers', or even 'It's just straight up and down!'

I love those famous old saws for appropriate occasions: Hirst and Rhodes: 'We'll get 'em in singles.' And there is another one, for the same sort of circumstances but in a broiling cauldron such as Melbourne, when our two heroes are observed meeting half-way from the pavilion. After the famous one-wicket victory one was asked what the other had said: 'Effing hot, aint it?'

The incoming batsman, for his part, if the circumstances remotely permit, should compliment the resident and, if he has been scoring at all well, assure him of all the strike he wants.

The strike is very important. In a defensive engagement it is usually much better for the batsmen to concentrate on keeping one bowler each. From the bowler's point of view the other player invariably looks easier to overcome than the one he is faced with. And in one sense that is correct, since it must be easier for each batsman to cope with only one set of problems.

In all other circumstances the opposite generally applies. Obviously, if one batsman is going really well, it is best for both of them to ensure that he receives as much of the strike as possible. It is often amazing, incidentally, how fast the support player can progress just in singles.

In normal 50:50 relationships it is a constant annoyance to the fielding side to have the strike changing. The field probably has to be altered, the bowlers are denied the opportunity of producing a tight pattern of deliveries in series and, of course, singles keep the score ticking along without undue risk.

In this context it is perfectly natural for each batsman at the start of an over to be looking for fours and then a single towards the end of it! They should therefore rib each other about 'counting well' if this happens from time to time, as it does remind one another to look for *all* the runs available, not just most of them.

There are some batsmen in a side, the clean hitters who score mainly in boundaries, or at least full hits, while others rely on a steady stream of singles being tucked away. The two types should complement each other. Yet very often they do not, because the hitter is not looking for the same sort of run. He is often unaware of the deftness of the soft nudge that will not reach short third man; he can even ignore his own mishit. He wants the strike, yet he is often unresponsive to the 'nudger's' ability to give it to him. Captain and batsmen have a positive duty to bridge this gap in attitude.

The captain can do a great deal to improve the running between the wickets of all his batsmen. Some players are bad judges of a run and little can be done about that. However, a side that bats with a feeling of mutual confidence and partnership can put ceaseless pressure on the fielding side and improve its own run rate.

A ball may be hit towards the boundary at long-on, for example. The striker calls 'Yes!' and, as he passes the non-striker, he says, 'There may be another.' The non-striker should answer, 'Hang on a moment,' or 'I'll have a look.' They both run, touch and turn, before the non-striker calls, 'Yes' or 'No'.

Without that mid-wicket exchange (a) the non-striker may not run his first run fast enough to take the second and (b) there is always the danger that the striker, expecting two runs, will turn and advance too far before being sent back by the non-striker fatally late.

Similarly, between overs, the batsmen should exchange information, such as, 'There's always two to third man, I think he's got a weak arm', or 'There's a run square on the leg side; mid-wicket is left-handed.' Or again, 'Now they've pushed mid-on back a bit even the hard hit to him is a run.' The opportunities are endless, the principle constant.

In all this endeavour to weld a batting side to a common purpose, one point must not be overlooked. The captain must try to exploit the individuality of each batsman. On no account should the stroke-players be curbed or the nudgers undervalued. Against some batting sides you can set a field for one batsman and it will remain more or less correct for all the others. The better batting sides set repeated problems for the fielding side because each one of them seems to have different strengths and methods.

A good captain manages to exploit the individual differences of his side and makes each member aware of his potential contribution to a successful unit. In setting his batting order and talking with his players he is providing an environment in which they can all flourish.

This is especially important when a new member joins the side. He will invariably be trying to show the others what a good player he is, rather than concentrating on the requirements of the team. A clear understanding of this predicament on the part of the captain is the first step in welding him into the whole. Otherwise a couple of failures by the new man can mean that the side is carrying a real passenger for several matches. Mike Gatting had just this personal barrier to surmount before the making of his first Test hundred gave him sufficient self-confidence to bat to his true ability. Club cricketers do not have to withstand the press sniping, but better management could have guided him through that particular wilderness far more quickly.

As with the hitter and the 'nudger', batsmen of one type frequently misunderstand the value of those with a different approach. Many opening batsmen in club cricket play a very limited number of shots, spend a long time at the crease and glean a huge amount of runs over the season. They often cause considerable frustration among their free-scoring teammates. They are of immense value to the stroke-players who follow them in providing a platform from which they can launch themselves; but they must be made aware of their limitations, learn to run well and, as the innings progresses, give the bulk of the strike to the more free-scoring players.

The dour opener, for his part, frequently takes the view that his colleagues just throw their wickets away. He must make sure that this is never through frustration caused by his own slowness. Of course, there will be occasions when the free-scorers might have curbed their natural instincts somewhat, but he will learn to be mighty glad of their extra range and weight of shots to take the pressure off him whenever he finds the going difficult.

This is a fairly characteristic problem, encountered in most sides, but it is really a question of communication. Similarly, if there is a batsman in your side with whom one or two others dislike batting, the only way to solve the problem is to get them to talk about it. They will end, almost certainly, by all being grateful for doing so, and become more complete performers as a result. Above all, they will enjoy their cricket more.

16

Limited-over cricket

Limited-over cricket was developed (a) to answer a desire for knock-out competition; (b) as a remedy for bad cricket, to prevent the dull draw; and (c) for financial purposes to attract less sophisticated crowds by instant excitement.

The technical expertise and sheer athleticism displayed now at the higher levels of one-day cricket are truly amazing. The limited-over game has undoubtedly improved the standards of fielding, of field-placing, of defensive bowling and of the batting of tail-enders. There can be no doubt either that batsmen have learnt to score runs at a fast and sustained rate in situations which, a few years back, would have been looked upon as impossible. It is not uncommon for sides in the Sunday League to score 16 runs off the last over of the match to win.

In good conditions, between teams of somewhere near equal strength, the result is usually mathematically close, which means that one bad over, especially towards the later stages of the game, can affect the result dramatically. The game is exciting and easy to follow.

However, between sides of *unequal* strength, or where conditions favour one side disproportionately, it is the most boring type of game imaginable. Even in a 'good' game there are few subtleties, no hidden depths, no rich contrasts. But, and it is a big but, in a knock-out you must win, so you have to keep calm and hold your wits about you, come what may.

As in real cricket, it is most important that you do your homework thoroughly – more so even, for if you get it wrong, there is no tomorrow. The rules of the competition dictate the number of bowlers you must have, but it is handy if you have sufficient all-rounders to enable you to carry an extra bowler in case of mishaps, whether brought on by injury or by opposing batsmen. Do not be afraid to play your spinners.

Poor John Mortimore, the Gloucestershire off-spinner, did his species a great disservice by being hit unceremoniously out of Lord's in the early days of the Gillette Cup, but spinners can, in truth, be just as effective as medium-paced trundlers. What you need are accurate bowlers who can bat a bit and field well; it is a demanding game.

As normally, find out all that you can about your opponents. Work out your batting order and your probable bowling pattern. Bowlers like to know if you are intending to give them three spells of four overs or expect to bowl them straight out (even if you do change your mind when the time comes). Similarly batsmen are happier during a long, hot session in the field if they know whether they have to get padded up straightaway or can put their feet up for a while.

Finally, fix it firmly in your team's minds that they are going to be fielding for a long time. There is nowhere to hide and relax. The real pressure comes in the last 5, 10, or 15 overs, or just before lunch; either way you will have spent 2 hours or more in the field on the trot. Do not allow them to relax when things are going well. Belligerent counter-attack can change the picture very rapidly indeed. Each man has a vital role to play; he should know what that is.

When you reach the ground, study carefully its size and shape and the speed of the outfield. It is easy on a new ground to give away needless runs because, for example, third man is too deep to save two, or because it has a strange shape, such as a square boundary so close that you have to settle for giving away some singles in order to save fours.

Fielding first. The first principle is, of course, that since you have to make whatever your opponents make, in a fixed time, there is no necessary advantage in bowling them out quickly. Your job is to keep them down to the lowest possible score. In general, therefore, you get them to commit suicide by keeping the game too tight for scoring comfortably. Attack by conventional means is highly dangerous.

Fielding second. I remember once having our opposition 0 for 4 in 2 overs, chasing 180. We thereupon had lots of slips and short-legs, close fielders who could have lost us the match. What we should have had was two third men and two long-legs!

Field-placing. With the new ball you might allow yourself, say, a 6/3 field; mid-on, short square-leg, long-leg, two slips, gulley, third man, cover, mid-off. Do not leave it like that for long, though, unless chances and few runs are coming; defend first and foremost.

The best defensive field for medium-pace is, of course, the saving-one ring, providing that no fours pierce it, i.e., as long as conditions and the batsmen allow you to get away with it. Third man, mid-wicket and long-leg will be the first to be put out on the boundary (see Diag. 15, p. 162).

The third-man area is one of the most complex of problems. The only way to block the arc from square cover to long-stop, as far as the faster bowlers are concerned, is to have three men: a fine third man on the fence is needed to cover the gap normally filled by the slips; then, of course, one can hardly do

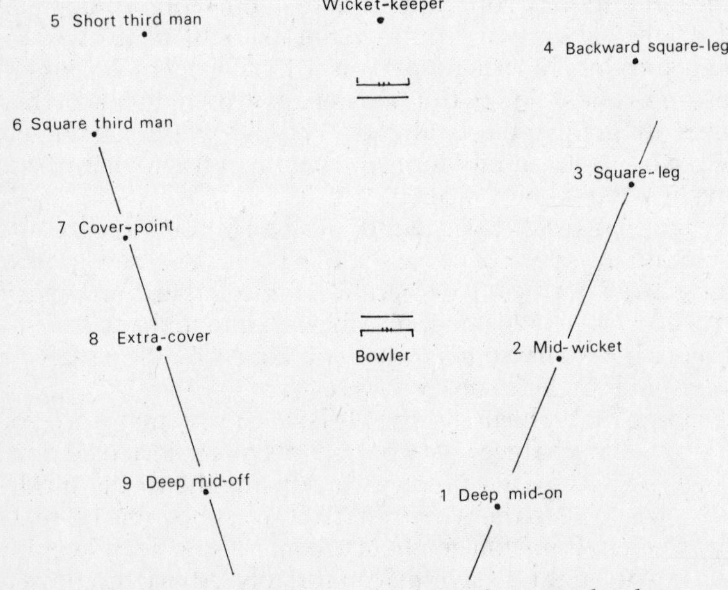

Diagram 17 – Limited-over ring for medium-pace bowlers

Back to the 'Big A', but you will not get away with this field in faster conditions, or with quicker bowlers; or against positive batting. Once the field is penetrated save the fours as well as singles.

without the standard squarish man on the edge to counter the square-cut and square-drive; finally, in limited-over cricket, short third man is given a lot of catches and without him there is a huge yawning gap, inviting singles.

This is reasonable since the strong arc at third man should be strictly necessary only for an off-side line. The trouble is that, if the bowling is not straight, the batsman has a free hit; if it is straight it can be worked away to the leg side.

The limited-over ring for medium-pace bowlers

Assumptions: slowish, typical club wicket with a little movement off the pitch or in the air, and slowish outfield to match. Right-hand batsman.

Go for this arrangement with your seam-up bowlers whenever possible.

There is a 4/5 split. Depending on which way the ball is being moved, this can be weighted to off or to leg.

Long-leg and third man can frequently be close enough to save the single if the combination of bowler's speed and conditions allow.

There are no singles available. The gaps are very small, so it takes a bad ball and good timing and placing to pierce this field in slow conditions. Expect to be hit over the top, straight, or to mid-wicket.

Under pressure, or with faster bowlers, or in faster conditions, the usual variations are as follows, in one combination or another:

1. *Bowling at leg stump.* Nos. 3 and 4 both on the boundary; nos. 6 or 7 moves to mid-wicket to join no. 2; no. 5 remains on the boundary, fairly fine.
2. *Bowling at off stump.* Place nos. 5 and 7 on the boundary. You can also move no. 3 across to join them if the bowler's accuracy and movement, and the batsman's lack of ability, will allow. No. 6 becomes short third man. No. 7 may well be behind square, too. Club batsmen do not move their feet the way Vivian Richards does, so do not fear to set the field for them, not for him.

Bowl a full length and a consistent line (no apologies for saying this yet again). Then nos. 1 and 9 can go as far back as you like, nos. 2 and 8 must stay straight, in line with the bowler's stumps, no. 3 in front of square, nos. 6 and 7 again on

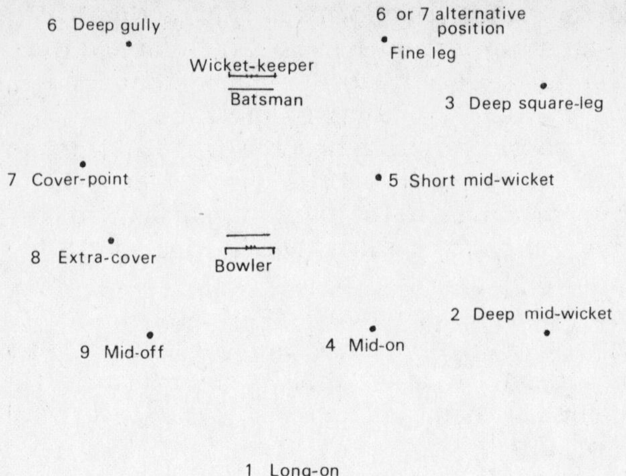

Diagram 18 – Limited-overs double-ring for spinners – right-hand batsman

the single. Do you now sense that no. 6 is spare? He can be used anywhere you fancy, on the slog at mid-wicket, or at deep square third man/cover point, or saving a single behind square on either side of the wicket. Yes, but it still requires a full length and line.

Limited-over double-ring for spinners
Assumptions: slowish conditions, as in previous example, but with some turn in the wicket.

The important points to realise, as distinct from field-settings for the faster bowlers, are these:

1. You no longer need to defend the arcs behind the wicket so assiduously.
2. You can usually put greater pressure on the single because of the lack of pace on the ball.
3. There is a greater danger of one really disastrous over.

For the *off-spinner* a 5/4 leg-side split is probably standard, with three men on the leg-side boundary (see Diag. 18). If there is enough turn, short third man or square cover point, nos. 6 or 7, can save the single behind on the leg side instead. The field is then split 6/3, which is stronger.

Always make sure that the gap between nos. 8 and 9 is minimal because there is no one behind them. Keep no. 8 level with the bowler's stumps. Under pressure mid-off, no. 9 can go out on the boundary as well, as indeed can no. 7, but never no. 8.

A useful variation is to bowl round the wicket, with a 6/3 leg-side split. Then three men plus the bowler will be placed to save the single on the leg side.

For the *left-arm spinner* there are similarly two main themes.

The classic method is to bowl off stump and outside to a 6/3 off-side split, with long-off and deep extra cover on the boundary, and four men saving the single. On the leg side a straight mid-wicket level with the bowler's stumps saves the single, with nos. 1 and 2 on the edge at long-on and mid-wicket. For this the bowler must bowl round the wicket, but from really close to the stumps.

The alternative is to bowl at leg stump and outside, either from round the wicket and at a wide angle, or from over the wicket. In either case there will probably be a relatively high proportion of arm-balls *vis-à-vis* the off-stump attack.

The field-placing will then be split 6/3 leg side if possible, 5/4 if you must, the same as for the off-spinner. Nos. 6 and 7 on the leg side will be kept extremely busy.

There is a dangerous mistake, now frequently to be seen in club limited-over matches, caused by slavishly copying the first-class performers.

If you were lucky enough to watch the last over of the 1985 NatWest final between Nottinghamshire and Essex, you will have seen Derek Randall achieve the well-nigh impossible by hitting 16 runs off the first five of Pringle's deliveries. Each ball was bowled well outside the leg stump and three of them were creamed for 4 through the covers.

Randall had thus left himself just 2 runs to score for victory and immortality off the last ball. Easy after what he had just managed! But being mortal, and dearly loved for it, he hit a full toss straight to mid-wicket!

Randall is a sort of genius. Club batsmen cannot begin to emulate him. So do not begin to think that you need three sweepers on the cover boundary when your bowlers are bowling outside the leg stump!

The serious point is this. You only need sweepers on the boundary on both sides of the ground if your bowlers are going to bowl on both sides of the wicket. Containing most club batsmen is easy because of their limited range of shots. Just because it is a limited-over match they will not develop new ones; but do observe the individual with your usual care. Concentrate on bottling up *his* shots, not someone else's.

Handling your bowling

Assuming that the conditions are such that it is likely the batting side will use all their allotted overs, it is most important to have your best (and preferably your fastest) bowlers available at the end. You are taking a risk, therefore, if you use up more than half their overs with the new ball. At the same time you do not want to change them both at once, so think in terms of, for example, 2 × 6 overs for one and 3 × 4 overs for the other.

The next sensible ploy is to get your spinner(s) on early. The batsmen are not so likely to go for an all-out assault in, say, the ninth over, especially if you have managed to take an early wicket or so, as they will be later. This means, therefore, that a spinner can risk giving the ball a little more air, which in turn gives him more variety and enables him to bowl better, while the batsman has a greater problem picking the ball to hit. You have to balance this against the amount of life and movement still available for your other change seamers.

In this form of cricket you are operating within a rather rigid framework, and so one ghastly problem recurs: unless you remember to slot in an odd number of overs from someone, or change ends at some time, you will find that one of your carefully preserved opening bowlers is left with the insurmountable problem of having to bowl two consecutive overs from opposite ends to finish the innings! There must be someone in the side good at mathematics. Get him to sort it out for you.

You should aim to break out of this rigid system as far as you can. Think in terms of short spells rather than long ones, unless you have the batsmen really bottled up tight. By doing so you are constantly probing for weaknesses and setting slightly different problems, never letting batsmen settle. You are also keeping your own options open for as long as possible. You want to postpone as long as you can the evil moment when a bowler is being hit to all parts and yet you have to keep him on.

Mike Gatting made a fascinating decision in this respect in the Benson and Hedges International series at Perth in January 1987 when England beat the West Indies. England were defending 228 which, in theory, was about 30 runs below par for the conditions. However, the demands of a full schedule on the Indian subcontinent had clearly taken their toll of the West Indian batsmen. Gladstone Small and Botham had bowled extremely well. When John Emburey removed Vivian Richards, Phil Edmonds and he operated in harness to make Logie and Dujon struggle hard to keep any sort of momentum going. With 20 overs to go, West Indies needed 120 runs and had 6 wickets in hand. Dilley had 6 overs left, Small 2, Edmonds 8 and Emburey 4.

The obvious standard plan would be to finish with Dilley and Small bowling the last 5 overs. The other consideration always is to attempt to guard against calamity by keeping all options open as long as possible. My thinking would therefore have been to keep the shackles on with the spinners so long as the batsmen allowed it, swopping then to Dilley with Edmonds, and being quite happy for Dilley to bowl two separate spells.

What did Gatting do? He split the spin partnership, before anything happened, and put on Small, thereby both losing an option and committing himself to ending with a spinner at one end. He may have intended to give Dilley two spells, but he bowled him straight through. As a result he finished with spin at both ends.

Convention suggests that Gatting played it completely wrong, but since Dilley bowled a perfect line and length with a touch of out-swing, he eased him off the hook. On the other hand perhaps it so confused the batsmen that they looked like novices?

As in any form of cricket it is vital that you know when you are winning. In 1984 and 1985 there were two extraordinary instances when Kent lost their final and England lost to Australia. The circumstances were strangely similar. In both cases left-arm spinners, Underwood and Edmonds, were winning the match for the side fielding second, but were taken off before they had used up their quota of overs. The game was then won easily off the quicker but plainer bowlers. Stupid captaincy.

There are several related matters that are worthy of note and comment.

Attacking new batsmen
Although attack in the normal sense is dangerous, negative attack can be as effective. A new batsman should be hemmed in to prevent his getting a single. Make him struggle to get off the mark, and especially when there is someone going well at the other end and the new man is desperate to get away from the bowling. With luck, too desperate.

Fielding second with insufficient runs
When your side has batted first, and failed to make enough runs, the likelihood is that you will not have to bowl all your allotted overs. In this case it is obviously important to make sure that your best men have every chance to bowl their full share. Apart from leaving out your 'bit' bowlers, which is no problem, do not hesitate to change anyone who is presenting less problems than you might have hoped.

By 'enough runs' I mean, of course, your view of the standard for that day in those conditions. Bearing in mind the state of the wicket, speed of outfield and size of ground, add to or subtract from a 'norm' of somewhere about four runs per over. Raymond Illingworth has commented that the biggest problem at county level is for the side batting first to establish the correct standard for that day. Your batsmen have largely to do that for you: make them think about it.

Conversely, where your side has made plenty of runs, you can help yourself further by using up your second-string bowlers at an early stage. Make sure you save all the fours with five or six men on the fence. Then your best bowlers really will have the whip-hand when the desperation stakes are run later.

Twelfth man
Many minor considerations can make a big difference. A twelfth man, a rarity in club cricket, can prove to be the difference between winning and losing a knock-out match. Just think: one man who is not even playing, between your club and that trophy. That makes him just as vital as the other eleven: if he realises that, he will be there.

Over rates

If you field first it is especially important to keep the game going. The fielders stay more alert and will be out there for a shorter time.

Rain

Do not bowl with a wet ball. There is no virtue, no morality about hurrying: the game will be shortened if need be. Make sure your bowlers keep the ball dry; stand at mid-off yourself with a rag. You do not want to field in the wet. The umpires will be quite happy to stay if there is plenty of action. They are human, in spite of everything, so they will soon get fed up watching you drying the ball while they are getting colder and wetter!

Make sure your bowlers keep the ball dry

Intervals

Do not allow your own batsmen to play for lunch or tea. On the contrary, the last few overs before an interval are precisely the time to cut loose if you can. The fielders will be at their tiredest and longing for the break. The moment to hit out is when your opponents are thinking that they have not done too badly.

Summary

What strikes me as particularly odd about limited-over cricket is that all the work seems to be done by the bowlers. Having bowled and fielded all day, they feel they can then sit back for a while and watch the batting stars enjoy themselves in their various ways. Then, suddenly, what happens? One of those poor old bowlers has to go out and hit his only ball, the last of the match, for four in order to win! A strange system, indeed. The important point, however, is that the crunch comes at the end. The pressure drifts towards the end of each innings very much more than in normal cricket.

At the end of the first innings it is difficult to keep the fielding side concentrating and working and controlling events. It requires constant pre-match emphasis and determination. The better the fielding side has performed earlier, the more difficult this is.

At the end of the second innings the attitude is different because there is a specific total in view. A well-organised fielding side, with its most defensive bowlers operating, should always be able to win against the last three or four batsmen when they need 20 or 30 runs off the last 5 overs.

Having offered all the foregoing advice, I must admit to one delightful occasion when I got it all wrong. In January 1975 I skippered our club side in a Mackeson Cup competition in Jamaica. Before we went there we had a few nets and some fielding practice in the rain on the fairway of a local golf course: better than nothing, perhaps, but not the ideal preparation. We also had an ideas-cum-briefing session during which I warned everyone that (a) the umpires would cheat and (b) we should be able to make up for our physical shortcomings by our intellectual superiority. Read on.

In the event the umpires were outstandingly good and fair; and mentally the Jamaicans were so far ahead of us in making the best use of their conditions that it was almost a contest between men and boys. We had, admittedly, to get used to the brilliant light, the heat (and the rum), the hard, gritty outfields, and the little plateau-like playing strip. Fielding there was totally different from anything we had practised in England!

We won one match. The other four all followed the same course. I lost the toss. The opposition locked themselves in their changing-room. We had a beer. The smallest Jamaican available was sent out with the message, 'You bat, man.'

We thereupon struggled against some alarming variations in bounce until the wicket dried out. This meant that we invariably failed by about 20 to 40 runs to set the home side the target we wanted to give them.

During the interval I would give our side my usual pep talk about keeping things really tight with the new ball, getting them behind the clock, and everything being 'even Stevens' again.

The Jamaicans simply knocked the ball down off the raised wicket into the dust and played tip and run. Coupled with the odd bad delivery this meant that after the first half-dozen overs they had scored 30 runs or more and the game was all over bar the shouting – of which there was plenty! It also made it very difficult to get our three best bowlers (all spinners) into action early enough to affect the outcome.

Once the shine was off, the locals usually proceeded to play themselves in, but on one occasion they managed to find room to disprove yet another of my theories.

We had scored 179 in our 45 overs. They were 128 for 8 after 27 overs. So, needing 52 to win with 18 overs to go, they were well ahead of the clock (as always), but there was surely no way in which nos. 8, 10 and 11 could survive. Progressing almost entirely in singles, they kept their heads relentlessly down until we managed to run one of them out with the scores level. No. 11 then promptly whacked his first ball unceremoniously for four.

Lovely cricket!

17

Nuts and bolts, and fair play

It has often been said that the fascination of cricket, and what gives the game such depth, is that it is life in microcosm. Sir Arthur Bryant put it beautifully:

> This is what, for Englishmen, cricket does. It draws together, in a little space of time and place, all the diverse arts of love and emulation, conflict and comradeship, patience and boldness, sunshine and shower, city and country, prose and poetry, and makes them one

In other words, there is much more to cricket than mere mechanics. It follows from this that the captain is responsible not only for what his players do, but how. The sort of club he represents, the way the players behave – especially under duress – and ultimately the enjoyment of everyone concerned, visitors and spectators included, depends on the quality of his leadership.

Captain's qualities and responsibilities

At the highest level, one can readily appreciate the differing personal qualities required of, say, an England captain for several long hot months on a tour of India and Pakistan, compared with a one-day series in England; and it would be strange if many people possessed all the presumed attributes of an ideal captain. One just has to do the best one can with one's own individual talents; learn to paper over the cracks and perhaps moderate one's vices. The club will survive (even be quietly grateful) if the captain upsets one or two people, but he will certainly have no success without a genuine relationship based on mutual respect, loyalty and affection.

We have all played in fixtures that are niggly and acrimonious. Conversely there are some clubs with whom one invariably has an entertaining and well-contested battle. The difference is not pure chance, but a question of attitude and of that time-honoured concept, sportsmanship.

While one cannot be too dogmatic about what constitutes good sportsmanship, most bad sportsmanship, bad manners, even cheating, arise from sloppy attitudes to the game. Such attitudes often show up under pressure. Since pressure is frequently put forward as an excuse for dubious behaviour, it is as well to examine these things before that point arises.

The demarcation between sloppiness and cheating is not always clear-cut. I offer a few examples and my own personal views.

Maradonna's behaviour in Argentina's World Cup win against England in 1986 was not questionable just because he handled the ball, nor even because he tried to reach it with his hand, but because he accepted the goal. No, not even that. What is the point of sport if its participants and spectators tolerate and exonerate the 'professional foul'? For here we had the best player in the world not only committing a foul that invalidated his goal, but accepting the goal, and apparently being prepared to be seen by about half the population of the world to be cheating. To crown that, the viewing public also seemed prepared to treat him, not with approbrium but with acclaim.

Cricketers mostly do not cheat, and they certainly 'get stick' when they do. What sort of 'professional foul' are they in danger of committing?

First, there is the question of catches at the wicket. In the past it has been accepted widely that catches behind the wicket were appealed for and the decision left to the umpire. Batsmen assumed that they would be given 'not out' to balls they had hit, often enough over a lifetime, to balance the opposite cases: a reasonable enough philosophy.

More recently many players have taken the view that a batsman who hits a catch to any fielder is out. Again, this is a good, honest, responsible attitude, and why should it be any different whether that fielder is mid-off or the wicket-keeper?

However, there have been various side-effects. First, the number of decisions made by umpires, and therefore the number of their mistakes, has decreased. It seems reasonable to assume that this has in some degree contributed to the undoubted improvement in the standard of umpiring in club cricket over the last twenty years. It must be admitted, though, that umpires often feel that they are being made to look foolish when a batsman walks out in spite of their verdict to the contrary.

Unfortunately, batsmen who still take the old-fashioned view – that they accept the umpire's decision whichever way it goes – tend to be abused for cheating, which they are not. Also, the batsman, having aimed a shot in one direction, does not always see the ball caught behind him. Naturally, no one is going to 'walk' unless he is satisfied that the ball has been fairly caught, but this again can give rise to unjust criticism. On the other hand, having built up a reputation as a 'walker', especially with his home umpire, it is very simple for a batsman to stand his ground in a vital match and pretend that he 'did not get a touch'. Then he is quite definitely cheating.

A further complication arises, though much more frequently in first-class cricket than in club cricket. When the spinners are operating in favourable conditions, fielders are clustered round, looking for bat-pad catches. It is very difficult for umpires to adjudicate on these. One reads that in India everyone appeals for every single ball that bounces up off the pads. Certainly Tony Greig, for example, used to appeal often and successfully when standing at silly point for Underwood. This sort of appealing seems to be an attempt to get a batsman given out off a ball which he did not hit. It is quite different from keeping the batsmen aware of the close catcher's presence. In my view it is cheating, pure and simple.

On England's tour to India in the winter of 1972–3, the cheating on both sides, and hence the umpiring, became so bad that the two captains and the tour manager met to call a truce. The captains were Tony Lewis and Ajit Wadekar, the England manager, Donald Carr. They then convened a meeting of all the players and, moreover, kept their word to each other for the remainder of the series. This was an object-lesson to all those who, in countless similar circumstances, would stand helplessly by and say that nothing could be done; and it provides yet another opportunity for you to ask yourself what sort of captain you are.

This is not to say that the blame in these cases lies entirely with the fielding side. One certainly is angry at a batsman who gives an obvious bat-pad catch, only to stand his ground and then be given not out; and there is a tremendous temptation to descend to the same level, especially for the professional with £X,000 at stake. The club cricketer, however, is playing only for glory or winning his league or whatever. There is not much glory to be had from cheating in any form, and two wrongs do not make a right, especially in cricket.

The sole exception I have heard of is the story of the famous Welsh rugby international who scored the final try to beat England, knowing that he had grounded the ball short of the line and pushed it over in the ensuing mêlée. When he died and approached the gates of heaven he was asked if he had committed any sin that might preclude his entry. He recited his unobserved action in the famous match, only to be told that it was no sin.

'But St Peter, I know I cheated deliberately.'

'Ah,' came the reply, 'but I'm not St Peter, I'm St David.'

Conversely, it is not uncommon to see a batsman given out lbw off a ball which all the close fieldsmen know he hit. On this, I believe that the fielding captain should ask the umpire's permission to withdraw the appeal and let the batsman continue. It requires tact, though!

Personally I can never see the point of those deafening appeals from all parts of the ground; and, for that matter, I dislike the players leaping about in delight when an appeal is upheld. The first is stupid while the second smacks of crowing over a fallen adversary. Both have an element of bad manners. Similar bad manners are often shown by stand-in umpires, who make me wonder sometimes if they are stone deaf, standing there absolutely mute in response to an appeal.

I have also seen a number of perfectly valid wickets thrown away by fielders appealing in ecstasy as they throw themselves full length to take catches inches off the ground. It naturally creates a doubt in the minds of the umpires even if they are not unsighted or asleep. Do not let your players do it. If you are in doubt as to the validity of a catch, one of yours or one of theirs, all you have to do is ask, 'Did you catch it, Fred?' If he says 'Yes', it is out; if he says, 'I think so' then it is not. In cricket there are few people who will look you in the eye and lie; and word quickly gets round about the one or two who will.

A most remarkable example of the importance of this took place during the third of the final series of one-day internationals between Australia and New Zealand in Melbourne on 2 February, 1981.

G. S. Chappell made 90 for Australia by courtesy of a certain M. C. Snedden, who caught him quite brilliantly when 58. The television pictures showed clearly that a fair catch had been made. The umpires managed to avoid looking in the direction of the ball; Chappell stood his ground and, in the absence of Snedden saying 'Yes, I caught it', carried on batting. This was the same match, incidentally, in which Trevor Chappell bowled that underhand grubber for the last ball, thereby depriving New Zealand of all possibility of the 6 runs they needed to win.

Handling the ball

Other instances of sloppy attitudes to the playing of the game come to mind. First, how often have you seen a batsman play the ball down at his feet and throw it back to the bowler? What is the point? The fielders are there to do that job; and I had a pleasant reward in one national knockout match for not responding to the close fielders' call of, 'thank you'. Gulley ran in, picked up the ball and threw it back to the bowler, who was not even looking and we ran two! 'Handled the ball' is an entirely unnecessary way of getting out, so why run the risk?

There are only two circumstances when I feel justified in appealing for it (although even then it would depend on the opposition and the personalities involved): first when the ball is still rolling or spinning in the general direction of the stumps. Second, if the batsman advances down the pitch to throw the ball back and then takes a short single, he is cheating, albeit without being aware of the fact. He is able to take the short single by putting the fielding side on their heels.

Do not forget that a fielder who did not hear the nick on to the pad and appeals 'for lbw' just as the ball is being handled will reap an inevitable reward. The umpire has no option but to give the batsman out.

On one dark, cold, wet day when we had no sight-screens,

one of the opposing batsmen received an inadvertent, slippery, head-high full toss which he lost sight of in the gloom. At the very last moment he fended it off with his left hand while still holding his bat in the other. Their umpire, at the bowler's end, looked at me. I grinned back. Nothing was said; but that evening in the bar we persuaded the batsman to buy us a pint.

Out-of-shape ball

Most club cricketers are mystified by the sight of first-class players complaining about the ball when it is only a few overs old. The occasional burst stitch, or suggestion of flattening, on an otherwise new ball seldom excites more than passing comment in club cricket. This is as it should be, nor is it any criticism of the professionals; they rightly expect to ply their chosen trade with first-quality equipment.

An area of slackness, where club cricketers are sometimes at fault, is when the ball swells to more than its prescribed size. The umpires are supposed to have a pair of brass gauges for measuring the size of the ball, which should pass through one, but not the other. It is not infrequent that the ball swells during play. This may be due to the internal cork or winding, to loose stitching of the cover, or to damp. In any event, a large soft ball is an advantage to the batting side, whereas a small hard one helps the bowlers.

You have to think twice before complaining if the ball is too big while you are fielding first; if the opposition does not notice, nor think, nor complain, then presumably it will become even easier for your own batsmen later in the day.

If you are fielding second, however, take a good look at the ball at the start of their innings and from time to time during it. If the bowlers are happy and you are controlling the match, do not even consider a complaint. But if you notice a lack of bounce and movement in the quicker bowlers, or of nip and snap about the spinners, suspect an oversize ball. It can make a great deal of difference.

Just ask the umpires to pass the ball through their 9⅟16-inch gauge for you. They almost certainly will not have one, but they will be aware that you know what you are talking about. In any case a swollen ball is obvious to the naked eye by comparison.

Overthrows

Overthrows are a subject about which I have recurrent arguments. In the first place, if a batsman, when running between the wickets, is struck by a throw-in and the ball then careers off over the boundary, the striker is awarded four extra runs. Had the batsman intercepted the ball deliberately the fielding side could appeal and the batsman would be out for 'obstructing the field'.

There is a convention in these circumstances that, if the ball hits a batsman and thereby he has the opportunity to take one or two runs only, he is unsporting in doing so. This strikes me as illogical and wrong.

Another aspect of overthrows is a different example of muddled thinking. I believe that, in a well-drilled side, any fielder should be able to shy at the stumps at either end – given a chance of a run-out – knowing that someone, or two, will always be backing up, and that the possible reward of a wicket outweighs the danger of giving away 4 runs.

A terrified cry of 'Steady' does not therefore help a fielder when he makes a throw for a run-out. Nor can it be correct to criticise him if he gives away overthrows.

Having said that, of course there will be tight situations when the fielders have to look around first, before having a shy. On the other hand, suppose you have just declared with a big total behind you. The batsman pushes into the covers, runs and could be out by a yard. Would you not be quite happy to lay four overthrows to a wicket when cover point throws to the bowler's end with no mid-on to back up? The miserable sight of the bowler intercepting a throw to his stumps, thereby preventing any chance of a run-out, always makes me furious. What would have happened if Joe Solomon had not had the confidence to throw the wicket down to finish the famous tied Test of 1961? If you want to set yourself the highest standards, you have only to ask yourself how you and your side would stand up to that sort of pressure.

There have been no better Test captains than Benaud and Worrell, so the standard is severe; but you can be relatively just as good at your own level in your own orbit. Your Solomon may miss the stumps, but in the same circumstances, in the deciding match of your league, will he be just as well-drilled and confident and be given the same blanket backing up behind the stumps? Those you can give him.

In saying that Benaud and Worrell are without peers as Test captains, I am not saying that they were the best of all time. Just as one cannot compare the batting of Bradman and W. G. Grace, so the varieties of context prevent any meaningful comparison of captaining in different eras. They are members of a select group of, quite simply, 'the best'.

It was, moreover, no coincidence that the second tied Test, between Australia and India in September 1986 at Madras, should also involve two excellent captains. Kapil Dev is well-known as a man who takes every cricketing challenge head-on and he has even in the past been dropped by India for recklessness. However, he had captained India quite beautifully in England in the previous English summer, being firm, subtle, concerned for his players and, of course, successful. He had even managed his own contributions correctly in the context of the requirements of the match. He certainly had no hesitation in attempting to score 348 to win.

Allan Border, for his part, had set up the tie by declaring before the start of the fifth day's play, to the surprise of most onlookers. Nor did he lose his nerve. India at one stage reached 331 for 6, but he kept the spinners, Bright and Matthews, going to the end. What a fitting indication of Border's excellence this Test match was.

When your particular crunch comes, the last thing you want is for your fielders to be covering new ground. If they have been in the habit of frequently having a shy at the stumps, they will be more practised, more accurate and more controlled. They will, therefore, be more likely to hit them. At the same time, when backing up becomes a habit, the fielders are more frequently involved and remain alert. This of itself may well have a further advantage in more catches being caught.

This sort of alertness and aggression is infectious and makes fielding much more fun. It also acts as a strong disincentive to the batting side. If the fielders always whack the ball back in, quickly and firmly, they pose a constant threat, and inhibit runs. They are repeatedly reminding the batsmen too that they are up against a very good side. After a while, both teams will believe it!

Dropped catches

Dropped catches, similarly, can cause abject misery and loss of confidence. The good captain can, of course, minimise such grisly events by selecting the right men for each position. (Anyone who doubts the importance of this should read of the terrifying retribution heaped upon the innocent head of poor Fred Tate in the Manchester Test of 1902.) When a catch is dropped, however, it is no good being annoyed, except when a fielder was not concentrating. If it was due to faulty technique you can do something about that for the future, but for the present you have to ensure that the next catch is caught. (Remember R. C. Robertson-Glasgow's little poem 'First Slip'?) So if the offender wishes to move to somewhere less onerous, move him. If, on the other hand, he is the sort of fellow who will automatically be that much more determined to catch the next chance, leave him be.

Lord Hawke is reputed to have had a man playing for him once who dropped several catches during the first innings of the match, to the noble lord's evident displeasure. When they went out to field for the second innings Lord Hawke set the field and simply ignored him entirely. He was thus forced to ask where he should position himself. 'Oh, just wander about where you like. There will be plenty of balls flying around. One or two might hit you.'

Collisions

The prospect of two fielders racing headlong into each other, when intent on making the same catch, is the subject of much humour and considerable chagrin, not to say pain. One day I was fielding at mid-off. A gently lofted catch was hit towards me, for which I did not have to move a single pace. As I was about to pouch the offering, I received a tackle of such superlative timing and ferocity as would have brought a Twickenham crowd to its feet. It was extra cover, no less, who remained laid out for some time having taken the ball full on the back of his head!

The lesson to be derived from such hilarity is that fielders must be aware of those around them. This sounds obvious, but it is the prerequisite of avoiding collisions. I am not a strong advocate of the captain shouting, 'Yours, John,' in hopeful fashion. By the time I have worked out how many

Johns there are playing, and they have all looked round to see if I called the right one . . . No, far better for one of the fielders concerned to call, 'Mine!' and let the others get out of the way. Moreover, he will not dare drop it then, will he? Indeed, if there is a high catch, safely caught, and no shout by the catcher, I give him a rocket.

Fast bowlers, courage and fair play

Most of this book has been concerned with the intellectual, psychological and technical aspects of cricket. Courage is another facet not to be ignored. I very much doubt, for example, if the sheer guts possessed by most Test players is widely enough understood. It cannot be much fun, to put it mildly, to find, in the first innings of a Test series, that Lillee and Thomson, or Larwood and Voce, or Gregory and MacDonald are simply too fast for you. The club cricketer may find that one or two bowlers in a season are too much of a handful, but they do not have to go back and face them over and over again.

Simply because a cricket ball can hurt, fast bowlers operate with a certain aura of power about them. As in any other walk of life, power tends to corrupt. The fast bowler is therefore a weapon to be used with care and discipline.

If this sounds pompous, there is a problem to be considered.

Fast bowlers have to learn to bowl fast. They should be aggressive and frightening. If batsmen are going to back off to the square-leg umpire and give their wickets away, so much the better. But there are different ways of using the weapon of speed. The classic system involved a full length, movement in the air, and subtle variations in pace and in angle of delivery. The other way is a barrage of bouncers and 'beamers' aimed to intimidate and maim.

These are extremes, of course. However, every captain will at some time in his life have a young fast bowler playing for him. He will then be faced with the problems of encouraging and helping the bowler to be as effective as possible under a variety of circumstances, of realising his full potential. At the same time the captain is the custodian of his club's reputation and standing. It is the captain who has to decide whether his players and, in this particular case, his fast bowler's behaviour is acceptable or not.

So this problem needs to be examined more closely. What about the 'beamer'? It cannot get a wicket. Its only object is to intimidate. An England fast bowler told me he had bowled one only in his life, whereupon his captain spoke to him at the end of the over: 'If I thought that was on purpose you would never play for the county again.' I share that captain's view.

The bouncer is a different case. Used sparingly it certainly is an effective wicket-taker. It also discourages the batsman from being too positive in coming right forward to full-length deliveries, thereby making them more telling as well. But, whacking the ball in short several times an over is a very different mode of attack. Again, the object is intimidation.

Speed is a relative term; relative to the wicket, relative to the ability of the batsman, and relative to the light. Therefore bowling that might be outright intimidation to one batsman can be meat and drink to another. Although one can argue that the umpires have the power to intervene in the former circumstances, they are surely admonishing the captain should they have to do so.

Although it is a long time ago now, the 1932–3 tour of Australia is well worth studying by any captain (or fast bowler, come to that) who wishes to decide for himself what is, or is not, acceptable. 'Body-line' raised such a furore that the documentation on the tour is enormous. The ill-feeling it aroused was tremendous. Whatever the rights and wrongs of body-line, I am sure that the crux of the matter is this: 'If the way you play cricket, or let your players behave, is such that people actively dislike you, or even hate you for it, then you cannot be playing it properly.'

One sublimely unequivocal attitude to this problem came from, of all places, Hawaii. We had the pleasure of entertaining (or, more correctly, being entertained by, for never have I met a side so absolutely determined to ensure the enjoyment of all concerned) the Californian Cricket Association on a tour of England. They were a cosmopolitan assortment from almost every cricketing corner of the globe, and their technical ability fell, shall we say, some way below the highest. One of their number was an Indian gentleman (and I use the word advisedly) whose fascinatingly varied life had brought him now to be a highly successful and respected civil engineer in Hawaii.

He had recently been captaining his club side when it had acquired the services of an itinerant fast bowler. This bowler apparently bowled one bouncer in his opening spell for the club, which thereupon came to an abrupt end: 'We don't want any of that, thank you very much. We play cricket to enjoy ourselves.'

Personally, while I endorse the attitude, I cannot entirely agree with the implied dichotomy. On a good wicket, and speaking as an opening batsman, I relish the challenge of the occasional bouncer and derive active pleasure from dealing with it successfully; I also respect the bowler. But this is in no sense the same as having to endure a short-pitched barrage on a green-top wicket.

The same argument applies to what the Australians call 'sledging': the oral abuse of batsmen. To my mind a certain amount of backchat between old adversaries who enjoy and respect each other is an integral part of 'the rich fabric of the game'. Swearing, however, is not my idea of chivalry.

The 1980 Laws have recognised this by enabling the

umpires to stop the game if the striker is 'incommoded' while he is receiving a ball. A delightful word: if you were facing Michael Holding advancing towards you, ball in hand, you would be in no doubt that this 'incommodation' included the bowler's run-up (Law 42.6).

For that matter it is now understood also that the batsman can obstruct the field by word as well as by action (Law 37.1).

The pressures of Test cricket are of course immense, but the pressures are just as real to those involved for a school side to beat its rivals, or for a club to win its last match to top its league or win its knockout final.

Concentrate on the essentials of winning

As the captain on such occasions, you will want to be able to concentrate on the essentials of winning. For your part you cannot afford to let the side down by being upset by gamesmanship or bad umpiring decisions. Similarly you do not want added pressure created by the fact that you have failed to train your side well enough. To give two examples:

1. It is crunch time: 4 runs to win and 1 wicket to fall, twelve balls to go. You have set your field with care. The batsman drives firmly but in the air, a head-high catch straight at mid-off. If he holds it you have won; if he drops it, the batsman gets a single and no. 11 faces. You look round, only to see that mid-off in his excitement has crept in so far that the ball goes for 4 and, as a result, you lose the match. In a better drilled side mid-off would have made a mark where you put him, walked back a further 5 yards or so and been on the mark at the moment of impact.
2. It is your club's first-ever knockout final. You field first. The umpires are independently appointed. Your best opening bowler is warned for running down the middle of the wicket in his first over, and in the second over you are ordered to take him off. You have only the five requisite bowlers under the competition rules, so a joker has to purvey eight overs: curtains.

   Your own club umpire never used to say anything because he did not want to cause a scene. The bowler always bowled from his end, downhill. You knew he ran on the wicket, but then the umpires are in charge, aren't they? No, *you are*.

Whatever your level of cricket, whatever the competition, the pressure tends to build up towards the end of the season. This has the advantage that it gives you time to prepare your side to handle it. But what of yourself? How can you be certain that when the time comes you, too, will be fully prepared to cope?

Nerves are the first hurdle to surmount, but essentially they are a manifestation of the body producing extra adrenalin to increase muscular efficiency. Looked at from this point of view, a feeling of nervousness is both necessary and good, nothing to be worried about.

In addition, the captain has too many other things to think about to be aware of nervousness. If he is concentrating his mind on all the positive means of making the best use of his resources he will be simply too busy.

Personally, I relish the high spots. The more tense the situation, the more excited everyone around me, the more certain I feel that my side is going to win, because I know I can keep cool and my brain working. How can one be so confident? For me the answer is an image I carry in my head, the image of one man, Frank Worrell.

The setting was that wonderful Lord's Test of 1963. The ascendancy had been wrested first by one side, then the other, over four and a half days of fierce unremitting gladiatorial combat. The final scene found England needing just over 60 runs to win with 90 minutes to go. West Indies wanted 5 wickets, including that of Cowdrey who had his broken arm in plaster. The light was appalling. Hall and Griffith were bowling with every ounce of energy, glistening with effort. Brian Close, taking a terrible battering about the body, was charging yards down the wicket to them. Pandemonium raged. As runs kept coming and wickets fell the equation grew tighter and tighter. In the midst of the fury and tumult, in the eye of the storm, cool and quiet, was Worrell. I was watching on television when the cameras suddenly showed him for a moment, clad in a long-sleeved sweater, with one hand in his trouser pocket, motioning some fielder a yard or so this way or that with the other.

A camera clicked in my brain at that moment and the image

will never fade. It matters not whether there was excessive time wasting: there was only one man in control of that match and it was not a batsman.

Time wasting

Time wasting is a difficult subject. The 20 overs in the last hour legislation has certainly cured the end-game problems in this respect. Why, though, has the average over rate in first-class cricket fallen so much over the last thirty years? Has the same happened in club cricket without anyone noticing?

The first-class game has been, and is, bedevilled by negative thinking. The general attitude seems to be to achieve the draw first and then advance from that comfortable platform in circumspect pursuit of victory. The simplest way of obtaining a draw is by reducing the length of the game; that can most easily be done by bowling fewer overs.

Conversely a side that is intent fully on winning, romps through its overs quickly; every ball bowled offers another chance of taking a wicket. Good sides are bored by draws. Good sides are not scared of losing.

It follows that a side intent on a draw will approach the game in a more leisurely fashion than one hell-bent on winning. This is natural and to be anticipated by any sensible captain.

There will also be occasions when a batting side gets itself into a tangle by going too slowly and the fielding side will wish to add to their problems. This is very much in the style of a good football team which controls and varies the pace of a match, or of a runner attempting to break his rivals by alternating slow laps with bursts of acceleration. But these are positive measures.

The sort of time-wasting that is cheating is a deliberate plan to play as little cricket as possible. I have played against sides who, expecting to lose, employed a whole series of medium-pace bowlers with inordinately long runs. They dawdle back to their marks chatting to the skipper the while. They frequently lose their step just as they reach the delivery stride and have to repeat the whole boring process again. At the start of each over they walk all the way in from long-leg to hand a sweater to the umpire and then have to retreat most of the way back again in order to bowl. Between each bowling change

Some sides employ medium-pace bowlers with inordinately long runs

there is a protracted discussion about field-placing; the result being identical with the one before. And so it goes on.

Club umpires have no authority to do anything about this. Personally, as captain, I take the only action open to me. In the bar afterwards I make sure that the opposing captain knows that I have observed every trick and that my side think he was cheating. If we lose the fixture as a result (which has not yet happened) I would not feel overwhelmingly deprived, but just sad that their committee did not have the courage to appoint someone else for their club captain. In a league you are unfortunately deprived of this sanction.

In the first-class game, and in particular Test cricket, there are two other factors that are pertinent as well. First, people have to pay to watch such rubbish. In the absence of any basic minimum overs agreement all sides are guilty: in the West Indies in 1985–6 England bowled just as few overs per hour as their hosts.

Second, the low over-rate system has been exploited to keep fast bowlers fresh. This of itself is not new. What is new is to have at a team's disposal four fast bowlers, all of whom are perpetually fresh. Twelve overs per hour equals 24 overs per session of play and 6 overs per bowler: two little bursts of 3 overs apiece and none of them is even sweating! Interval for lunch, and then the same routine starts again in the afternoon.

This system is not simply negative. It aims at winning the match through the explosive power of the fast bowlers. No doubt Clive Lloyd or Vivian Richards would explain it from the other direction: the four best bowlers happen to be fast, and fast bowlers need long runs which result in slow over rates. Personally, I believe the argument is spurious and that the system is not only against the spirit but against the Laws of the game as they stand at the moment. There may be an argument in favour of changing the Laws, but that is another matter.

Law 42, Unfair Play, contains the following apposite sections:

> 1. Responsibility of Captains.
> The captains are responsible at all times for ensuring that play is conducted within the spirit of the game as well as within the Laws.
> 8. The Bowling of Fast Short-Pitched Balls.
> The bowling of fast short-pitched balls is unfair if, in the opinion of the umpire at the bowler's end, it constitutes an attempt to intimidate the striker.
> Umpires shall consider intimidation to be the deliberate bowling of fast short-pitched balls which by their length, height and direction are intended or likely to inflict physical injury on the striker. The relative skill of the striker shall also be taken into consideration.
> 10. Time Wasting.
> Any form of time wasting is unfair.

I believe that a system of bowling which entails all the bowlers bowling fast short-pitched balls, as standard, to be unfair. Law 42, section 13(d) defines such a ball (as a guide) as one that passed or would have passed above shoulder height of the striker standing in a normal batting stance at the crease.

If the fast bowlers aim to bowl slightly short of a length, expecting movement off the pitch, steep lift to chest height and speed to produce the edge chances, this sounds perfectly fair. And it would be if the bowlers were medium-pacers. When the bowlers are the four fastest in the world, with two or more of similar pace waiting in the wings in case of injury or loss of form, it looks more like systematic intimidation. It is not in the least like one bowler in one club fixture each season being 'a bit of a handful'. Surely, in a five-Test series, ten innings, the batsmen are going to get hit frequently and they are going to be dismissed frequently by the 13(d) ball, which is so similar to the others that the batsman is forced to play it. Is that not intimidation?

The authorities have been woefully weak in making any attempt to come to grips with this problem. Yet there are plenty of options open to them, e.g.:

1. Insist not only on a minimum number of overs per day, but also a minimum per session.
2. A new ball after considerably more than the present 85 overs.
3. A new ball after so many runs rather than overs.
4. No second new ball in an innings.
5. Making the 13(d) ball a wide.
6. Bowlers are stronger and fitter than in the past and they already have to deliver from behind the popping crease instead of a yard in front of it. Maybe the next move should be to lengthen the pitch?
7. Limit the number of fielders behind the wicket on the off side, as well as on the leg side.
8. Provide that the wicket-keeper has to stand up to the stumps for a proportion of the match.
9. Draw a line across the pitch short of which the ball must not land.

The first requirement is that the authorities should face up to the facts: (a) that the bowling of only 12 overs an hour is illegal, not just regrettable; (b) that a game consisting entirely of fast short-pitched bowling is not only illegal, but boring and ultimately therefore suicidal to the first-class game.

These remarks are not as out of place here as they may seem. For you, as captain of your team or club, are now the custodian of cricket in your environment, jointly with all the players around you and your committee. You have a responsibility, therefore, for the nature of the game within that orbit, however limited that orbit may be. If those responsible for the higher and wider reaches of the game fail to do their job, that probably increases, rather than decreases, the onus upon you.

The more you consider these problems as the game changes with each generation, the better the understanding you will develop of the intrinsic nature of cricket.

18

The joys of captaincy

I have tried to provide in this book plenty of ideas and food for thought for both aspiring and practising cricket captains. I also hope that I have begun to fill the gap I sensed among the memoirs of famous captains and the volumes of cricket instruction; and shown, too, in answer to my initial question, that the captain, so far from being a figurehead, is the man who should be in control of a game.

One famous former captain, however, has written some observations which are directly relevant and helpful. Not surprisingly, this is Richie Benaud who, in *A Tale of Two Tests*, says:

> Most important of all, he (the captain) must believe with conviction that the team comes before all else.
>
> If there was ever one point of captaincy that should be underlined ad infinitum it is: never, never tell your team something that is patently not correct.
>
> One of the secrets of successful captaincy is to make the most of the material with which you have been blessed.
>
> When a lucky break comes your way you must grab it with both hands and look for the opportunity to use it to the best advantage.

In other words, captaincy requires boundless enthusiasm, total honesty and a positive approach.

Cricket should be fun, and captaincy is such a large part of the game that it should be the greatest fun of all, transcending as it does all the other arts of the game. Yet the opportunities for learning it, for practice, are so limited. One cannot go and watch and copy in the same way as one can study a first-class batsman, bowler or wicket-keeper. For that matter, not all county or national captains are good, let alone great. So how can one start?

Even that well-trodden path of learning by one's mistakes ensures a fairly unpleasant time both for yourself and for the rest of the side. Lack of confidence is also sure to lead to mistakes; and mistakes in their turn cause a lack of confidence.

Those delightful humorists at dinners, who relate how they followed their captains out of sheer curiosity and witnessed defeat being plucked from the very jaws of victory, are using wit as the ultimate defence. Such gems are forged only out of abject misery.

The source of misery for a cricketer in the final analysis is, I believe, a failure of communication. Most of the equations a captain has to solve have no absolute right or wrong answer. That same answer can be found from several different directions. It is a question of probabilities and even possibilities.

The first and perhaps only vital requirement of a captain is, therefore, not simply that he should get the answer right, but that his team should understand what he is attempting to do and why. Certainly there should be discussion as to a given line of approach. There should also be some divergence of view, but in the end the team has to arrive at a common purpose which the captain has to direct.

In the broadest possible terms, every team has to decide if it is going to attempt to win as its primary objective. Conversely, is it going to make certain of a draw first and then hope that sometimes a win will materialise from there?

Many teams never even make that decision consciously. In many other sides the troops have made one decision, the captain another: result purgatory.

Captaincy is, therefore, both personal and collective. To be successful it has to be open, honest, intelligent and affectionate. It involves discipline and debate. It entails the motivation and welding of the multifarious gifts of the individuals into a stronger, more effective whole.

The games, therefore, that give the greatest satisfaction are those in which these qualities are put to the test. Matches against technically stronger opponents, or where the luck of the toss and the weather give them a huge advantage, cannot be won without the corporate whole being stronger than its individual components.

Captain and players have to think, and accept discipline; without those qualities even great skill is likely to be fruitless.

Exactly the same mental toughness and agility are often needed, as I have shown, to beat a much weaker side rather than allow them the draw which is the height of their ambition. It is not easy to declare when one of your friends has his first hundred well within his grasp, nor to change the bowling when someone is performing beautifully without taking wickets. It is far from easy for them to accept that personal achievements must be secondary to the success of the team.

The trouble with, and joy of, captaincy is that so much is subjective. 'Will A bowl more effectively than B?' You cannot know. You may be given indications, but in fact you do not know. Even if they both bowl, A can be instrumental in obtaining wickets for B.

Ian Peebles tells an hilarious story of how, in one match for Middlesex against Kent, Walter Robins gave the finest exhibition of leg-spin bowling he could imagine, on a good wicket, to no effect whatever. When Peebles came on himself some sort of demon took control of events. A whole succession of long hops and full tosses was either unaccountably missed completely or hit in the air to fielders who had forgotten to move from the previous over. He bowled arrant rubbish and took seven wickets for nothing much.

After a match everyone has his own divergent views on what should have happened, which is understandable. What is more surprising is the difference of opinion that can be found as to what actually did happen. The rights and wrongs of the way the game was handled can be, and are, argued for hours. For example, my analysis of what happened, why and how, in those two Test matches described at the beginning of this book is, of course, only my opinion. It is not fact. The scores may be fact, but the matter of their creation is not. Similarly, my view of any match we play at home will certainly be quite different from that of the visiting skipper. Let me give an example.

You have an opening bowler, no more than medium-pace, who bowls in-swingers. Sometimes, when the ball is new and the conditions right, they really move a long way.

One day a left-hander opens the batting and he plays at and misses by a comfortable distance each ball of the first over, all outside the off stump. Who is winning?

The bowler trundles off to third man thinking of quips, such as, 'I'll give you a clue, it's red.' He is happy.

The batsman, on the other hand, has simply played up and down the line of the stumps. He has not had to commit himself, because each delivery has been on a length, but not, by the time it reached him, on the line. He could go on playing like that all day.

Next over the bowler pitches it a little further up and the batsman promptly squeezes two fours, mostly off the middle of the bat, between gulley and cover point. Who has won that over?

The bowler irritably gestures to his captain that he wants a square third man and stalks off.

The batsman is still having an easy ride, but the captain has seen enough to persuade him to have a word with the bowler. He is convinced the bowler is winning. So, next over, he places the square third man and two gulleys. The first ball is slashed through them for 4 more. Now the batsman feels *he* is on top.

At long last the bowler manages to pitch a near half-volley straight enough to be hitting off stump. The batsman, forced to play a positive shot, but without room to get the leverage he needs, is comfortably caught at gulley.

So here we had the ball beating the bat, yet the batsman winning: the batsman hitting boundaries yet the bowler winning. You can imagine the batsman not thinking the bowler very good: only one delivery both on length and on line. You can also imagine the fielding captain feeling sure of winning that little contest repeatedly. Meanwhile, the bowler believed the boundaries came off the edge!

My other favourite example of these problems of interpretation was encountered while I was fielding somnambulantly on the boundary one gloriously hot sunny day. An ancient rustic of rubicund countenance sat near me and, at the fall of a wicket, we engaged in the following conversation:

'Fabulous weather, isn't it? You ought to be playing yourself on a day like this.'

'Me? Oh no, lad,' and he chuckled away in the depths of his bright blue eyes beneath bushy white eyebrows. 'I'm 83 and I last played 51 years ago June past.'

'You were only a boy yourself then. Why did you give up?'

'On this very ground it was.' A wistful, sad look clouded his mirthful gaze as he surveyed the scene.

'I used to play for the village, Haythorpe, in them days. Well, we'd had a longish dry spell and it was the local Derby match against Towerton. Wicket was a beauty. Like concrete she wur. 'Course blooming skipper lost the toss and we fielded. Never looked like getting any one of them out and come tea they declared at 240 some odd.

'Then the worst happened; thunderstorm. Cor bless me it did rain. Great round drops like sovereigns. Only lasted for about quarter of an hour. Then we wasted a bit of time making out it was too wet. Anyhow there was nothing for it, we had to play eventually. Well, you can imagine what it was like, can't you? Ball flew orf that wicket like I dunno what.'

He broke off for a moment in sheer disbelief.

'Well I went in number four and I dunno, but I reckon I batted about the best of my life. Hour and forty minutes I stayed there. Then at last I caught one. Straight between the eyes. Orf I went. Joined the others in hospital.

'Well, that warn't the end of it. We got away with a draw somehow; 27 for 9 we was at close of play. But now listen,' and he put a strong old hand on my arm to retain my attention. 'I can laugh at it now, but my goodness I was angry at the time. Come Friday the account was in the local paper, you see. Top match in the district it wur, and there were these big headlines all across the top of the back page: HAYTHORPE SAVED BY RAIN.

'No, dammit. Never played again.'

If there can be that much divergence of view on what actually did happen in a match, it is hardly surprising that there is frequently a variety of ideas as to what should have happened.

It is my experience that any match played between two sides hell-bent on beating one another, will produce an enjoyable game of cricket. The games that die are those where one side or the other loses its nerve. There may, of course, be several perfectly understandable reasons for this: some niggle left behind from the same fixture last time; or the feeling that you have done all the work and you are not going to give them the match after their lack of effort; or you may have lost last week in much the same circumstances. There may even be a perfectly genuine misunderstanding as to what is or is not a practicable proposition. Even so, the root cause of dull cricket, or ill-tempered cricket for that matter, is that the captain does not know how to win. One could go further: there are surprisingly frequent circumstances when the captain does not know whether he is winning or losing!

The subjects I have covered in this book have been mostly directed at club and school cricket; the environments, after all, where most cricket is played. The fact that I have quoted examples from Test matches is no contradiction, nor, I hope, is it presumptuous.

In the first place the Tests are, if not familiar to all, well documented and therefore available sources of further study. Second, they differ from club cricket only in degree; the players are more skilful and the playing time is longer – but both of these aspects expose deficiencies and mistakes in the most ruthless fashion.

Believe me, Test sides have often been badly captained, or badly managed or badly selected – sometimes all three. Really good Test skippers are rare, which is natural enough when one thinks about it. First the pool of players with the necessary playing ability is small. Second, the age group within which that playing standard can be maintained is short; and third, the external pressures created by quixotic selectors, or constant tours abroad, or the news media, or the demands of county duties and benefit seasons, further reduce the active life of a Test captain. The turnover rate of captains is in fact higher than seems desirable.

It is logical to conclude, therefore, that there are probably many club captains who are better at their job than the majority of their Test counterparts. Personally I find that both a comforting and a humbling thought. And so is this. You may never become a Test player, but there is nothing to prevent your becoming a Test-class captain.

'Well, I declare'

Appendixes

I. The Laws of Cricket
II. Limpsfield Cricket Club results, 1959–76
III. Sources and further reading
IV. Index

Every captain should know The Laws of Cricket

I

The Laws of Cricket

(1980 CODE)

Contents

Law 1. The Players

1. Number of Players and Captain

A match is played between two sides each of eleven players, one of whom shall be captain. In the event of the captain not being available at any time, a deputy shall act for him.

2. Nomination of Players

Before the toss for innings, the captain shall nominate his players, who may not thereafter be changed without the consent of the opposing captain.

Note

(a) More or Less than Eleven Players a Side
A match may be played by agreement between sides of more or less than eleven players, but not more than eleven players may field.

Law 2. Substitutes and Runners: Batsman or Fieldsman Leaving the Field: Batsman Retiring: Batsman Commencing Innings

1. *Substitutes*

Substitutes shall be allowed by right to field for any player who during the match is incapacitated by illness or injury. The consent of the opposing captain must be obtained for the use of a substitute if any player is prevented from fielding for any other reason.

Experimental Law: In normal circumstances, a substitute shall be allowed to field only for a player who satisfies the umpires that he has become injured or become ill during the match. However, in very exceptional circumstances, the umpires may use their discretion to allow a substitute for a player who has to leave the field or does not take the field for other wholly acceptable reasons, subject to consent being given by the opposing captain. If a player wishes to change his shirt, boots etc., he may leave the field to do so (no changing on the field), but no substitute will be allowed.

2. *Objection to Substitutes*

The opposing captain shall have no right of objection to any player acting as substitute in the field, nor as to where he shall field, although he may object to the substitute acting as wicket-keeper.

3. *Substitute Not to Bat or Bowl*

A substitute shall not be allowed to bat or bowl.

4. *A Player for whom a Substitute has Acted*

A player may bat, bowl or field even though a substitute has acted for him.

5. *Runner*

A runner shall be allowed for a batsman who, during the match, is incapacitated by illness or injury. The person acting as runner shall be a member of the batting side and shall, if possible, have already batted in that innings.

6. *Runner's Equipment*

The person acting as runner for an injured batsman shall wear batting gloves and pads if the injured batsman is so equipped.

Experimental Law: The player acting as runner for an injured batsman shall wear the same external clothing and external protective equipment as the injured batsman.

7. *Transgression of the Laws by an Injured Batsman or Runner*

An injured batsman may be out should his runner break any one of Laws 33 (Handled the Ball), 37 (Obstructing the Field) or 38 (Run Out). As striker he remains himself subject to the Laws. Furthermore, should he be out of his ground for any purpose and the wicket at the wicket-keeper's end be put down he shall be out under Law 38 (Run Out) or Law 39 (Stumped) irrespective of the position of the other batsman or the runner, and no runs shall be scored.

When not the striker, the injured batsman is out of the game and shall stand where he does not interfere with the play. Should he bring himself into the game in any way, then he shall suffer the penalties that any transgression of the Laws demands.

8. Fieldsman Leaving the Field

No fieldsman shall leave the field or return during a session of play without the consent of the umpire at the bowler's end. The umpire's consent is also necessary if a substitute is required for a fieldsman, when his side returns to the field after an interval. If a member of the fielding side leaves the field or fails to return after an interval and is absent from the field for longer than fifteen minutes, he shall not be permitted to bowl after his return until he has been on the field for at least that length of playing time for which he was absent. This restriction shall not apply at the start of a new day's play.

9. Batsman Leaving the Field or Retiring

A batsman may leave the field or retire at any time owing to illness, injury or other unavoidable cause, having previously notified the umpire at the bowler's end. He may resume his innings at the fall of a wicket, which for the purposes of this Law shall include the retirement of another batsman.

If he leaves the field or retires for any other reason he may only resume his innings with the consent of the opposing captain.

When a batsman has left the field or retired and is unable to return owing to illness, injury or other unavoidable cause, his innings is to be recorded as 'retired, not out'. Otherwise it is to be recorded as 'retired, out'.

10. Commencement of a Batsman's Innings

A batsman shall be considered to have commenced his innings once he has stepped on to the field of play.

Notes

(a) Substitutes and Runners

For the purpose of these Laws, allowable illnesses or injuries are those which occur at any time after the nomination by the captains of their teams.

Law 3. The Umpires

1. Appointment

Before the toss for innings, two umpires shall be appointed, one for each end, to control the game with absolute impartiality as required by the Laws.

2. Change of Umpires

No umpire shall be changed during a match without the consent of both captains.

3. Special Conditions

Before the toss for innings, the umpires shall agree with both captains on any special conditions affecting the conduct of the match.

4. The Wickets

The umpires shall satisfy themselves before the start of the match that the wickets are properly pitched.

5. Clock or Watch

The umpires shall agree between themselves and inform both captains before the start of the match on the watch or clock to be followed during the match.

6. Conduct and Implements

Before and during a match the umpires shall ensure that the conduct of the game and the implements used are strictly in accordance with the Laws.

7. Fair and Unfair Play

The umpires shall be the sole judges of fair and unfair play.

8. Fitness of Ground, Weather and Light

(a) The umpires shall be the sole judges of the fitness of the ground, weather and light for play.

(i) However, before deciding to suspend play, or not to start play, or not to resume play after an interval or stoppage, the umpires shall establish whether both captains (the batsmen at the wicket may deputise for their captain) wish to commence or continue in the prevailing conditions; if so, their wishes shall be met.

(ii) In addition, if during play the umpires decide that the light is unfit, only the batting side shall have the option of continuing play. After agreeing to continue to play in unfit light conditions, the captain of the batting side (or a batsman at the wicket) may appeal against the light to the umpires, who shall uphold the appeal only if, in their opinion, the light has deteriorated since the agreement to continue was made.

(b) After any suspension of play, the umpires, unaccompanied by any of the players or officials, shall, on their own initiative, carry out an inspection immediately the conditions improve and shall continue to inspect at intervals. Immediately the umpires decide that play is possible they shall call upon the players to resume the game.

9. *Exceptional Circumstances*

In exceptional circumstances, other than those of weather, ground or light, the umpires may decide to suspend or abandon play. Before making such a decision the umpires shall establish, if the circumstances allow, whether both captains (the batsmen at the wicket may deputise for their captain) wish to continue in the prevailing conditions; if so, their wishes shall be met.

10. *Position of Umpires*

The umpires shall stand where they can best see any act upon which their decision may be required.

Subject to this over-riding consideration, the umpire at the bowler's end shall stand where he does not interfere with either the bowler's run-up or the striker's view.

The umpire at the striker's end may elect to stand on the off instead of the leg side of the pitch, provided he informs the captain of the fielding side and the striker of his intention to do so.

11. *Umpires Changing Ends*

The umpires shall change ends after each side has had one innings.

12. *Disputes*

All disputes shall be determined by the umpires, and if they disagree the actual state of things shall continue.

13. *Signals*

The following code of signals shall be used by umpires who will wait until a signal has been answered by a scorer before allowing the game to proceed.

Boundary – by waving the arm from side to side.
Boundary 6 – by raising both arms above the head.
Bye – by raising an open hand above the head.
Dead Ball – by crossing and re-crossing the wrists below the waist.
Leg-bye – by touching a raised knee with the hand.
No-ball – by extending one arm horizontally.

Out	– by raising the index finger above the head. If not out, the umpire shall call 'not out'.
Short run	– by bending the arm upwards and by touching the nearer shoulder with the tips of the fingers.
Wide	– by extending both arms horizontally.

14. *Correctness of Scores*

The umpires shall be responsible for satisfying themselves on the correctness of the scores throughout and at the conclusion of the match. See Law 21.6 (Correctness of Result).

Notes

(a) Attendance of Umpires
The umpires should be present on the ground and report to the ground executive or the equivalent at least thirty minutes before the start of a day's play.

(b) Consultation between Umpires and Scorers
Consultation between umpires and scorers over doubtful points is essential.

(c) Fitness of Ground
The umpires shall consider the ground as unfit for play when it is so wet or slippery as to deprive the bowlers of a reasonable foothold, the fieldsmen, other than the deep-fielders, of the power of free movement, or the batsmen of the ability to play their strokes or to run between the wickets. Play should not be suspended merely because the grass and the ball are wet and slippery.

(d) Fitness of Weather and Light
The umpires should suspend play only when they consider that the conditions are so bad that it is unreasonable or dangerous to continue.

Law 4. The Scorers

1. *Recording Runs*

All runs scored shall be recorded by scorers appointed for the purpose. Where there are two scorers they shall frequently check to ensure that the score sheets agree.

2. *Acknowledging Signals*

The scorers shall accept and immediately acknowledge all instructions and signals given to them by the umpires.

Law 5. The Ball

1. Weight and Size

The ball, when new, shall weigh not less than 5½ ounces/155.9g, nor more than 5¾ ounces/163g; and shall measure not less than 8 13/16 inches/22.4cm, nor more than 9 inches/22.9cm in circumference.

2. Approval of Balls

All balls used in matches shall be approved by the umpires and captains before the start of the match.

3. New Ball

Subject to agreement to the contrary, having been made before the toss, either captain may demand a new ball at the start of each innings.

4. New Ball in Match of Three or More Days' Duration

In a match of three or more days' duration, the captain of the fielding side may demand a new ball after the prescribed number of overs has been bowled with the old one. The governing body for cricket in the country concerned shall decide the number of overs applicable in that country, which shall be not less than 75 six-ball overs (55 eight-ball overs).

5. Ball Lost or Becoming Unfit for Play

In the event of a ball during play being lost or, in the opinion of the umpires, becoming unfit for play, the umpires shall allow it to be replaced by one that in their opinion has had a similar amount of wear. If a ball is to be replaced, the umpires shall inform the batsman.

Notes

(a) Specifications

The specifications, as described in 1 above, shall apply to top-grade balls only. The following degrees of tolerance will be acceptable for other grades of ball.

(i) *Men's Grades 2–4*
Weight: 5 5/16 ounces/150g to 5 13/16 ounces/165g.
Size: 8 11/16 inches/22.0cm to 9 1/16 inches/23.0cm.

(ii) *Women's*
Weight: 4 15/16 ounces/140g to 5 5/16 ounces/150g.
Size: 8¼ inches/21.0cm to 8⅞ inches/22.5cm.

(iii) *Junior*
Weight: 4 5/16 ounces/133g to 5 1/16 ounces/143g.
Size: 8 1/16 inches/20.5cm to 8 11/16 inches/22.0cm.

Law 6. The Bat

1. *Width and Length*

The bat overall shall not be more than 38 inches/96.5cm in length; the blade of the bat shall be made of wood and shall not exceed 4¼ inches/10.8cm at the widest part.

Notes

(a) The blade of the bat may be covered with material for protection, strengthening or repair. Such material shall not exceed 1⁄16 inch/1.56mm in thickness.

Law 7. The Pitch

1. *Area of Pitch*

The pitch is the area between the bowling creases – see Law 9 (The Bowling, Popping and Return Creases). It shall measure 5ft/1.52m in width on either side of a line joining the centre of the middle stumps of the wickets – see Law 8 (The Wickets).

2. *Selection and Preparation*

Before the toss for innings, the executive of the ground shall be responsible for the selection and preparation of the pitch; thereafter the umpires shall control its use and maintenance.

3. *Changing Pitch*

The pitch shall not be changed during a match unless it becomes unfit for play, and then only with the consent of both captains.

4. *Non-Turf Pitches*

In the event of a non-turf pitch being used, the following shall apply:

(a) Length: That of the playing surface to a minimum of 58ft/17.68m.
(b) Width: That of the playing surface to a minimum of 6ft/1.83m.

See Law 10 (Rolling, Sweeping, Mowing, Watering the Pitch and Re-marking of Creases) Note (a).

Law 8. The Wickets

1. Width and Pitching

Two sets of wickets, each 9 inches/22.86cm wide, and consisting of three wooden stumps with two wooden bails upon the top, shall be pitched opposite and parallel to each other at a distance of 22 yards/20.12m between the centres of the two middle stumps.

2. Size of Stumps

The stumps shall be of equal and sufficient size to prevent the ball from passing between them. Their tops shall be 28 inches/71.1cm above the ground, and shall be dome-shaped except for the bail grooves.

3. Size of Bails

The bails shall be each 4⅜ inches/11.1cm in length and when in position on the top of the stumps shall not project more than ½ inch/1.3cm above them.

Notes

(a) Dispensing with Bails
In a high wind the umpires may decide to dispense with the use of bails.

(b) Junior Cricket
For junior cricket, as defined by the local governing body, the following measurements for the wickets shall apply:

Width – 8 inches/20.32cm.
Pitched – 21 yards/19.20m.
Height – 27 inches/68.58cm.
Bails – each 3⅞ inches/9.84cm in length and should not project more than ½ inch/1.3cm above the stumps.

Law 9. The Bowling, Popping and Return Creases

1. The Bowling Crease

The bowling crease shall be marked in line with the stumps at each end and shall be 8 feet 8 inches/2.64m in length, with the stumps in the centre.

2. The Popping Crease

The popping crease, which is the back edge of the crease marking, shall be in front of and parallel with the bowling crease. It shall have the back edge of the crease marking 4 feet/1.22m from the centre of the stumps and shall extend to a minimum of 6 feet/1.83m on either side of the line of the wicket.

The popping crease shall be considered to be unlimited in length.

3. The Return Crease

The return crease marking, of which the inside edge is the crease, shall be at each end of the bowling crease and at right angles to it. The return crease shall be marked to a minimum of 4 feet/1.22m behind the wicket and shall be considered to be unlimited in length. A forward extension shall be marked to the popping crease.

Law 10. Rolling, Sweeping, Mowing, Watering the Pitch and Re-marking of Creases

1. Rolling

During the match the pitch may be rolled at the request of the captain of the batting side, for a period of not more than seven minutes before the start of each innings, other than the first innings of the match, and before the start of each day's play. In addition, if, after the toss and before the first innings of the match, the start is delayed, the captain of the batting side shall have the right to have the pitch rolled for not more than seven minutes.

The pitch shall not otherwise be rolled during the match.

The seven minutes' rolling permitted before the start of a day's play shall take place not earlier than half an hour before the start of play and the captain of the batting side may delay such rolling until ten minutes before the start of play should he so desire.

If a captain declares an innings closed less than fifteen minutes before the resumption of play, and the other captain is thereby prevented from exercising his option of seven minutes' rolling or if he is so prevented for any other reason, the time for rolling shall be taken out of the normal playing time.

2. Sweeping

Such sweeping of the pitch as is necessary during the match shall be done so that the seven minutes allowed for rolling the pitch, provided for in 1 above, is not affected.

3. Mowing

(a) Responsibilities of Ground Authority and of Umpires
All mowings which are carried out before the toss for innings shall be the responsibility of the ground authority; thereafter they shall be carried out under the supervision of the umpires. See Law 7.2 (Selection and Preparation).

(b) Initial Mowing
The pitch shall be mown before play begins on the day the match is scheduled to start, or in the case of a delayed start on the day the match is expected to start. See 3(a) above (Responsibilities of Ground Authority and of Umpires).

(c) Subsequent Mowings in a Match of Two or More Days' Duration
In a match of two or more days' duration, the pitch shall be mown daily before play begins. Should this mowing not take place because of weather conditions, rest days or other reasons, the pitch shall be mown on the first day on which the match is resumed.

(d) Mowing of the Outfield in a Match of Two or More Days' Duration
In order to ensure that conditions are as similar as possible for both sides, the outfield shall normally be mown before the commencement of play on each day of the match, if ground and weather conditions allow. See Note (b) to this Law.

4. Watering

The pitch shall not be watered during a match.

5. Re-marking Creases

Whenever possible the creases shall be re-marked.

6. Maintenance of Foot Holes

In wet weather, the umpires shall ensure that the holes made by the bowlers and batsmen are cleaned out and dried whenever necessary to facilitate play. In matches of two or more days' duration, the umpires shall allow, if necessary, the re-turfing of foot-holes made by the bowler in his delivery stride, or the use of quick-setting fillings for the same purpose, before the start of each day's play.

7. Securing of Footholds and Maintenance of Pitch

During play, the umpires shall allow either batsman to beat the pitch with his bat and players to secure their footholds by the use of sawdust, provided that no damage to the pitch is so caused, and Law 42 (Unfair Play) is not contravened.

Notes

(a) Non-turf Pitches
The above Law 10 applies to turf pitches.

The game is played on non-turf pitches in many countries at various levels. Whilst the conduct of the game on these surfaces should always be in accordance with the Laws of Cricket, it is recognised that it may sometimes be necessary for governing bodies to lay down special playing conditions to suit the type of non-turf pitch used in their country.

In matches played against touring teams, any special playing conditions should be agreed in advance by both parties.

(b) Mowing of the Outfield in a Match of Two or More Days' Duration
If, for reasons other than ground and weather conditions, daily and complete mowing is not possible, the ground authority shall notify the

captains and umpires, before the toss for innings, of the procedure to be adopted for such mowing during the match.

(c) Choice of Roller
If there is more than one roller available, the captain of the batting side shall have a choice.

Law 11. Covering the Pitch

1. *Before the Start of a Match*

Before the start of a match, complete covering of the pitch shall be allowed.

2. *During a Match*

The pitch shall not be completely covered during a match unless prior arrangement or regulations so provide.

3. *Covering Bowlers' Run-up*

Whenever possible, the bowlers' run-up shall be covered, but the covers so used shall not extend further than 4 feet/1.22m in front of the popping crease.

Notes

(a) Removal of Covers
The covers should be removed as promptly as possible whenever the weather permits.

Law 12. Innings

1. *Number of Innings*

A match shall be of one or two innings of each side according to agreement reached before the start of play.

2. *Alternate Innings*

In a two-innings match each side shall take their innings alternately except in the case provided for in Law 13 (The Follow-on).

3. *The Toss*

The captains shall toss for the choice of innings on the field of play not later than fifteen minutes before the time scheduled for the match to start, or before the time agreed upon for play to start.

4. Choice of Innings

The winner of the toss shall notify his decision to bat or to field to the opposing captain not later than ten minutes before the time scheduled for the match to start, or before the time agreed upon for play to start. The decision shall not thereafter be altered.

5. Continuation after One Innings of Each Side

Despite the terms of 1 above, in a one-innings match, when a result has been reached on the first innings, the captains may agree to the continuation of play if, in their opinion, there is a prospect of carrying the game to a further issue in the time left. See Law 21 (Result).

Notes

(a) Limited Innings – One-innings Match
In a one-innings match, each innings may, by agreement, be limited by a number of overs or by a period of time.

(b) Limited Innings – Two-innings Match
In a two-innings match the first innings of each side may, by agreement, be limited to a number of overs or by a period of time.

Law 13. The Follow-on

1. Lead on First Innings

In a two-innings match the side which bats first and leads by 200 runs in a match of five days or more, by 150 runs in a three-day or four-day match, by 100 runs in a two-day match, or by 75 runs in a one-day match, shall have the option of requiring the other side to follow their innings.

2. Day's Play Lost

If no play takes place on the first day of a match of two or more days' duration, 1 above shall apply in accordance with the number of days' play remaining from the actual start of the match.

Law 14. Declarations

1. Time of Declaration

The captain of the batting side may declare an innings closed at any time during a match, irrespective of its duration.

2. Forfeiture of Second Innings

A captain may forfeit his second innings, provided his decision to do so is notified to the opposing captain and umpires in sufficient time to allow seven minutes' rolling of the pitch. See Law 10 (Rolling, Sweeping, Mowing, Watering the Pitch and Re-marking of Creases). The normal ten-minute interval between innings shall be applied.

Law 15. Start of Play

1. Call of Play

At the start of each innings and of each day's play, and on the resumption of play after any interval or interruption, the umpire at the bowler's end shall call 'play'.

2. Practice on the Field

At no time on any day of the match shall there be any bowling or batting practice on the pitch.

No practice may take place on the field if, in the opinion of the umpires, it could result in a waste of time.

3. Trial Run-up

No bowler shall have a trial run-up after 'play' has been called in any session of play, except at the fall of a wicket when an umpire may allow such a trial run-up if he is satisfied that it will not cause any waste of time.

Law 16. Intervals

1. Length

The umpire shall allow such intervals as have been agreed upon for meals, and ten minutes between each innings.

2. Luncheon Interval – Innings Ending or Stoppage within Ten Minutes of Interval

If an innings ends or there is a stoppage caused by weather or bad light within ten minutes of the agreed time for the luncheon interval, the interval shall be taken immediately.

The time remaining in the session of play shall be added to the agreed length of the interval but no extra allowance shall be made for the ten-minute interval between innings.

3. Tea Interval – Innings Ending or Stoppage within Thirty Minutes of Interval

If an innings ends or there is a stoppage caused by weather or bad light within thirty minutes of the agreed time for the tea interval, the interval shall be taken immediately.

The interval shall be of the agreed length and, if applicable, shall include the ten-minute interval between innings.

4. Tea Interval – Continuation of Play

If, at the agreed time for the tea interval, nine wickets are down, play shall continue for a period not exceeding thirty minutes or until the innings is concluded.

5. Tea Interval – Agreement to Forego

At any time during the match, the captains may agree to forego a tea interval.

6. Intervals for Drinks

If both captains agree before the start of a match that intervals for drinks may be taken, the option to take such intervals shall be available to either side. These intervals shall be restricted to one per session, shall be kept as short as possible, shall not be taken in the last hour of the match, and in any case shall not exceed five minutes.

The agreed times for these intervals shall be strictly adhered to, except that if a wicket falls within five minutes of the agreed time then drinks shall be taken out immediately.

If an innings ends or there is a stoppage caused by weather or bad light within thirty minutes of the agreed time for a drinks interval, there will be no interval for drinks in that session.

At any time during the match the captains may agree to forego any such drinks interval.

Notes

(a) Tea Interval – One-day Match
In a one-day match, a specific time for the tea interval need not necessarily be arranged, and it may be agreed to take this interval between the innings of a one-innings match.

(b) Changing the Agreed Time of Intervals
In the event of the ground, weather or light conditions causing a suspension of play, the umpires, after consultation with the captains, may decide in the interests of time-saving to bring forward the time of the luncheon or tea interval.

Law 17. Cessation of Play

1. *Call of Time*

The umpire at the bowler's end shall call 'time' on the cessation of play before any interval or interruption of play, at the end of each day's play, and at the conclusion of the match. See Law 27 (Appeals).

2. *Removal of Bails*

After the call of 'time', the umpires shall remove the bails from both wickets.

3. *Starting a Last Over*

The last over before an interval or the close of play shall be started provided the umpire, after walking at his normal pace, has arrived at his position behind the stumps at the bowler's end before time has been reached.

4. *Completion of the Last Over of a Session*

The last over before an interval or the close of play shall be completed unless a batsman is out or retires during that over within two minutes of the interval or the close of play or unless the players have occasion to leave the field.

5. *Completion of the Last Over of a Match*

An over in progress at the close of play on the final day of a match shall be completed at the request of either captain, even if a wicket falls after time has been reached.

If, during the last over, the players have occasion to leave the field, the umpires shall call 'time' and there shall be no resumption of play and the match shall be at an end.

6. *Last Hour of Match – Number of Overs*

The umpires shall indicate when one hour of playing time of the match remains according to the agreed hours of play. The next over after that moment shall be the first of a minimum of 20 six-ball overs (15 eight-ball overs), provided a result is not reached earlier or there is no interval or interruption of play.

7. *Last Hour of Match – Intervals between Innings and Interruptions of Play*

If, at the commencement of the last hour of the match, an interval or interruption of play is in progress or if, during the last hour, there is an interval between innings or an interruption of play, the minimum number of overs to be bowled on the resumption of play shall be reduced in proportion to the duration, within the last hour of the match, of any such interval or interruption.

The minimum number of overs to be bowled after the resumption of play shall be calculated as follows:

(a) In the case of an interval or interruption of play being in progress at the commencement of the last hour of the match, or in the case of a first interval or interruption, a deduction shall be made from the minimum of 20 six-ball overs (or 15 eight-ball overs).

(b) If there is a later interval or interruption, a further deduction shall be made from the minimum number of overs which should have been bowled following the last resumption of play.

(c) These deductions shall be based on the following factors:

- (i) The number of overs already bowled in the last hour of the match or, in the case of a later interval or interruption, in the last session of play.
- (ii) The number of overs lost as a result of the interval or interruption allowing one six-ball over for every full three minutes (or one eight-ball over for every full four minutes) of interval or interruption.
- (iii) Any over left uncompleted at the end of an innings to be excluded from these calculations.
- (iv) Any over left uncompleted at the start of an interruption of play to be completed when play is resumed and to count as one over bowled.
- (v) An interval to start with the end of an innings and to end ten minutes later; an interruption to start on the call of 'time' and to end on the call of 'play'.

(d) In the event of an innings being completed and a new innings commencing during the last hour of the match, the number of overs to be bowled in the new innings shall be calculated on the basis of one six-ball over for every three minutes or part thereof remaining for play (or one eight-ball over for every four minutes or part thereof remaining for play); or alternatively on the basis that sufficient overs be bowled to enable the full minimum quota of overs to be completed under circumstances governed by (a), (b) and (c) above. In all such cases the alternative which allows the greater number of overs shall be employed.

8. Bowler Unable to Complete an Over during Last Hour of the Match

If, for any reason, a bowler is unable to complete an over during the period of play referred to in 6 above, Law 22.7 (Bowler Incapacitated or Suspended during an Over) shall apply.

Law 18. Scoring

1. A Run

The score shall be reckoned by runs. A run is scored:

(a) So often as the batsmen, after a hit or at any time while the ball is in play, shall have crossed and made good their ground from end to end.
(b) When a boundary is scored. See Law 19 (Boundaries).
(c) When penalty runs are awarded. See 6 below.

2. Short Runs

(a) If either batsman runs a short run, the umpire shall call and signal 'one short' as soon as the ball becomes dead and that run shall not be scored. A run is short if a batsman fails to make good his ground on turning for a further run.
(b) Although a short run shortens the succeeding one, the latter, if completed, shall count.
(c) If either or both batsmen deliberately run short the umpire shall, as soon as he sees that the fielding side have no chance of dismissing either batsman, call and signal 'dead ball' and disallow any runs attempted or previously scored. The batsmen shall return to their original ends.
(d) If both batsmen run short in one and the same run, only one run shall be deducted.
(e) Only if 3 or more runs are attempted can more than one be short and then, subject to (c) and (d) above, all runs so called shall be disallowed. If there has been more than one short run the umpires shall instruct the scorers as to the number of runs disallowed.

3. Striker Caught

If the striker is caught, no run shall be scored.

4. Batsman Run Out

If a batsman is run out, only that run which was being attempted shall not be scored. If, however, an injured striker himself is run out, no runs shall be scored. See Law 2.7 (Transgression of the Laws by an Injured Batsman or Runner).

5. Batsman Obstructing the Field

If a batsman is out Obstructing the Field, any runs completed before the obstruction occurs shall be scored unless such obstruction prevents a catch being made, in which case no runs shall be scored.

6. Runs Scored for Penalties

Runs shall be scored for penalties under Laws 20 (Lost Ball), 24 (No-ball), 25 (Wide-ball), 41.1 (Fielding the Ball) and for boundary allowances under Law 19 (Boundaries).

7. Batsman Returning to Wicket he has Left

If, while the ball is in play, the batsmen have crossed in running, neither shall return to the wicket he has left, even though a short run has been called or no run has been scored as in the case of a catch. Batsmen, however, shall return to the wickets they originally left in the case of a boundary and of any disallowance of runs and of an injured batsman being, himself, run out. See Law 2.7 (Transgression by an Injured Batsman or Runner).

Notes

(a) Short Run

A striker taking stance in front of his popping crease may run from that point without penalty.

Law 19. Boundaries

1. The Boundary of the Playing Area

Before the toss for innings, the umpires shall agree with both captains on the boundary of the playing area. The boundary shall, if possible, be marked by a white line, a rope laid on the ground, or a fence. If flags or posts only are used to mark a boundary, the imaginary line joining such points shall be regarded as the boundary. An obstacle, or person, within the playing area shall not be regarded as a boundary unless so decided by the umpires before the toss for innings. Sightscreens within, or partially within, the playing area shall be regarded as the boundary and when the ball strikes or passes within or under or directly over any part of the screen, a boundary shall be scored.

2. Runs Scored for Boundaries

Before the toss for innings, the umpires shall agree with both captains the runs to be allowed for boundaries, and in deciding the allowance for them, the umpires and captains shall be guided by the prevailing custom of the ground. The allowance for a boundary shall normally be 4 runs, and 6 runs for all hits pitching over and clear of the boundary line or fence, even though the ball has been previously touched by a fieldsman. 6 runs shall also be scored if a fieldsman, after catching a ball, carries it over the boundary. See Law 32 (Caught) Note (a). 6 runs shall not be scored when a ball struck by the striker hits a sightscreen full pitch if the screen is within, or partially within, the playing area, but if the ball is struck directly over a sightscreen so situated, 6 runs shall be scored.

3. A Boundary

A boundary shall be scored and signalled by the umpire at the bowler's end whenever, in his opinion:

(a) A ball in play touches or crosses the boundary, however marked.
(b) A fieldsman with ball in hand touches or grounds any part of his person on or over a boundary line.
(c) A fieldsman with ball in hand grounds any part of his person over a boundary fence or board. This allows the fieldsman to touch or lean on or over a boundary fence or board in preventing a boundary.

4. Runs Exceeding Boundary Allowance

The runs completed at the instant the ball reaches the boundary shall count if they exceed the boundary allowance.

5. Overthrows or Wilful Act of a Fieldsman

If the boundary results from an overthrow or from the wilful act of a fieldsman, any runs already completed and the allowance shall be added to the score. The run in progress shall count provided that the batsmen have crossed at the instant of the throw or act.

Notes

(a) Position of Sightscreens
Sightscreens should, if possible, be positioned wholly outside the playing area, as near as possible to the boundary line.

Law 20. Lost Ball

1. Runs Scored

If a ball in play cannot be found or recovered, any fieldsman may call 'lost ball' when 6 runs shall be added to the score; but if more than 6 have been run before 'lost ball' is called, as many runs as have been completed shall be scored. The run in progress shall count provided that the batsmen have crossed at the instant of the call of 'lost ball'.

2. How Scored

The runs shall be added to the score of the striker if the ball has been struck, but otherwise to the score of byes, leg-byes, no-balls or wides as the case may be.

Law 21. The Result

1. *A Win – Two-innings Matches*

The side which has scored a total of runs in excess of that scored by the opposing side in its two completed innings shall be the winners.

2. *A Win – One-innings Matches*

(a) One-innings matches, unless played out as in 1 above, shall be decided on the first innings, but see Law 12.5 (Continuation after One Innings of Each Side).
(b) If the captains agree to continue play after the completion of one innings of each side in accordance with Law 12.5 (Continuation after One Innings of Each Side) and a result is not achieved on the second innings, the first innings shall stand.

3. *Umpires Awarding a Match*

(a) A match shall be lost by a side which, during the match, (i) refuses to play, or (ii) concedes defeat, and the umpires shall award the match to the other side.
(b) Should both batsmen at the wickets or the fielding side leave the field at any time without the agreement of the umpires, this shall constitute a refusal to play and, on appeal, the umpires shall award the match to the other side in accordance with (a) above.

4. *A Tie*

The result of a match shall be a tie when the scores are equal at the conclusion of play, but only if the side batting last has completed its innings.
If the scores of the completed first innings of a one-day match are equal, it shall be a tie but only if the match has not been played out to a further conclusion.

5. *A Draw*

A match not determined in any of the ways as in 1, 2, 3 and 4 above shall count as a draw.

6. *Correctness of Result*

Any decision as to the correctness of the scores shall be the responsibility of the umpires. See Law 3.14 (Correctness of Scores).
If, after the umpires and players have left the field in the belief that the match has been concluded, the umpires decide that a mistake in scoring has occurred, which affects the result, and provided time has not been reached, they shall order play to resume and to continue until the agreed finishing time unless a result is reached earlier.

If the umpires decide that a mistake has occurred and time has been reached, the umpires shall immediately inform both captains of the necessary corrections to the scores and, if applicable, to the result.

7. *Acceptance of Result*

In accepting the scores as notified by the scorers and agreed by the umpires, the captains of both sides thereby accept the result.

Notes

(a) Statement of Results
The result of a finished match is stated as a win by runs, except in the case of a win by the side batting last when it is by the number of wickets still then to fall.

(b) Winning Hit or Extras
As soon as the side has won, see 1 and 2 above, the umpire shall call 'time', the match is finished, and nothing that happens thereafter other than as a result of a mistake in scoring (see 6 above) shall be regarded as part of the match.

However, if a boundary constitutes the winning hit – or extras – and the boundary allowance exceeds the number of runs required to win the match, such runs scored shall be credited to the side's total and, in the case of a hit, to the striker's score.

Law 22. The Over

1. *Number of Balls*

The ball shall be bowled from each wicket alternately in overs of either six or eight balls according to agreement before the match.

2. *Call of 'Over'*

When the agreed number of balls has been bowled, and as the ball becomes dead or when it becomes clear to the umpire at the bowler's end that both the fielding side and the batsmen at the wicket have ceased to regard the ball as in play, the umpire shall call 'over' before leaving the wicket.

3. *No-ball or Wide-ball*

Neither a no-ball nor a wide-ball shall be reckoned as one of the over.

4. *Umpire Miscounting*

If an umpire miscounts the number of balls, the over as counted by the umpire shall stand.

5. Bowler Changing Ends

A bowler shall be allowed to change ends as often as desired, provided only that he does not bowl two overs consecutively in an innings.

6. The Bowler Finishing an Over

A bowler shall finish an over in progress unless he be incapacitated or be suspended under Law 42.8 (The Bowling of Fast Short-pitched Balls), 9 (The Bowling of Fast High Full Pitches), 10 (Time Wasting) and 11 (Players Damaging the Pitch). If an over is left incomplete for any reason at the start of an interval or interruption of play, it shall be finished on the resumption of play.

7. Bowler Incapacitated or Suspended during an Over

If, for any reason, a bowler is incapacitated while running up to bowl the first ball of an over, or is incapacitated or suspended during an over, the umpire shall call and signal 'dead ball' and another bowler shall be allowed to bowl or complete the over from the same end, provided only that he shall not bowl two overs, or part thereof, consecutively in one innings.

8. Position of Non-striker

The batsman at the bowler's end shall normally stand on the opposite side of the wicket to that from which the ball is being delivered, unless a request to do otherwise is granted by the umpire.

Law 23. Dead Ball

1. The Ball Becomes Dead

When:

(a) It is finally settled in the hands of the wicket-keeper or the bowler.
(b) It reaches or pitches over the boundary.
(c) A batsman is out.
(d) Whether played or not, it lodges in the clothing or equipment of a batsman or the clothing of an umpire.
(e) A ball lodges in a protective helmet worn by a member of the fielding side.
(f) A penalty is awarded under Law 20 (Lost Ball) or Law 41.1 (Fielding the Ball).
(g) The umpire calls 'over' or 'time'.

2. Either Umpire Shall Call and Signal 'Dead Ball'

When:

(a) He intervenes in a case of unfair play.
(b) A serious injury to a player or umpire occurs.
(c) He is satisfied that, for an adequate reason, the striker is not ready to receive the ball and makes no attempt to play it.
(d) The bowler drops the ball accidentally before delivery, or the ball does not leave his hand for any reason.
(e) One or both bails fall from the striker's wicket before he receives delivery.
(f) He leaves his normal position for consultation.
(g) He is required to do so under Law 26.3 (Disallowance of Leg-byes).

3. The Ball Ceases to be Dead

When:

(a) The bowler starts his run-up or bowling action.

4. The Ball is Not Dead

When:

(a) It strikes an umpire (unless it lodges in his dress).
(b) The wicket is broken or struck down (unless a batsman is out thereby).
(c) An unsuccessful appeal is made.
(d) The wicket is broken accidentally either by the bowler during his delivery or by a batsman in running.
(e) The umpire has called 'no-ball' or 'wide'.

Notes

(a) Ball Finally Settled
Whether the ball is finally settled or not – see (a) above – must be a question for the umpires alone to decide.

(b) Action on Call of 'Dead Ball'
(i) If 'dead ball' is called prior to the striker receiving a delivery, the bowler shall be allowed an additional ball.
(ii) If 'dead ball' is called after the striker receives a delivery, the bowler shall not be allowed an additional ball, unless a 'no-ball' or 'wide' has been called.

Law 24. No-ball

1. Mode of Delivery

The umpire shall indicate to the striker whether the bowler intends to bowl over or round the wicket, overarm or underarm, right- or left-handed. Failure on the part of the bowler to indicate in advance a change in his mode of delivery is unfair and the umpire shall call and signal 'no-ball'.

2. *Fair Delivery – The Arm*

For a delivery to be fair the ball must be bowled, not thrown – see Note (a) below. If either umpire is not entirely satisfied with the absolute fairness of a delivery in this respect he shall call and signal 'no-ball' instantly upon delivery.

3. *Fair Delivery – The Feet*

The umpire at the bowler's wicket shall call and signal 'no-ball' if he is not satisfied that in the delivery stride:

(a) The bowler's back foot has landed within and not touching the return crease or its forward extension; or
(b) Some part of the front foot whether grounded or raised was behind the popping crease.

4. *Bowler Throwing at Striker's Wicket before Delivery*

If the bowler, before delivering the ball, throws it at the striker's wicket in an attempt to run him out, the umpire shall call and signal 'no-ball'. See Law 42.12 (Batsman Unfairly Stealing a Run) and Law 38 (Run Out).

5. *Bowler Attempting to Run Out Non-striker before Delivery*

If the bowler, before delivering the ball, attempts to run out the non-striker, any runs which result shall be allowed and shall be scored as no-balls. Such an attempt shall not count as a ball in the over. The umpire shall not call 'no-ball'. See Law 42.12 (Batsman Unfairly Stealing a Run).

6. *Infringement of Laws by a Wicket-keeper or a Fieldsman*

The umpire shall call and signal 'no-ball' in the event of the wicket-keeper infringing Law 40.1 (Position of Wicket-keeper) or a fieldsman infringing Law 41.2 (Limitation of On-side Fieldsmen) or Law 41.3 (Position of Fieldsmen).

7. *Revoking a Call*

An umpire shall revoke the call 'no-ball' if the ball does not leave the bowler's hand for any reason. See Law 23.2 (Either Umpire Shall Call and Signal 'Dead Ball').

8. *Penalty*

A penalty of 1 run for a no-ball shall be scored if no runs are made otherwise.

9. Runs from a No-ball

The striker may hit a no-ball and whatever runs result shall be added to his score. Runs made otherwise from a no-ball shall be scored no-balls.

10. Out from a No-ball

The striker shall be out from a no-ball if he breaks Law 34 (Hit the Ball Twice) and either batsman may be run out or shall be given out if either breaks Law 33 (Handled the Ball) or Law 37 (Obstructing the Field).

11. Batsman Given Out off a No-ball

Should a batsman be given out off a no-ball the penalty for bowling it shall stand unless runs are otherwise scored.

Notes

(a) Definition of a Throw
A ball shall be deemed to have been thrown if, in the opinion of either umpire, the process of straightening the bowling arm, whether it be partial or complete, takes place during that part of the delivery swing which directly precedes the ball leaving the hand. This definition shall not debar a bowler from the use of the wrist in the delivery swing.

(b) No-ball Not Counting in Over
A no-ball shall not be reckoned as one of the over. See Law 22.3 (No-ball or Wide-ball).

Law 25. Wide-ball

1. Judging a Wide

If the bowler bowls the ball so high over or so wide of the wicket that, in the opinion of the umpire, it passes out of the reach of the striker, standing in a normal guard position, the umpire shall call and signal 'wide-ball' as soon as it has passed the line of the striker's wicket.

The umpire shall not adjudge a ball as being wide if:

(a) The striker, by moving from his guard position, causes the ball to pass out of his reach.
(b) The striker moves and thus brings the ball within his reach.

2. Penalty

A penalty of 1 run for a wide shall be scored if no runs are made otherwise.

3. Ball Coming to Rest in Front of the Striker

If a ball which the umpire considers to have been delivered comes to rest in front of the line of the striker's wicket, 'wide' shall not be called. The striker has a right, without interference from the fielding side, to make one attempt to hit the ball. If the fielding side interfere, the umpire shall replace the ball where it came to rest and shall order the fieldsmen to resume the places they occupied in the field before the ball was delivered.

The umpire shall call and signal 'dead ball' as soon as it is clear that the striker does not intend to hit the ball, or after the striker has made an unsuccessful attempt to hit the ball.

4. Revoking a Call

The umpire shall revoke the call if the striker hits a ball which has been called 'wide'.

5. Ball Not Dead

The ball does not become dead on the call of 'wide-ball' – see Law 23.4 (The Ball is Not Dead).

6. Runs Resulting from a Wide

All runs which are run or result from a wide-ball which is not a no-ball shall be scored wide-balls, and if no runs are made 1 shall be scored.

7. Out from a Wide

The striker shall be out from a wide-ball if he breaks Law 35 (Hit Wicket), or Law 39 (Stumped). Either batsman may be run out and shall be out if he breaks Law 33 (Handled the Ball), or Law 37 (Obstructing the Field).

8. Batsman Given Out off a Wide

Should a batsman be given out off a wide, the penalty for bowling it shall stand unless runs are otherwise made.

Notes

(a) Wide-ball Not Counting in Over

A wide-ball shall not be reckoned as one of the over – see Law 22.3 (No-ball or Wide-ball).

Law 26. Bye and Leg-bye

1. Byes

If the ball, not having been called 'wide' or 'no-ball', passes the striker without touching his bat or person, and any runs are obtained, the umpire shall signal 'bye' and the run or runs shall be credited as such to the batting side.

2. Leg-byes

If the ball, not having been called 'wide' or 'no-ball', is unintentionally deflected by the striker's dress or person, except a hand holding the bat, and any runs are obtained the umpire shall signal 'leg-bye' and the run or runs so scored shall be credited as such to the batting side.

Such leg-byes shall be scored only if, in the opinion of the umpire, the striker has:

(a) Attempted to play the ball with his bat; or
(b) Tried to avoid being hit by the ball.

3. Disallowance of Leg-byes

In the case of a deflection by the striker's person, other than in 2(a) and (b) above, the umpire shall call and signal 'dead ball' as soon as 1 run has been completed or when it is clear that a run is not being attempted, or the ball has reached the boundary.

On the call and signal of 'dead ball' the batsmen shall return to their original ends and no runs shall be allowed.

Law 27. Appeals

1. Time of Appeals

The umpires shall not give a batsman out unless appealed to by the other side which shall be done prior to the bowler beginning his run-up or bowling action to deliver the next ball. Under Law 23.1(f) (The Ball Becomes Dead), the ball is dead on 'over' being called; this does not, however, invalidate an appeal made prior to the first ball of the following over provided 'time' has not been called – see 17.1 (Call of Time).

2. An Appeal 'How's That?'

An appeal 'How's That?' shall cover all ways of being out.

3. Answering Appeals

The umpire at the bowler's wicket shall answer appeals before the other umpire in all cases except those arising out of Law 35 (Hit Wicket) or Law 39 (Stumped) or Law 38 (Run Out) when this occurs at the striker's wicket.

When either umpire has given a batsman not out, the other umpire shall, within his jurisdiction, answer the appeal or a further appeal, provided it is made in time in accordance with 1 above (Time of Appeals).

4. Consultation by Umpires

An umpire may consult with the other umpire on a point of fact which the latter may have been in a better position to see and shall then give his decision. If, after consultation, there is still doubt remaining the decision shall be in favour of the batsman.

5. Batsman Leaving his Wicket under a Misapprehension

The umpires shall intervene if satisfied that a batsman, not having been given out, has left his wicket under a misapprehension that he has been dismissed.

6. Umpire's Decision

The umpire's decision is final. He may alter his decision, provided that such alteration is made promptly.

7. Withdrawal of an Appeal

In exceptional circumstances the captain of the fielding side may seek permission of the umpire to withdraw an appeal provided the outgoing batsman has not left the playing area. If this is allowed, the umpire shall cancel his decision.

Law 28. The Wicket is Down

1. Wicket Down

The wicket is down if:

(a) Either the ball or the striker's bat or person completely removes either bail from the top of the stumps. A disturbance of a bail, whether temporary or not, shall not constitute a complete removal, but the wicket is down if a bail in falling lodges between two of the stumps.
(b) Any player completely removes with his hand or arm a bail from the top of the stumps, provided that the ball is held in that hand or in the hand of the arm so used.
(c) When both bails are off, a stump is struck out of the ground by the ball, or a player strikes or pulls a stump out of the ground, provided that the ball is held in the hand(s) or in the hand of the arm so used.

2. One Bail Off

If one bail is off, it shall be sufficient for the purpose of putting the wicket down to remove the remaining bail, or to strike or pull any of the three stumps out of the ground in any of the ways stated in 1 above.

3. All the Stumps Out of the Ground

If all the stumps are out of the ground, the fielding side shall be allowed to put back one or more stumps in order to have an opportunity of putting the wicket down.

4. Dispensing with Bails

If owing to the strength of the wind, it has been agreed to dispense with the bails in accordance with Law 8, Note (a) (Dispensing with Bails), the decision as to when the wicket is down is one for the umpires to decide on the facts before them. In such circumstances and if the umpires so decide, the wicket shall be held to be down even though a stump has not been struck out of the ground.

Notes

(a) Remaking the Wicket
If the wicket is broken while the ball is in play, it is not the umpire's duty to remake the wicket until the ball has become dead – see Law 23 (Dead Ball). A member of the fielding side, however, may remake the wicket in such circumstances.

Law 29. Batsman Out of His Ground

1. When out of his Ground

A batsman shall be considered to be out of his ground unless some part of his bat in his hand or of his person is grounded behind the line of the popping crease.

Law 30. Bowled

1. Out Bowled

The striker shall be out bowled if:

(a) His wicket is bowled down, even if the ball first touches his bat or person.
(b) He breaks his wicket by hitting or kicking the ball on to it before the completion of a stroke, or as a result of attempting to guard his wicket. See Law 34.1 (Out Hit the Ball Twice).

Notes

(a) Out Bowled – Not lbw
The striker is out bowled if the ball is deflected on to his wicket even though a decision against him would be justified under Law 36 (lbw).

Law 31. Timed Out

1. Out Timed Out

An incoming batsman shall be out Timed Out if he wilfully takes more than two minutes to come in – the two minutes being timed from the moment a wicket falls until the new batsman steps on to the field of play.

If this is not complied with and if the umpire is satisfied that the delay was wilful and if an appeal is made, the new batsman shall be given out by the umpire at the bowler's end.

2. Time to be Added

The time taken by the umpires to investigate the cause of the delay shall be added at the normal close of play.

Notes

(a) Entry in Scorebook
The correct entry in the scorebook when a batsman is given out under this Law is 'timed out', and the bowler does not get credit for the wicket.

(b) Batsmen Crossing on the Field of Play
It is an essential duty of the captains to ensure that the in-going batsman passes the out-going one before the latter leaves the field of play.

Law 32. Caught

1. Out Caught

The striker shall be out Caught if the ball touches his bat or if it touches below his wrist his hand or glove, holding the bat, and is subsequently held by a fieldsman before it touches the ground.

2. A Fair Catch

A catch shall be considered to have been fairly made if:

(a) The fieldsman is within the field of play throughout the act of making the catch.

(i) The act of making the catch shall start from the time when the fieldsman first handles the ball and shall end when he both retains complete control over the further disposal of the ball and remains within the field of play.

(ii) In order to be within the field of play, the fieldsman may not touch or ground any part of his person on or over a boundary line. When the boundary is marked by a fence or board the fieldsman may not ground any part of his person over the boundary fence or board, but may touch or lean over the boundary fence or board in completing the catch.

(b) The ball is hugged to the body of the catcher or accidentally lodges in his dress or, in the case of the wicket-keeper, in his pads. However, a striker may not be caught if a ball lodges in a protective helmet worn by a fieldsman, in which case the umpire shall call and signal 'dead ball'. See Law 23 (Dead Ball).
(c) The ball does not touch the ground even though a hand holding it does so in effecting the catch.
(d) A fieldsman catches the ball, after it has been lawfully played a second time by the striker, but only if the ball has not touched the ground since being first struck.
(e) A fieldsman catches the ball after it has touched an umpire, another fieldsman or the other batsman. However, a striker may not be caught if a ball has touched a protective helmet worn by a fieldsman.
(f) The ball is caught off an obstruction within the boundary provided it has not previously been agreed to regard the obstruction as a boundary.

3. *Scoring of Runs*

If a striker is caught, no run shall be scored.

Notes

(a) Scoring from an Attempted Catch
When a fieldsman carrying the ball touches or grounds any part of his person on or over a boundary marked by a line, 6 runs shall be scored.

(b) Ball Still in Play
If a fieldsman releases the ball before he crosses the boundary, the ball will be considered to be still in play and it may be caught by another fieldsman. However, if the original fieldsman returns to the field of play and handles the ball, a catch may not be made.

Law 33. Handled the Ball

1. *Out Handled the Ball*

Either batsman on appeal shall be out *Handled the Ball* if he wilfully touches the ball while in play with the hand not holding the bat unless he does so with the consent of the opposite side.

Notes

(a) Entry in Scorebook
The correct entry in the scorebook when a batsman is given out under this Law is 'handled the ball', and the bowler does not get credit for the wicket.

Law 34. Hit the Ball Twice

1. Out Hit the Ball Twice

The striker, on appeal, shall be out Hit the Ball Twice if, after the ball is struck or is stopped by any part of his person, he wilfully strikes it again with his bat or person except for the sole purpose of guarding his wicket: this he may do with his bat or any part of his person other than his hands, but see Law 37.2 (Obstructing a Ball From Being Caught).

For the purpose of this Law, a hand holding the bat shall be regarded as part of the bat.

2. Returning the Ball to a Fieldsman

The striker, on appeal, shall be out under this Law if, without the consent of the opposite side, he uses his bat or person to return the ball to any of the fielding side.

3. Runs from Ball Lawfully Struck Twice

No runs except those which result from an overthrow or penalty – see Law 41 (The Fieldsman) – shall be scored from a ball lawfully struck twice.

Notes

(a) Entry in Scorebook
The correct entry in the scorebook when the striker is given out under this Law is 'hit the ball twice', and the bowler does not get credit for the wicket.

(b) Runs Credited to the Batsman
Any runs awarded under 3 above as a result of an overthrow or penalty shall be credited to the striker, provided the ball in the first instance has touched the bat, or, if otherwise, as extras.

Law 35. Hit Wicket

1. Out Hit Wicket

The striker shall be out Hit Wicket if, while the ball is in play:

(a) His wicket is broken with any part of his person, dress, or equipment as a result of any action taken by him in preparing to receive or in receiving a delivery, or in setting off for his first run, immediately after playing, or playing at, the ball. (b) He hits down his wicket whilst lawfully making a second stroke for the purpose of guarding his wicket within the provisions of Law 34.1 (Out Hit the Ball Twice).

Notes

(a) Not Out Hit Wicket

A batsman is not out under this Law should his wicket be broken in any of the ways referred to in 1(a) above if:

(i) It occurs while he is in the act of running, other than in setting off for his first run immediately after playing at the ball, or while he is avoiding being run out or stumped.

(ii) The bowler after starting his run-up or bowling action does not deliver the ball; in which case the umpire shall immediately call and signal 'dead ball'.

(iii) It occurs whilst he is avoiding a throw-in at any time.

Law 36. Leg Before Wicket

1. *Out lbw*

The striker shall be out lbw in the circumstances set out below:

(a) Striker Attempting to Play the Ball

The striker shall be out lbw if he first intercepts with any part of his person, dress or equipment a fair ball which would have hit the wicket and which has not previously touched his bat or a hand holding the bat, provided that:

(i) The ball pitched in a straight line between wicket and wicket or on the off side of the striker's wicket, or in the case of a ball intercepted full pitch would have pitched in a straight line between wicket and wicket; and

(ii) The point of impact is in a straight line between wicket and wicket, even if above the level of the bails.

(b) Striker Making No Attempt to Play the Ball

The striker shall be out lbw even if the ball is intercepted outside the line of the off stump if, in the opinion of the umpire, he has made no genuine attempt to play the ball with his bat, but has intercepted the ball with some part of his person and if the circumstances set out in (a) above apply.

Law 37. Obstructing the Field

1. *Wilful Obstruction*

Either batsman, on appeal, shall be out Obstructing the Field if he wilfully obstructs the opposite side by word or action.

2. *Obstructing a Ball From Being Caught*

The striker, on appeal, shall be out should wilful obstruction by either batsman prevent a catch being made.

This shall apply even though the striker causes the obstruction in lawfully guarding his wicket under the provisions of Law 34. See Law 34.1 (Out Hit the Ball Twice).

Notes

(a) Accidental Obstruction
The umpires must decide whether the obstruction was wilful or not. The accidental interception of a throw-in by a batsman while running does not break this Law.

(b) Entry in Scorebook
The correct entry in the scorebook when a batsman is given out under this Law is 'obstructing the field', and the bowler does not get credit for the wicket.

Law 38. Run Out

1. *Out Run Out*

Either batsman shall be Run Out if in running or at any time while the ball is in play – except in the circumstances described in Law 39 (Stumped) – he is out of his ground and his wicket is put down by the opposite side. If, however, a batsman in running makes good his ground he shall not be out run out if he subsequently leaves his ground, in order to avoid injury, and the wicket is put down.

2. *'No-ball' Called*

If a no-ball has been called, the striker shall not be given run out unless he attempts to run.

3. *Which Batsman Is Out*

If the batsmen have crossed in running, he who runs for the wicket which is put down shall be out; if they have not crossed, he who has left the wicket which is put down shall be out. If a batsman remains in his ground or returns to his ground and the other batsman joins him there, the latter shall be out if his wicket is put down.

4. *Scoring of Runs*

If a batsman is run out, only that run which is being attempted shall not be scored. If, however, an injured striker himself is run out, no runs shall be scored. See Law 2.7 (Transgression of the Laws by an Injured Batsman or Runner).

Notes

(a) Ball Played on to Opposite Wicket
If the ball is played on to the opposite wicket, neither batsman is liable to be run out unless the ball has been touched by a fieldsman before the wicket is broken.

(b) Entry in Scorebook
The correct entry in the scorebook when a batsman is given out under this Law is 'run out', and the bowler does not get credit for the wicket.

Law 39. Stumped

1. *Out Stumped*

The striker shall be out Stumped if, in receiving the ball, not being a no-ball, he is out of his ground otherwise than in attempting a run and the wicket is put down by the wicket-keeper without the intervention of another fieldsman.

2. *Action by the Wicket-keeper*

The wicket-keeper may take the ball in front of the wicket in an attempt to stump the striker only if the ball has touched the bat or person of the striker.

Note

(a) Ball Rebounding from Wicket-keeper's Person
The striker may be out stumped if, in the circumstances stated in 1 above, the wicket is broken by a ball rebounding from the wicket-keeper's person or equipment or is kicked or thrown by the wicket-keeper on to the wicket.

Law 40. The Wicket-keeper

1. *Position of Wicket-keeper*

The wicket-keeper shall remain wholly behind the wicket until a ball delivered by the bowler touches the bat or person of the striker, or passes the wicket, or until the striker attempts a run.

In the event of the wicket-keeper contravening this Law, the umpire at the striker's end shall call and signal 'no-ball' at the instant of delivery or as soon as possible thereafter.

2. *Restriction on Actions of the Wicket-keeper*

If the wicket-keeper interferes with the striker's right to play the ball and to guard his wicket, the striker shall not be out except under Laws 33 (Handled the Ball), 34 (Hit the Ball Twice), 37 (Obstructing the Field), 38 (Run Out).

3. Interference with the Wicket-keeper by the Striker

If in the legitimate defence of his wicket, the striker interferes with the wicket-keeper, he shall not be out, except as provided for in Law 37.2 (Obstructing a Ball From Being Caught).

Law 41. The Fieldsman

1. Fielding the Ball

The fieldsman may stop the ball with any part of his person, but if he wilfully stops it otherwise, 5 runs shall be added to the runs already scored; if no run has been scored 5 penalty runs shall be awarded. The run in progress shall count provided that the batsmen have crossed at the instant of the act. If the ball has been struck, the penalty shall be added to the score of the striker, but otherwise to the scores of byes, leg-byes, no-balls or wides as the case may be.

2. Limitation of On-side Fieldsmen

The number of on-side fieldsmen behind the popping crease at the instant of the bowler's delivery shall not exceed two. In the event of infringement by the fielding side the umpire at the striker's end shall call and signal 'no-ball' at the instant of delivery or as soon as possible thereafter.

3. Position of Fieldsmen

Whilst the ball is in play and until the ball has made contact with the bat or the striker's person or has passed his bat, no fieldsman, other than the bowler, may stand on or have any part of his person extended over the pitch (measuring 22 yards/20.12m × 10 feet/3.05m). In the event of a fieldsman contravening this Law, the umpire at the bowler's end shall call and signal 'no-ball' at the instant of delivery or as soon as possible thereafter. See Law 40.1 (Position of Wicket-keeper).

4. Fieldsmen's Protective Helmets

Protective helmets, when not in use by members of the fielding side, shall only be placed, if above the surface, on the ground behind the wicket-keeper. In the event of the ball, when in play, striking a helmet whilst in this position, five penalty runs shall be awarded as laid down in Law 41.1 and Note (a).

Note

(a) Batsmen Changing Ends

The 5 runs referred to in 1 and 4 above (and the Experimental Law) are a penalty and the batsmen do not change ends solely by reason of this penalty.

Law 42. Unfair Play

1. Responsibility of Captains

The captains are responsible at all times for ensuring that play is conducted within the spirit of the game as well as within the Laws.

2. Responsibility of Umpires

The umpires are the sole judges of fair and unfair play.

3. Intervention by the Umpire

The umpires shall intervene without appeal by calling and signalling 'dead ball' in the case of unfair play, but should not otherwise interfere with the progress of the game except as required to do so by the Laws.

4. Lifting the Seam

A player shall not lift the seam of the ball for any reason. Should this be done, the umpires shall change the ball for one of similar condition to that in use prior to the contravention. See Note (a).

5. Changing the Condition of the Ball

Any member of the fielding side may polish the ball provided that such polishing wastes no time and that no artificial substance is used. No-one shall rub the ball on the ground or use any artificial substance or take any other action to alter the condition of the ball.

In the event of a contravention of this Law, the umpires, after consultation, shall change the ball for one of similar condition to that in use prior to the contravention.

This Law does not prevent a member of the fielding side from drying a wet ball, or removing mud from the ball. See Note (b).

6. Incommoding the Striker

An umpire is justified in intervening under this Law and shall call and signal 'dead ball' if, in his opinion, any player of the fielding side incommodes the striker by any noise or action while he is receiving the ball.

7. Obstruction of a Batsman in Running

It shall be considered unfair if any fieldsman wilfully obstructs a batsman in running. In these circumstances the umpire shall call and signal 'dead ball' and allow any completed runs and the run in progress, or alternatively any boundary scored.

8. The Bowling of Fast Short-pitched Balls

The bowling of fast short-pitched balls is unfair if, in the opinion of the umpire at the bowler's end, it constitutes an attempt to intimidate the striker. See Note (d).

Umpires shall consider intimidation to be the deliberate bowling of fast short-pitched balls which by their length, height and direction are intended or likely to inflict physical injury on the striker. The relative skill of the striker shall also be taken into consideration.

In the event of such unfair bowling, the umpire at the bowler's end shall adopt the following procedure:

(a) In the first instance the umpire shall call and signal 'no-ball', caution the bowler and inform the other umpire, the captain of the fielding side and the batsmen of what has occurred.
(b) If this caution is ineffective, he shall repeat the above procedure and indicate to the bowler that this is a final warning.
(c) Both the above caution and final warning shall continue to apply even though the bowler may later change ends.
(d) Should the above warnings prove ineffective the umpire at the bowler's end shall:

- (i) At the first repetition call and signal 'no-ball' and when the ball is dead direct the captain to take the bowler off forthwith and to complete the over with another bowler, provided that the bowler does not bowl two overs or part thereof consecutively. See Law 22.7 (Bowler Incapacitated or Suspended during an Over).
- (ii) Not allow the bowler, thus taken off, to bowl again in the same innings.
- (iii) Report the occurrence to the captain of the batting side as soon as the players leave the field for an interval.
- (iv) Report the occurrence to the executive of the fielding side and to any governing body responsible for the match, who shall take any further action which is considered to be appropriate against the bowler concerned.

9. The Bowling of Fast High Full Pitches

The bowling of fast high full pitches is unfair. See Note (e).

In the event of such unfair bowling the umpire at the bowler's end shall adopt the procedures of caution, final warnings, action against the bowler and reporting as set out in 8 above.

10. Time Wasting

Any form of time wasting is unfair.

(a) In the event of the captain of the fielding side wasting time or allowing any member of his side to waste time, the umpire at the bowler's end shall adopt the following procedure:
- (i) In the first instance he shall caution the captain of the fielding side and inform the other umpire of what has occurred.
- (ii) If this caution is ineffective he shall repeat the above procedure and indicate to the captain that this is a final warning.
- (iii) The umpire shall report the occurrence to the captain of the batting side as soon as the players leave the field for an interval.
- (iv) Should the above procedure prove ineffective the umpire shall report the occurrence to the executive of the fielding side and to any governing body responsible for that match, who shall take appropriate action against the captain and the players concerned.

(b) In the event of a bowler taking unnecessarily long to bowl an over the umpire at the bowler's end shall adopt the procedures, other than the calling of 'no-ball', of caution, final warning, action against the bowler and reporting.

(c) In the event of a batsman wasting time (See Note (f)) other than in the manner described in Law 31 (Timed Out), the umpire at the bowler's end shall adopt the following procedure:
- (i) In the first instance he shall caution the batsman and inform the other umpire at once, and the captain of the batting side, as soon as the players leave the field for an interval, of what has occurred.
- (ii) If this proves ineffective, he shall repeat the caution, indicate to the batsman that this is a final warning and inform the other umpire.
- (iii) The umpire shall report the occurrence to both captains as soon as the players leave the field for an interval.
- (iv) Should the above procedure prove ineffective, the umpire shall report the occurrence to the executive of the batting side and to any governing body responsible for that match, who shall take appropriate action against the player concerned.

11. *Players Damaging the Pitch*

The umpires shall intervene and prevent players from causing damage to the pitch which may assist the bowlers of either side. See Note (c).

(a) In the event of any member of the fielding side damaging the pitch, the umpire shall follow the procedure of caution, final warning, and reporting as set out in 10(a) above.

(b) In the event of a bowler contravening this Law by running down the pitch after delivering the ball, the umpire at the bowler's end shall first caution the bowler. If this caution is ineffective the umpire shall adopt the procedures, other than the calling of 'no-ball', of final warning, action against the bowler and reporting.

(c) In the event of a batsman damaging the pitch the umpire at the bowler's end shall follow the procedures of caution, final warning and reporting as set out in 10(c) above.

12. Batsman Unfairly Stealing a Run

Any attempt by the batsman to steal a run during the bowler's run-up is unfair. Unless the bowler attempts to run out either batsman – see Law 24.4 (Bowler Throwing at Striker's Wicket before Delivery) and Law 24.5 (Bowler Attempting to Run Out Non-striker before Delivery) – the umpire shall call and signal 'dead ball' as soon as the batsmen cross in any such attempt to run. The batsmen shall then return to their original wickets.

13. Player's Conduct

In the event of a player failing to comply with the instructions of an umpire, criticising his decisions by word or action, or showing dissent, or generally behaving in a manner which might bring the game into disrepute, the umpire concerned shall, in the first place, report the matter to the other umpire and to the player's captain requesting the latter to take action. If this proves ineffective, the umpire shall report the incident as soon as possible to the executive of the player's team and to any governing body responsible for the match, who shall take any further action which is considered appropriate against the player or players concerned.

Notes

(a) The Condition of the Ball
Umpires shall make frequent and irregular inspections of the condition of the ball.

(b) Drying of a Wet Ball
A wet ball may be dried on a towel or with sawdust.

(c) Danger Area
The danger area on the pitch, which must be protected from damage by a bowler, shall be regarded by the umpires as the area contained by an imaginary line 4 feet/1.22m from the popping crease, and parallel to it, and within two imaginary and parallel lines drawn down the pitch from the points on that line 1 foot/30.48cm on either side of the middle stump.

(d) Fast Short-pitched Balls
As a guide, a fast short-pitched ball is one which pitches short and passes, or would have passed, above the shoulder height of the striker standing in a normal batting stance at the crease.

(e) The Bowling of Fast Full Pitches
The bowling of one fast, high full pitch shall be considered to be unfair if, in the opinion of the umpire, it is deliberate, bowled at the striker, and if it passes or would have passed above the shoulder height of the striker when standing in a normal batting stance at the crease.

(f) Time Wasting by Batsmen
Other than in exceptional circumstances, the batsman should always be ready to take strike when the bowler is ready to start his run-up.

II

Limpsfield Cricket Club results, 1959–1976

Captain	Year	Played	Won	Drawn	Lost	Abandoned
J. M. Davies	1959	31	10	8	13	–
	1960	35	22	8	5	–
	1961	44	28	10	4	2
	1962	51	35	3	9	4
	1963	48	29	9	10	4
	1964	49	22	7	17	3
	1965	46	24	3	12	7
E. M. Rose	1966	47	26	10	8	3
	1967	43	23	10	7	3
	1968	38	18	8	6	6
	1969	45	23	7	14	1
	1970	44	25	10	7	2
	1971	40	22	8	10	–
R. H. Neve	1972	42	24	6	7	6
J. I. Garrard	1973	45	22	10	12	1
	1974	44	20	9	7	8
E. M. Rose	1975	48	35	7	5	1
	1976	48	34	6	7	1
Totals	18 Seasons	P	W	D	L	A
		793	442	139	160	52

III

Sources and further reading

Arlott, John (Ed.)	Cricket: the Great Captains (1971)
Barnes, Simon	A Singular Man (1986)
Benaud, Richie	A Tale of Two Tests (1962)
Bradman, Donald	Farewell to Cricket (1950)
Bradman, Donald	The Art of Cricket (1958)
Brearley, Mike	The Ashes Retained (1978)
Brearley, Mike	The Ashes Regained (1979)
Brearley, Mike	The Art of Captaincy (1985)
Buchanan, Handasyde (Ed.)	Great Cricket Matches (1962)
Cardus, Neville	Days in the Sun (1924)
Cowdrey, Colin	M.C.C.: the autobiography of a cricketer (1976)
Day, Harvey	Luck of the Toss (1970)
Dollery, H. E.	Professional Captain (1952)
Fender, P. G. H.	The Turn of the Wheel (1929)

Books, books

Fingleton, Jack	The Greatest Test of All (1961)
Gibson, Alan	The Cricket Captains of England (1979)
Illingworth, Ray	Captaincy (1980)
Jardine, D. R.	In Quest of the Ashes (1933)
Larwood, Harold	Bodyline? (1933)
M.C.C.	M.C.C. Cricket Coaching Book (1952)
Noble, M. A.	The Game's the Thing (1926)
Marriott, C. S.	The Complete Leg-Break Bowler (1968)
Ross, Alan	Australia 55 (1955)
Smith, T. E.	Cricket Umpiring & Scoring (1980)
Swanton, E. W.	Swanton in Australia (1975)
Thomson, A. A.	Cricket: The Great Captains (1965)
Warner, P. F.	How We Recovered the Ashes 1904 (1905)
Warner, P. F.	My Cricketing Life (1921)

IV

Select Index